YALE HISTORICAL PUBLICATIONS

David Horne, Editor

MISCELLANY 75

Published under the direction
of the Department of History
with assistance from the income
of the Frederick John Kingsbury
Memorial Fund

H. G. WELLS
and the WORLD STATE

by W. Warren Wagar

NEW HAVEN, YALE UNIVERSITY PRESS, 1961

TO DOROTHY

ACKNOWLEDGMENTS

WHEN I FIRST PROBED into the possibility of a doctoral dissertation on H. G. Wells in 1954, popular and scholarly interest in Wells was practically extinct. In his delightful Introduction to Geoffrey West's biography, Wells had waved "the striving immortals onward," and now it seemed as if they really were going on, leaving H.G. stranded somewhere back in the 1930's. But then a number of important articles began appearing in the journals on Wells. Dr. Gordon N. Ray acquired Wells' papers for the University of Illinois and announced a forthcoming full-length study of Wells' life. The University of Illinois Press is publishing his correspondence. As this book is in the press, news comes from Nottingham of the organization of an H. G. Wells Society (Acting Secretary, John R. Hammond, 39 Rugby Road, West Bridgford). The wheels are turning. It is not too much to hope that by 1966, the centennial of Wells' birth, he will have caught up with the striving immortals of the twentieth century in spite of himself. A little later on, I suspect he will even be joining the leaders of that spectral procession. The heyday of the symbol-mongers and the literary technicians cannot last much longer; it is time again for Wells.

My thanks are due, first of all, to Dr. Ray, who most kindly gave me full and free access to the Wells Archive at Urbana, and also to Mrs. Charles H. Shattuck, who catalogued the collection and gave me much help in locating materials. I am also in the debt of Dr. William Gaines and the United States Educational Commission in the United Kingdom for a profitable year of writing and research in London in 1957–58 as a Fulbright grantee. During my stay in London, I had useful talks with many people, including Professor G. P. Wells and Mrs. Marjorie Wells, for many years Wells' secretary. Professor and Mrs. Wells and Mr. F. R. Wells, the executors of Wells' estate, graciously supplied me with all the necessary permissions to quote from Wells' published and unpublished work. Many thanks are in order, too, for my adviser in London, Professor J. Isaacs of Queen Mary College in the University of London, who gave generously and good humoredly of his time and wisdom.

Several members of the faculty of the Graduate School of Yale University served on my dissertation committee, and I had the benefit of their criticism when the present study was in its formative stages. I should like to mention in particular Lewis P. Curtis, the late Cecil H. Driver, and John Morton Blum. I am especially grateful for the constant advice, criticism, and encouragement of Franklin Le Van Baumer, my adviser at Yale, who has kept in close touch with the book since he first urged me, nearly five years ago, to write it. Finally, for her patience with peevishness and impatience with idleness, and her unflagging love and loyalty, I thank my wife.

W.W.W.

Wellesley, Massachusetts
November 1960

CONTENTS

Introduction:

H. G. WELLS AND THE
INTELLECTUAL HISTORIAN

From the scholarly point of view, H. G. Wells was one of
the twentieth century's queerest ducks. There is no lack of
testimonials to his importance. "He has stimulated more
people into hard thinking," said Harold Laski in 1930,
"than any other living writer of English prose."[1] But most
academic specialists will not have him. For students of English literature he has shrunk to the dimensions of a minor
novelist, fit for sweeping into the literary dustbin nowadays
shared by Hilaire Belloc, Arnold Bennett, and John Galsworthy. In all the fields he invaded for his adventures in
journalism and *vulgarisation,* from history and biology to
economics and education, he is either completely ignored
or tolerated with contempt.

But one kind of scholar should be more than grateful for
Wells. To the intellectual historian, attempting to trace
patterns of thought and describe climates of opinion, he is
primary source material. He linked insights, articulated
hopes and fears, educated masses, expressed the temper of

1. "H. G. Wells," *Daily Herald* (1930), reprinted in *Living Age,*
339 (1930), 287.

an age. No other writer of his generation so completely bridged the gap between the man in the library and laboratory and the man in the street. Journalist, teacher, preacher, and prophet on the grandest possible scale, Wells gives the intellectual historian abundant help in answering the basic problems of his discipline: how ideas in a society get into circulation, become fashionable, and are broadly disseminated through whole populations. The most profoundly original of philosophers could not legitimately attract the intellectual historian more than Wells.

It is not easy to speak with authority of a man who tried his hand at so many literary trades. To explain his range and productivity requires the thesis in Alan Wood's biography of another tireless modern—Bertrand Russell—that "all great human achievement can be resolved, in the last resort, to some superabundant source of energy."[2] No man with the usual reserves of energy, though twice as brilliant as Wells, could have managed to hurl himself into so many projects and enjoy so rich and full a private life to boot. A dozen or more entirely distinct occupations might be listed after Wells' name in a reference book:

For some literate children of the twentieth century, he was a writer of fantastic short stories and short novels. He counts as the father of science-fiction among its devotees; his science fantasies still introduce thousands of readers each year to that peculiarly modern species of fabling. In stories like "The Country of the Blind" and in romances like *The Time Machine* and *The War of the Worlds*, he furnished the genre with imperishable classics. Others knew him best as a social novelist, a writer who used his knowledge and experience of the southeastern counties of England to document the decay of the Victorian social order and to create, in passing, wonderfully comic portraits of petty bourgeois

2. Wood, *Bertrand Russell: The Passionate Sceptic* (London, Allen and Unwin, 1957), p. 241.

Englishmen caught up in the maelstrom of change; critics still like *Tono-Bungay* and *The History of Mr. Polly*. In the days when only Bernard Shaw could rival his popularity, Wells was also known as the twentieth century's most representative utopian; in *A Modern Utopia, Men Like Gods,* and *The Shape of Things to Come,* he anticipated a scientifically organized world society that mankind could attain only by mobilizing its collective will. He ranked high among the prophets of socialism; he was the author of *New Worlds for Old,* the most widely read socialist tract of the Edwardian era, and he pumped fresh blood into the Fabian Society. Still another and even larger number of readers encountered him as a journalist, a contributor to hundreds of popular newspapers and magazines on a prodigious range of subjects, from sex, politics, and religion to simplified science. The general public heard him on the B.B.C. or on lecture tours in America and Australia, and it found him in the cinema as the author of films like *Things to Come.* He reached millions with his educational books, his outlines of history, biology, and the social sciences. There was Wells the popularizer of pragmatism in *First and Last Things,* Wells the apostle of a deified humanity in *God the Invisible King,* Wells the world revolutionist in *The Open Conspiracy,* and more Wellses still: in all, 110 books and several hundred unreprinted articles in the press. More than twelve million words were published under his name, over a span of more than fifty years.

All through his career, Wells' admirers and critics could not make up their minds whether to label his work a distillation of the world-view of the late nineteenth century, a mirror of contemporary thought, or a body of prophetic wisdom well ahead of its time. It was perhaps less than any of these, but an extraordinary number of ideas did crowd through Wells' mind and, stamped into the familiar shapes of his thought, they did tumble out into his books. He retained all his life the absorptive curiosity of a puppy or a small child. Many things caught his eye; they were usually the things that interested other people; and whatever he had on his mind he hurried into print. Most of his best books overflow with ideas (that remarkable "novel" *The World of William Clissold* is a choice example), supplying the intellectual historian with invaluable clues to the mental climate of the years of their publication. Wells called himself in 1939 "the trace of the flow of thought during the past half century,"[3] and he was not far from right.

In the abundance of his writing, in the variety of his interests, in his role as a popularizer of ideas and an encyclopedist of general knowledge, and in the satirical virulence of his social criticism, Wells belonged to a species of intellectual almost extinct in our time but familiar to students of the French Enlightenment. As Voltaire and d'Alembert were *philosophes* of an age under the spell of Newtonian physics, so Wells was a philosophe of the Darwinian age. He differed from them on scores of issues, but he was the same sort of intellectual. "They were not philosophers in the technical and academic sense," writes one intellectual historian of the philosophes, and his description fits Wells perfectly:

> Neither were they scholars or specialists, nor courtiers or "gentlemen." They were emphatically not of the ivory tower. Literary men, popularizers, propagandists, they made their appeal to a newly awakened public opinion, against the powers that be, against the learned world of church and university. Fontenelle was their prototype, but they went further than Fontenelle, for they wished not only to advance knowledge but to change society—the educational and religious system,

3. Wells, *The Fate of Man* (New York, 1939), pp. 67–68. Hereafter, unless otherwise designated, all works cited in footnotes are by Wells.

the economic and social system, eventually even the political system.[4]

Like the philosophes, Wells was a popularizer, a social reformer, a foe of an *ancien régime*. Like the philosophes, he sought to educate a newly literate public, although this public—the "quarter-educated" of George Gissing's *New Grub Street,* the beneficiaries of the state school systems that sprang up everywhere in Europe and North America toward the close of the nineteenth century—was much larger than the public reached by the philosophes. But like the philosophes, Wells had high hopes for the power of education to transform mankind, and he favored practical education in modern and utilitarian subjects over the traditional educational disciplines. Like most of the pre-Jacobin philosophes, he was a cosmopolitan with hardly a trace of sympathy for patriotism or popular democracy. He shared, at least a little, the eighteenth-century classicist's disdain for deeply emotional art, mystical experience, and natural beauty. He worshiped the future with all the quasi-religious feeling Diderot ascribed to the philosophes, and like them he was an irreverent mocker of privilege, a zealot for common sense, and a dedicated humanist.[5] "Mr. Wells is not Voltaire," Carl Becker once wrote, in his review of *The Outline of History,* "but his *rôle* is much the same: like Voltaire he is a versatile man of letters, with warm human sympathies, interested in all the knowledge of his day; like

4. Franklin Le Van Baumer, in Baumer, ed., *Main Currents of Western Thought* (New York, Knopf, 1952), p. 358.
5. "Humanist" is an exasperating word. It can be, and has been, applied to existentialists, Marxists, positivists, neo-Thomists, and half a dozen other competing schools of thought. See, e.g., Auguste Etcheverry, *Le Conflit actuel des humanismes,* Paris, 1955. But as it will be used in the present study with reference to Wells, a "humanist" is what Corliss Lamont tries to define in his *Humanism as a Philosophy,* New York, 1949.

Voltaire he is a man of faith, who believes that men may be made more enlightened and more humane; like Voltaire he is enlisted in the war on *l'Infâme*—on hypocrisy, superstition, fanaticism, tyranny."[6]

Of course Wells was not the only public teacher of his generation. Frank Swinnerton brackets him with three of his contemporaries who were also popular pundits: Bernard Shaw, G. K. Chesterton, and Hilaire Belloc; and a useful study could be made of all four of them with special reference to the years 1901–14.[7] Bertrand Russell has been a philosophe in his way, as well as a philosopher; and among American writers, Lewis Mumford has performed similar services. But none of them covered more ground or reached more readers than Wells. He was the most serious of the popular writers of his time, and the most popular of the serious.

The casual reader who found himself colliding with Wells now and then in one or more of his several literary roles might have failed to grasp the inner unity of Wells' work. Wells did not write for the sheer joy of writing; he did not enlighten for enlightenment's sake. He was a man with a mission, or rather two intimately connected missions, each with material enough for a full-length study done from the peculiar angle of approach of the intellectual historian.

In the last chapter of his *Experiment in Autobiography*, entitled "The Idea of a Planned World," Wells described

6. Becker, "Mr. Wells and the New History," *Everyman His Own Historian* (New York, Crofts, 1935), p. 190; cf. Albert Guérard, "The 'New History': H. G. Wells and Voltaire," *Scribner's Magazine, 76* (1924), 476–84, and Arnaud Dandieu, "Wells et Diderot," *Mercure de France, 194* (1927), 513–36.

7. See especially Swinnerton's *The Georgian Literary Scene*, London, 1935. Shaw, Wells, Belloc, and Chesterton together wrote about 400 books.

the "structural frame of my life" as the propaganda of "a world-wide 'Open Conspiracy' to rescue human society from the net of tradition in which it is entangled and to reconstruct it upon planetary lines."[8] Here, as plainly as he could, he provided his biographers and critics with at least the conscious purposes behind all the immense volume of his work. On the one hand, he campaigned against the Victorian social order and successfully challenged nineteenth-century values in education, sexual behavior, religion, and government. He accustomed a whole generation to believe in the inevitable smash-up of the Victorian way of life, through the agency of inevitable technological change. With Bernard Shaw and Bertrand Russell, in the end he helped to liberate the twentieth-century mind from a wide assortment of Victorian prejudices. The victories of socialism, the waning of the classical tradition in education, the attenuation of the Victorian moral code, and the new role of women in public life all illustrate social changes in which Wells' influence was potent. And, on the other hand, he was nearly all his life a prophet of world order. As eagerly as he helped to pull down the Victorian synthesis, he turned with obsessive enthusiasm to the task of outlining the requirements for world synthesis. His contest with the Victorian social order suggests the theme of one study. His response to the economic, political, and spiritual world crisis of the twentieth century suggests another.

The present study is at least an anticipation of the second of these two possible projects. The anti-Victorian element in Wells' work has already been explored at some length in a number of other books and academic dissertations; and, although none of these works is definitive, they provide together a useful commentary on the earlier phases of his career. Three works published in the 1920's surveyed

8. *Experiment in Autobiography* (New York, 1934), p. 549.

the course of his thinking down to that time: Edouard
Guyot's *H.-G. Wells* (Paris, 1920), Georges Connes' *Etude
sur la pensée de Wells* (Strasbourg, 1926), and F. H. Doughty's *H. G. Wells: Educationist,* London, 1926. More recently, several dissertations in the field of English literary
criticism have touched on Wells' thought, for the most part
stressing his earlier work.[9] But Wells' career as a prophet
of world order, which closed only with his death in 1946,
could hardly be studied until now and remains more or less
virgin territory. It is just this aspect of his work which most
clearly relates him to the main currents of Western thought
in the past four decades.

After the first World War the intellectual avant-garde
branded him as a spokesman of old-fashioned scientific
rationalism; but it is too often overlooked that he was also
one of the first prophets of the world crisis of the twentieth
century. Above all in the minds of the general reading
public, he awakened the now painfully familiar feeling that
modern man is on the road to racial disaster. He shocked—
or entertained—millions of readers with prophecies of im-
aginary world wars in which the whole fabric of civilization
disintegrated. The intelligentsia often missed the impact
of his warnings, because Wells to many of them was inex-
tricably associated with the confident materialism of the
Edwardian generation in which he had risen to world prom-
inence. To many of them he symbolized the old prewar
intoxication with "progress." Although Wells had never
accepted the conventional Victorian and Edwardian for-

9. Otto Barber, *H. G. Wells' Verhältnis zum Darwinismus,* Leipzig, 1934; Heinz Mattick, *H. G. Wells als Sozialreformer,* Leipzig,
1935; Ullrich Sonnemann, *Der soziale Gedanke im Werk von H. G.
Wells,* Berlin, 1935; Robert P. Weeks, "H. G. Wells as a Sociological
Novelist," dissertation, University of Michigan, 1952; and Moses W.
Steinberg, "Formative Influences on the Thought of H. G. Wells,"
dissertation, University of Toronto, 1952.

mulas on the prospects of mankind, it was easy to imagine that he had, and to expose him as a victim of the delusion of "inevitable progress." But at least for the general reading public Wells dramatized the twentieth-century world crisis. He scolded and warned. The Joshua who had stormed the walls of the Victorian Jericho became now, for the majority of his readers, a wailing Jeremiah. And, with Jeremiah, he was not content to complain and diagnose and threaten. He offered a comprehensive scheme of proposals to bring mankind to world unity. Wells' work gave popular currency to a need increasingly felt by the intellectual leaders of Western civilization for political, social, moral, and educational synthesis. If he broadcasted, though on another wavelength, Spengler's warning of the imminent collapse of the West, he also anticipated the pleas of Toynbee, Northrop, and Mumford in the mid-twentieth century for an integrated world civilization.

The growth of Wells' obsession with the sickness of civilization can best be measured by the changing character of his fiction. The shift from novels primarily in the Edwardian literary tradition and primarily devoted to destructive analysis of English society to novels of ideas whose heroes were self-conscious pioneers in world-rebuilding set in even before the outbreak of the first World War. In the end he deliberately burned his literary boats. As he admitted in his autobiography, he dropped "below the habitual novel reader's horizon . . . for good" when he paused to write *The Outline of History* in 1919.[10] He did not stop writing novels —sixteen were published in the years between 1922 and 1941—but critics stopped expecting him to write great novels. In general, he made no serious effort to surprise them.

Wells' concern for the future of civilization ate away his

10. *Experiment in Autobiography*, p. 614.

disposition to look on life bravely. But it also preserved him from trying to ring endless changes on old triumphs, which plagues the writer who never recovers from the exhilaration of his first successes. The critics chorused for another *Kipps,* another *History of Mr. Polly;* Wells did not oblige them. For surrendering his claim to a place among the literary giants that he never really wanted, he deserves no medals. He may have seriously impaired his effectiveness as a prophetic voice by not placing a higher value on rhetoric and artistic integrity. But when the history of the twentieth century is written, his honesty and courage will command respect. And if the world crisis he sought to convert into world order is survived successfully, it will be his sense of dreadful urgency that animates the survivors.

Expounding Wells' social philosophy in some sort of logical and compact order is a hazardous enterprise, because he never seriously tried at any time to work his thought into a concise system. Although he remained all his life a reasonably consistent thinker, his emphases, moods, and alliances shifted from year to year, and his social thought is distributed through the pages of seven or eight dozen books written over a period of fifty years. Most of these books were not, to say the very least, written for posterity; they are often loosely reasoned, carelessly constructed, and intellectually slippery and shallow, so that any study of his thought is likely to display much more of *l'esprit systématique* than Wells ever did. To trace every casual or deliberate shift of emphasis from book to book and year to year would be fruitless and tiresome.

On the other hand, Wells was consistent enough in the spirit if not in the letter of his work to make an interpretative synthesis possible. The present study opens with a short biographical account of Wells' prophetic career and his diagnosis of the twentieth-century world crisis. The second chapter is an analysis of the ideas on which his social thought was based. The next three chapters offer a step-by-step discussion and criticism of his theory of world revolution: his program for a renaissance in education, his idea of an "open conspiracy," and his vision of world order in being. In the last chapter an attempt is made to analyze both his success and his failure as a prophet. I suspect that in another generation or two, when some of the rough edges and awkward gaps in his thought will no longer be so glaringly obvious and when the anguished disillusionment of mid-century men has ripened into sober resolution, H. G. Wells will be acknowledged as a crucial intermediary between the intellectual inheritance of the West and the coming world civilization.

Chapter One:

THE PROPHETIC OFFICE

THE PROPHET

Old and tired, broken in health and spirit, sickened by an aimless world war then in its sixth year, H. G. Wells surprised his readers in 1945 by prophesying the imminent extinction of civilized life on earth. After a half century of hopefulness, he now suddenly surrendered to despair. "This world," he wrote, "is at the end of its tether. The end of everything we call life is close at hand and cannot be evaded." Some unsuspected limit to human adaptability had been reached. Before man could bring his affairs under the control of informed intelligence, the human race had arrived at an impasse. "The writer is convinced that there is no way out or round or through the impasse. It is the end." Civilization was an anthill being kicked to pieces by an implacable cosmic enemy. "The stars in their courses" had turned against man, "and he has to give place to some other animal better adapted to face the fate that closes in more and more swiftly upon mankind."[1]

Wells entitled this last book *Mind at the End of Its Tether:* in just forty-one barely coherent pages it seemed to cancel the message he had taken such pains to convey in nearly all his writing. There was no shape of things to come, after all; no possibility of Utopia, or even survival; the

---

1. *Mind at the End of Its Tether* (New York, 1946), pp. 1, 4, 18.

pattern of the past, disclosed in *The Outline of History,* no longer had any bearing on the future. "Hitherto," he wrote, "events had been held together by a certain logical consistency, as heavenly bodies . . . have been held together by the pull, the golden cord, of Gravitation."[2] Now the cord had snapped. The old apparent relationship between the evolving mind of humanity and the implacable will of the cosmos had dissolved. The human phase of evolution was over.

Nor did Wells ever recover his faith in man's capacity for survival and salvation. Written in the late summer and autumn of 1944, *Mind at the End of Its Tether* was his last published book, but he experienced no change of heart or mind down to his death in August 1946.[3] And perhaps

2. Ibid., p. 5.

3. Through 1944 and 1945 Wells worked sporadically on another book, "Exasperations: The Last Testament of H. G. Wells," composed mainly of articles published in 1944 but with some unpublished material in the mood of *Mind at the End of Its Tether.* Chapter 10, e.g., "The Mills of God with the Brakes Off," teems with apocalyptic images. The typescript is in the Wells Archive at the University of Illinois. The Archive also has an unpublished appendix to *Mind at the End of Its Tether,* a collection of seven brief "Aesop's Fables"— about men, instead of animals, since men are nowadays "the most foolish vermin that have ever overrun the earth." And in May 1946 he drafted a short letter, a copy of which is in the Archive, for some of his old friends and associates, advising them that he was at work on a new film scenario, to bring his 1935 film *Things to Come* up to date. He would call it "The Way the World Is Going," and he hoped it would help men face their "culminating destiny with dignity and mutual aid and charity." Nothing survives of the scenario, if, indeed, it was ever begun. His last substantial publication, "The Betterave Papers; Harold Swansdown up to Date, and Exposé of H. G. Wells," *Cornhill Magazine, 161* (1945), 349–63, adds nothing of value to the record of the last years; it appeared in the United States in the *Virginia Quarterly Review, 21* (1945). 413–33. Wells also published one final vitriolic attack on the English monarchy, less than two months before his death: "That Mosley Money!" *New Leader,* July 6, 1946.

with good cause. He had dedicated most of his life to the service of propaganda for world order. He had suggested one project after another for achieving, directly or indirectly, a world state. None had ever been tried. Now the world seemed sinking deeper and deeper into confusion, and the prophet himself, who had made its sorrows his own, was dying. Wells had always lived with a terrible intensity in the world here and now around him. The tragedy of his own approaching death, presaged by a breakdown in 1942; the tragedy of racial suicide being played in all the arenas of the twentieth century's second world war; and the still greater tragedy of the ineffectual truce likely to follow—all conspired to exhaust his courage.

Sir Arthur Salter describes *Mind at the End of Its Tether* as a bitter cry in Wells' Gethsemane,[4] which may seem a little extravagant at first glance. In his own person, Wells never cut a prophetic, much less a messianic, figure. A plump, jaunty, extraverted, irascible little man with the moral instincts of a Cockney Don Juan, he had always relished—like his hero Richard Remington in *The New Machiavelli*—"naked bodies and the jolly smells of things."[5] He could not be solemn, other-worldly, or doleful. His squeaky voice failed him embarrassingly on the lecture platform. Rather, he sparkled and crackled like a Roman candle, always at his best in conversation, at parties, in games. He lacked all the stock properties and virtues of prophets. Yet, as he reached his public, especially through his books, he was one of the most conscientious and deeply committed social prophets of the century. Although he knew the world and its ways only imperfectly, he ministered to the whole world; and when, at the last, it seemed to turn against him and fail him beyond all chance of recovery, he felt betrayed.

4. Salter, "H. G. Wells, Apostle of a World Society," *Personality in Politics* (London, Faber and Faber, 1947), p. 137.

5. *The New Machiavelli* (New York, 1910), p. 241.

Mind at the End of Its Tether was a howl of anguish. Its sincerity and intensity cannot be questioned: and at the same time it recalls, in its terse exasperation, all the years of warning and urging and prophesying, the books and articles, lectures and broadcasts, by the hundreds and thousands, in which it culminated.

The prophet who finally despaired of the world had started life poor in the world's goods. Wells was born in 1866 in Bromley, Kent, now a suburb of London, the son of a shopkeeper and a former lady's maid. No one is ever likely to improve on the chapters of his *Experiment in Autobiography* which record his progress, so much like the progress of any earnest Victorian aspiring to better himself, from lower middle-class Bromley schoolboy to draper's apprentice to worshipful student of T. H. Huxley to science teacher and finally London journalist, writing for Frank Harris and William Ernest Henley. One career led to another. The journalist became a writer of scientific romances, beginning with *The Time Machine* in 1895. The scientific romancer became a serious novelist in the Edwardian decade, the author of *Love and Mr. Lewisham, Kipps, Tono-Bungay, Ann Veronica,* and *The History of Mr. Polly,* which were simultaneously frontal attacks, slashed with Dickensian humor, on the mores, beliefs, and institutions of Victorian England. And at the same time, romancer and social novelist combined to produce the prophet of world reconstruction, the author of *Anticipations,* published in 1902, a seminal statement of Wells' social philosophy and, in his own words, "the keystone to the main arch of my work."[6]

What immediately sets Wells off from most of the prophets of world order who followed him, in the generation

6. *Experiment in Autobiography,* p. 549.

of Arnold J. Toynbee and Pitirim A. Sorokin, is of course his far deeper debt to the thought-world of the late nineteenth century. Had he been born twenty, or perhaps even ten, years later, his career could have taken a radically different turn. Instead, many of his fundamental convictions and much of his response to the twentieth-century world crisis betray his late Victorian origins. His analysis of the predicament of modern man, to choose a crucial example, developed by a perfectly natural sequence of ideas from his analysis of the disintegration of nineteenth-century English society. For most of his earlier readers it was just this destructive analysis, this alternately whimsical and savage indictment of the Victorian *ancien régime*, which made him worth reading.

The Victorian order was already far gone in decay, and ripe for concerted assault, when Wells and his generation began writing near the turn of the century. "The balance of educated intelligence," according to J. M. Robertson, had already turned against one of its chief props, Evangelical Protestantism, in the 1870's.[7] The evidence of the natural sciences, the penetrating biblical scholarship of the German "Higher Critics," and the Positivist movement had lured many of the best minds to some species of unbelief; others were returning penitent to Rome. Still another prop of the Victorian social order, its staunchly individualistic political philosophy, grounded in the thinking of Jeremy Bentham and J. S. Mill, had come under attack from the socialists, on the one hand, and the new imperialists, on the other, both demanding commitment to collectivistic ideals fundamentally alien to the Victorian liberal conscience. The Victorian moral code was being challenged by partisans of Algernon Swinburne, Edward FitzGerald's Omar Khayyam, and Friedrich Nietzsche; by the *fin-de-*

7. Robertson, *A History of Freethought in the Nineteenth Century* (2 vols. London, Watts, 1929), 2, 391.

siècle dandyism of Oscar Wilde and Aubrey Beardsley; by the fatalism of Thomas Hardy, the satire of Samuel Butler, the feminism of George Meredith, the social Darwinism of Benjamin Kidd. Most of the late Victorians were in some significant sense anti-Victorians. Even if the thinkers had been loyal to their society, larger forces beyond their control would have been rapidly undermining the Victorian way of life. Changes in the European balance of power, keener competition in world trade, the inexorable upward thrust of the working classes, and continuing revolutions in technology doomed the Victorian order to a premature death. Wells himself had no reason to defend it. He had escaped, but only narrowly, the fate usually reserved for sons of poor lower middle-class fathers. Years of penury, hat-tipping, sexual humiliation, missed chances, and ill health had left him wry and rebellious. As a matter of course he turned enthusiastically to the creeds of the intellectual avant-garde of his adolescence and early manhood. He could not embrace them all: then, as now, there were too many. But he read omnivorously. To judge from his early writing, by 1900 he had assimilated or consciously rejected most of the ideologies and faiths competing for young minds in the intellectual milieu of late nineteenth-century England. His experience as a science student in London in the 1880's confirmed him as a life-long votary of something he liked to call Science, with a capital, and of all the philosophical interpretations of Darwin he had no use for any but T. H. Huxley's. The rationalists made him a resolute atheist, and the Positivists infected him with the idea of an evolving "racial Being." From the Fabians, whose first public meetings in London he attended during his student days, and from the Utopian socialists—French, British, and American —he acquired a lasting conviction of the need for social planning on the broadest possible scale, and a taste for Utopias which never left him. The world-view he assembled from the ideas current in his formative years may seem emphatically Victorian to mid-twentieth-century critics; but it involved him in outspoken rejection of much of the structure of belief in which the older generations of his own time habitually lived and worked.

In the end, no critic of Victorian society reached so wide an audience or assailed the old order at so many vulnerable points. Especially in his best Edwardian novels, Wells became the most influential spokesman in the decade before the first World War of the liberal-socialist younger generation. No one caught the spirit of the times more successfully. He was the champion *par excellence* of socialism, science, and moral emancipation. He challenged the Establishment, and Christianity itself; he described and applauded the decline of the landed gentry and inveighed against robber-baron capitalists; he attacked the tyranny of the classics, the universities, and the public schools; he defended the New Woman and preached sexual equality and sexual freedom. The more he was damned by clergymen, schoolmasters, and conservative editors, the more he became, as he described himself in 1911, "a symbol against the authoritative, the dull, the presumptuously established, against all that is hateful and hostile to youth and tomorrow."[8]

It is difficult for anyone not then alive to appreciate Wells' grip on the imaginations of young people. George Orwell doubted, shortly before his death,

> whether anyone who was writing books between 1900 and 1920, at any rate in the English language, influenced the young so much. The minds of all of us, and therefore the physical world, would be perceptibly different if Wells had never existed. . . . Back in the nineteen-hundreds it was a wonderful experience for

8. "My Lucky Moment," *View* (April 29, 1911), quoted in Vincent Brome, *H. G. Wells* (London, Longmans, Green, 1951), p. 115.

a boy to discover H. G. Wells. There you were, in a
world of pedants, clergymen, and golfers, with your
future employers exhorting you to "get on or get out,"
your parents systematically warping your sexual life,
and your dull-witted schoolmasters sniggering over
their Latin tags; and here was this wonderful man who
could tell you about the inhabitants of the planets and
the bottom of the sea, and who *knew* that the future
was not going to be what respectable people imagined.[9]

Wells' books were also appearing in translation on the Con-
tinent, where they probably reached a much wider audience
than those of any other contemporary British writer; and
Eric Goldman finds him easily the most influential of the
British political writers in the United States during the
Progressive Era.[10]
And of course the Wells who wielded an angry pen
against the dead weight of the past was entirely in tune with
his times. He articulated the ambitions and frustrations of
the radical avant-garde in an era of radical ascendancy. He
was an integral part of the world of Keir Hardie, David
Lloyd George, Robert LaFollette, and Woodrow Wilson.
With his fellow radicals on both sides of the Atlantic, with
the Webbs, Graham Wallas, Bernard Shaw, Bertrand Russell, John Dewey, and Thorstein Veblen, he bears much

9. Orwell, "Wells, Hitler and the World State," *Critical Essays*
(London, Secker and Warburg, 1946), p. 87.
10. Goldman, *Rendezvous with Destiny: A History of Modern
American Reform* (New York, 1952), p. 230. "Think of the serious
young men in their first years of college back in 1910," Harrison Smith
recalled just fifteen years later, "arguing with downy hair on their
flushed cheeks about *The New Machiavelli, Ann Veronica* and *Tono-
Bungay* over their beer mugs and in their dormitories—talking until
dawn": Smith, "The Mind of the Race," in William A. Drake, ed.,
American Criticism, 1926 (New York, Harcourt, Brace, 1926), p. 244.

responsibility for the contents and contours of the modern mind.[11]

But where Wells differed from most of his generation, so much that he could imagine himself a sort of reincarnation of Roger Bacon,[12] a lonely pioneer rather than a popular giant-killer, was in his intuition of the twentieth-century world crisis and his prescription of an organic world commonwealth as the cure. Here he was a pathfinder.

Although this pathfinder Wells did not mature as a prophet of world crisis and world order until after the catastrophe of 1914, the history of his prophetic career cannot be rehearsed, even in the few pages available here, without looking once again at his life and work before 1914. In fact he owed much of his appeal in the Edwardian era precisely to his unique ability not only to knock the old order to pieces but also to offer a comprehensive vision of the new world that might rise, whole and hale, in its place. The leaders of the Fabian Society looked into the future, but by design the Fabian imagination did not stretch beyond the limits of local and national social and political reform. By the first decade of the twentieth century the best Utopian socialists of the nineteenth were sadly superannuated. The need was for someone with an expansive imagination to put wings on the modern socialist creed, to send it soaring into the future, to make it seem radiant with promise, to work it into a larger historical scheme than could be provided by the conventions of socialist economic analysis. The task suited Wells exactly.

11. Wells understood the United States almost as well as he understood Britain in the Edwardian era. He made sparing use of this knowledge in his novels, but *The Future in America* (New York, 1906) is one of the most penetrating studies ever made of American problems by a British writer.

12. *Experiment in Autobiography*, pp. 622–23.

Perhaps because of his scientific training, he had been tempted from the first to deal with life on a grand scale. He took all humanity for his subject: not the genteel "humanity" of classical humanism or the hollow "humanity" of political oratory, but the living organic biological species, the culminating event in the evolution of life in space and time. When he was only nineteen, in a letter to his college friend A. T. Simmons, he had drawn a sketch of himself "meditating on his future," surrounded by books entitled "Secret of the Kosmos," "Key to Politics," "All about God," and "Wells Design for a New Framework for Society."[13] It was a cartoon. But the humor thinly veiled an authentic ambition to think and write on the largest possible scale, which he never outgrew.

Wells' taste for large ideas and panoramic views took especially the form, very early in his literary life, of speculation about the future of civilization, and at first, in the fashion of *fin-de-siècle* romance, of dispirited speculation. One of his earliest published pieces was a melancholy sketch entitled "The Man of the Year Million," and his first scientific romance, *The Time Machine,* 1895, explored the decaying world of A.D. 802,701, in a vein that suggests Max Nordau's *Degeneration,* published just two years before.[14] A later set of stories, including one book-length romance, *When the Sleeper Wakes* (1899), described in detail the world of the twenty-second century; again Wells chose to give events a tragic turn. But in a pair of Huxleyan articles published in 1896–97 in *The Fortnightly Review,* Wells argued that science, socialism, and education could just as easily enable man to overthrow nature and direct the course

13. Reproduced in Geoffrey West, *H. G. Wells: A Sketch for a Portrait* (London, Howe, 1930), p. 59.
14. Although the final version was not published until 1895 in book form, Wells had been working on *The Time Machine* since 1888. See the full history of it in West, *H. G. Wells,* pp. 289–95.

of his own evolution. Whether the human prospect was decadence or triumph depended on the collective human will.[15]

A few years later, in the same Promethean key in the same journal, Wells took advantage of the turn of the century to produce his first serious full-scale essay in social philosophy, a set of nine prophetic papers, collected in book form in 1902 under the title, *Anticipations of the Reaction of Mechanical and Scientific Progress upon Human Life and Thought.* In the first several chapters he played the artful journalist using the arrival of the new century to dilate on the marvels of modern science. He predicted aviation, truck transport, the suburbanization of rural areas connecting great cities, prefabricated housing, modern household appliances, revolutions in military technology, and so forth. But in the heart of the book he probed deeply into the social implications of technological change. The lesson he drew from his analysis was clear. The scale and pace of life in the twentieth century would vastly increase; the old barriers of distance would fall; a planned world order would have to replace the existing nation-state system. And the deeper he probed, the more he yielded to his prophetic instincts. The planned order of the future would not create itself. Scanning the political horizon, he prophesied the imminent breakdown of the old order through a series of convulsive wars, but also the beginnings of a revolutionary movement, the "New Republic," which would seize control of the degenerate governments of the old world and lead humanity to the universal state. *Anticipations* was a virtuoso performance: nearly everything he was ever to write about social change and reconstruction appeared there in embryo. The last entry in Beatrice Webb's diary

15. "Human Evolution, an Artificial Process," *Fortnightly Review,* 66 (1896), 590–95; and "Morals and Civilisation," ibid., 67 (1897), 263–68.

for 1901 duly noted that *Anticipations* was "the most remarkable book of the year."[16]

The success of *Anticipations* encouraged Wells to think of himself not only as a novelist but also as a sociological and prophetic writer. Like many literary men, he reached the peak of his powers in his late thirties and early forties. His best novels belong to these years, between the publication of *Anticipations* in 1902 and the death of Edward VII in 1910. But he did not neglect the audience he had attracted with *Anticipations*. *Mankind in the Making* (1903) was a sequel designed expressly for the English-speaking world, expanding on the theme of a possible "New Republican" movement in Britain and America, with special attention to educational reform. *The Food of the Gods* (1904) burlesqued to serious purpose the idea advanced in *Anticipations* that life on earth was undergoing a tremendous change in scale as a result of scientific and technical progress. And in 1905 he assembled an imaginative synthesis of all his thoughts on world reconstruction in the form of a Utopia. In the self-consciously "modern" spirit of the times he called it *A Modern Utopia*.

Like all such, *A Modern Utopia* is a criticism of contemporary society, as pungent and effective in its way as *Kipps* or *Tono-Bungay* or any of Wells' Edwardian social novels. But it also developed a social philosophy, half in lyrical glimpses of a clean, orderly, dynamic, ideal society, half in hard-headed expositions of Wells' socialism. Fundamentally a moralist rather than a scientist, he was at his best in the lyrical glimpses, and sometimes unhelpfully vague in the hard, practical details. He lacked above all the zest for public administration of his Fabian colleagues. Still, on the whole, *A Modern Utopia* tended to convince. It an-

16. Webb, *Our Partnership,* ed. Barbara Drake and Margaret I. Cole (London, Longmans, Green, 1948), p. 226.

swered with honesty and courage a question most of the radical thinkers of Wells' generation evaded. Doing away with the public schools, the sexual mores, the armies, the foreign offices, the churches, and the governing classes could be justified only if the reformers knew what kind of world they wanted ultimately to set in place of the old one. *A Modern Utopia* supplied Wells' answer.

It would have to be, he said, one world. Societies cohered because all their parts fit together, and to tamper with any one part was to risk precipitating change in every other. Planned change might produce Paradise, but uncoordinated tinkering would end in a social corpse. The new world, he went on, could be made a viable social organism only if it spanned the entire planet, to adjust to the change of scale effected in modern life by the revolution in transport. The state of the future would be a world state, and the society of the future would be a collectivized world society. In the place of state churches and hereditary or elected governing classes, the modern Utopia would be managed by a self-perpetuating elite of "volunteer noblemen," inaptly styled the Samurai. Composed essentially of the professional classes—the specially trained, highly educated, and unusually gifted—the Order would maintain its own discipline through spiritual exercises and strictly enforced codes of conduct, fix its own membership requirements, and assume all responsibility for the planning and coordination of public life.

Flushed with the success of *A Modern Utopia* and the satisfying public and critical reception of his novel *Kipps* in the same year, Wells decided to try his hand at politics, selecting as his target naturally enough the Fabian Society (which he had joined, sponsored by Bernard Shaw and Graham Wallas, with the blessings of the Webbs, in 1903). He launched a movement in 1906 to revolutionize Fabian strategy from top to bottom, to bring the Society into politics and education, to increase its membership from 700 to 10,000—to convert it, in effect, "into the beginnings of an order, akin to [the] Samurai in *A Modern Utopia.* . . . I envisaged that reconditioned Fabian Society as becoming, by means of vigorous propaganda, mainly carried on by young people, the directive element of a reorganized socialist party. We would attack the coming generation at the high school, technical college and university stage, and our organization would quicken into a constructive social stratum."[17]

The story of Wells' campaign has been told too many times to need re-telling here.[18] Like most of his later efforts to translate his ideas into action, it failed, partly because he had no talent for leadership, partly because his approach to socialism would have forced the Fabians to renounce Fabianism itself. Wells saw the future in large, dramatically integrated wholes; he believed in wholesale spontaneous social reconstruction. Men were to demolish the old order with one hand and build the new, as a single planned world society, with the other. The Webbs and most of the Fabian old guard looked on the Fabian Society as a compact, unobtrusive, patient, molelike organism, whose destiny was to guide Britain to socialism by methodical, practical planning and research and by winning over and infiltrating the governing classes. Wells would have turned the Fabians into a militant revolutionary party, with ambitions far more grandiose than the capture of any one country for socialism.

17. *Experiment in Autobiography,* p. 564.
18. Consult Edward R. Pease, *The History of the Fabian Society* (London, 1916), pp. 163–84; West, *H. G. Wells,* pp. 157–67; and Mattick, *H. G. Wells als Sozialreformer,* pp. 95–127. Wells' *Faults of the Fabian* (London, 1906) is reprinted in Mattick, pp. 142–57. Copies of the original pamphlet, which had been privately printed for members of the Fabian Society only, are scarce. It contains Wells' whole program for Fabian reconstruction.

The Webbs wanted to make socialism respectable in Britain; Wells would have made it a world religion.

Unable to rally a majority of the Fabian membership to his cause, Wells resigned, fingers burned, in 1908. But his defeat in the Fabian Society did not discourage him from pursuing his prophetic career. Articles, novels, and tracts continued to pour out, as if by an irresistible impulse from an inexhaustible source.

Wells' later prewar work, although it yielded no prophetic books on a plane with *Anticipations* and *A Modern Utopia,* was significant in two ways. It was marked by a growing uneasiness over the prospects of Western civilization and by a change, after 1911, in the character of his novels. Both developments anticipated the direction his career took after the outbreak of war in 1914. Both suggest that even if no war had occurred, he would not have been content to live out his life as a Grand Old Man of English literature.

The likelihood of a catastrophic world war loomed largest in Wells' imagination, a war of unprecedented dimensions that would either wreck civilization or move the survivors to reorganize the whole structure of society. When it came, he pointed out in *Anticipations,* it would be not a polite scrimmage between professional armies on nineteenth-century lines but rather "a monstrous thrust and pressure of people against people." The distinction between combatants and noncombatants would be hopelessly blurred, and each belligerent state would be "organized as a whole to fight as a whole."[19] "No man," he added in 1908, "can mark the limits of the destruction of a great European conflict were it to occur at the present time."[20]

19. *Anticipations of the Reaction of Mechanical and Scientific Progress upon Human Life and Thought* (New York, 1902), pp. 200, 203.

20. *First and Last Things* (New York, 1908), p. 223.

But it was through the medium of the scientific romance that he delivered most of his warnings before 1914 on the implications of war for twentieth-century man. *In the Days of the Comet* (1906) included a fine apocalyptic scene of Europe at war, France and England against Germany, just before the tail of a comet collided with the earth's atmosphere and miraculously brought men to their senses. Two later romances, *The War in the Air* (1908) and *The World Set Free* (1914, first published serially, December 1913 to May 1914), recorded disastrous world wars. In both books most of the countries of the world were eventually involved in war. Heavy bombing by military aircraft, financial and economic ruin, and the failure of civilian morale resulted in the breakdown of civilization. *The World Set Free* actually chronicled a world war fought with atomic bombs, manufactured from an artificial element, an idea suggested to Wells by Soddy's books on radioactivity.

As Wells' historian from the remote future in *The War in the Air* explained, early twentieth-century people had blundered into catastrophe in the best of spirits, confident that they were secure from all real harm:

> Progress had marched as it seemed invincible about the earth, never now to rest again. For three hundred years and more the long, steadily accelerated diastole of Europeanised civilisation had been in progress: towns had been multiplying, populations increasing, values rising, new countries developing; thought, literature, knowledge unfolding and spreading. It seemed but a part of the process that every year the instruments of war were vaster and more powerful, and that armies and explosives outgrew all other growing things. . . .
>
> Three hundred years of diastole, and then came the swift and unexpected systole, like the closing of a fist. They could not understand it was a systole.

They could not think of it as anything but a jolt, a hitch, a mere oscillatory indication of the swiftness of their progress. Collapse, though it happened all about them, remained incredible. Presently some falling mass smote them down, or the ground opened beneath their feet. They died incredulous.[21]

The lesson was clear, and it could be read in many other scattered premonitions, in the consumptive socialist Masterman's diatribe on the "Sickness of the World" in *Kipps,* in George Ponderevo's fear in *Tono-Bungay* that humanity —like radium—might spin out its career in "atomic decay," in an essay first published in 1909 that warned of the dangers of total war and a collapse of the world's "unscientific" system of currency and finance.[22] Measured against what most scholars and experts were thinking in the early years of the century, Wells' uncannily accurate prophecies are a disturbing reminder to the specialized intelligence of the advantages of amateurism in social analysis. With no training and only random reading, he managed to outguess the professors.[23] His imagination was more elastic, his vision broader, and he had a wider variety of sources of information to check one against the other.

Wells' preoccupation in prewar years with the coming world crisis can also be studied in the changing character

21. *The War in the Air* (New York, 1908), pp. 341–42; cf. the similar passage in *The World Set Free* (New York, 1914), pp. 117–19.

22. *Kipps* (New York, 1905), pp. 327–33; *Tono-Bungay* (New York, 1909), pp. 386–87; "The Possible Collapse of Civilisation," in *Social Forces in England and America* (New York, 1914), pp. 383–89.

23. Cf., e.g., the papers in Wells' *Social Forces in England and America,* written between 1904 and 1914 and published in the spring of 1914, and the twelfth volume of the *Cambridge Modern History* (1910), with its embarrassing predictions of the progress of Russian democracy, the blessings of arms races, Germany's stabilizing role in central Europe, and the rosy future of Western civilization.

of his novels after 1911. His earlier heroes, much as events in their lives were often borrowed from Wells' own life, did not necessarily share his thoughts. But with Richard Remington in *The New Machiavelli* in 1911 the typical Wellsian hero began to think and talk more and more like his creator; all of Wells' later novels are populated with mouthpieces, faithful spokesmen of his current views on world reconstruction. They succeed or fail, from the artistic point of view, as they succeed or fail in soaking up a semblance of reality from Wells' own intensely vital personality.[24] By this criterion, none of the heroes invented between 1911 and 1914 succeeded. But most of them reflected Wells' increasing impatience with the drift of world affairs: Remington, the young politician sickened by the aimlessness of British political life in *The New Machiavelli;* Stratton, the publisher in *The Passionate Friends,* determined to awaken the world-mind by an encyclopedic integration of all knowledge; and Benham, the apostle of spiritual aristocracy and world brotherhood in *The Research Magnificent.* Each was a missionary soulfully resolved to rescue humanity from a

24. Throughout the present book lines delivered by characters in Wells' fiction will often be used to represent Wells' own views. All of his later novels and half the earlier ones are equipped with at least one obvious mouthpiece. Aldous Huxley and more recent novelists of ideas follow the same practice, usually with more skill and subtlety than Wells. To ascertain whether a character is speaking for Wells requires only the briefest check with nonfiction titles written about the same time, and a general familiarity with Wells' social philosophy. Some of the most important and consistent spokesmen of Wells in his novels are Remington in *The New Machiavelli,* Stratton in *The Passionate Friends,* Benham in *The Research Magnificent,* Britling in *Mr. Britling Sees It Through,* Huss in *The Undying Fire,* Hardy in *The Secret Places of the Heart,* Barnstaple in *Men Like Gods,* Clissold in *The World of William Clissold,* Steele in *The Anatomy of Frustration,* Wilbeck in *Apropos of Dolores,* and Uncle Robert Kentlake in *Babes in the Darkling Wood.*

decadent traditional way of life that had lost its meaning. But each went his own uncertain way. In the variety of their schemes for salvation may be seen Wells' own sense of frustration after the failure of his attempt to convert the Fabian Society and after it became clear that the "New Republic" prophesied in *Anticipations* and *Mankind in the Making*, or anything remotely like it, was not after all likely to materialize. Wells the successful literary man was enjoying life to the full. Contemporary descriptions find him overflowing with animal spirits and good humor.[25] But Wells the prophet—speaking now through one fictitious hero, and now another—was already searching restlessly for a cause dynamic enough to bring his thoughts and energies into new focus.

The prophet's search did not last long. In 1914 the world went to war, and the conflagration that followed met all his requirements.

The spiritual history of the first World War remains to be written. What E. M. Forster says of G. Lowes Dickinson might be said of thousands of Western minds: the "shock broke something in him which was never mended, and when at the close of his life he again functioned he had evolved a new apparatus, not repaired the old."[26] As Wells himself wrote years later, "No intelligent brain that passed through the experience of the Great War emerged without being profoundly changed. Our vision of life was revised in

25. One of the best is in A. G. Gardiner, *The Pillars of Society* (London, 1916), pp. 285–92. Wells faithfully rendered life at Easton Glebe, his Essex country home, in *Mr. Britling Sees It Through,* New York, 1916. See also, for homely details, the reminiscences of the Wells' Swiss governess, Mathilde M. Meyer, in *H. G. Wells and His Family,* Edinburgh, 1956.

26. Forster, *Goldsworthy Lowes Dickinson* (London, Arnold, 1934), p. 155.

outline and detail alike."[27] But a few random quotations cannot convey the quality of the change. The war crushed hopes, raised fears of the futility of Western civilization, set off a revival of religious feeling, killed outright half a generation of European youth, and discredited much of the thought and many of the thinkers of the prewar generation. Writers who matured before the war are divided from writers who matured after the war by the same gulf that separates Herodotus from Thucydides and Erasmus from Luther. As the shadow of the first World War lengthens, the more it seems to deserve its old title, "the Great War." All the world's disasters since 1918 have flowed inevitably from that first cause with the furious logic of classical tragedy.

The war found Wells on the brink of forty-eight, too old and too well prepared for it intellectually to be made over again, but young enough to be deeply affected.[28] Between 1914 and 1918 a major shift in emphasis occurred in his writing. A new sense of urgency invaded all his work, and within a few years he had transformed himself from a successful social novelist (who was also, by the way, a Utopian socialist) into a fully committed prophet of world order, who still wrote novels, but used them almost exclusively as vehicles for propaganda. In his own words he was one of those people "who were violently roused by the Great War. I feel that I have been coming awake and finding out things ever since that tremendous shock of August 1914. I had what I may call a *sense of change* before, but my sense of

27. *Experiment in Autobiography*, p. 569; cf. *The Bulpington of Blup* (New York, 1933), p. 192.

28. "I will confess I was taken by surprise by the Great War. Yet I saw long ahead how it could happen, and wove fantastic stories about it, I let my imagination play about it, but at the bottom of my heart I did not feel and believe it would really be let happen": *The Way the World Is Going* (Garden City, N.Y., 1929), p. 169.

change was enormously quickened by that illuminating catastrophe and its desolating consequences. And it turned me away from imaginative literature into a new direction."[29] The role Wells chose for himself altered his public, as it altered his work. It lost him one kind of reader and gained him another. He began to reach a wider but less select audience. His influence grew increasingly less personal and more diffuse. The world, by degrees, swallowed him up.[30]

The best index to the intensity of Wells' commitment to a prophetic career after 1914 is, of course, the subject matter of his books. With an old journalist's reverence for punctuality, he continued to produce as many books, on schedule, as before, but save for rare occasional pages and chapters the writing of his last thirty years was devoted, with an obsessive enthusiasm incomprehensible to most of his critics, to the task of saving Western civilization from its sins. The very directness of his approach, his determination to educate and preach and guide, spoiled his art. A great reputation was laid waste. But enough has been written of his interests before 1914 to suggest why the first World War, although it was in itself less climactic and apocalyptic than Wells had prophesied it would be, should have driven him to the extreme of sacrificing his literary ambitions on the altar of his social philosophy. H. L. Mencken detected the change in orientation even before the war had ended. Wells

29. *After Democracy* (London, 1932), pp. 73–74.

30. See, e.g., the self-conscious acceptance of the prophetic role in *Washington and the Riddle of Peace* (New York, 1922), p. 312: "My moods have fluctuated between hope and despair. But I know that I believe so firmly in this great World at Peace that lies so close to our own, ready to come into being as our wills turn towards it, that I must needs go about this present world of disorder and darkness like an exile doing such feeble things as I can towards the world of my desire, now hopefully, now bitterly, as the moods may happen, until I die."

suffered, he said, "from a messianic delusion—and once a man begins to suffer from a messianic delusion his days as a serious artist are ended." His ego bloated by his popularity, Wells had deserted greatness to become a "merchant of banal pedagogics . . . a hawker of sociological liver-pills."[31]

Milked of its venom, Mencken's diagnosis was fairly sound. Wells wrote more than twenty novels after the outbreak of the first World War, of which nearly a dozen concerned Wellsian heroes who had dedicated their lives, in one way or another, to the achievement of a world state. Three were Utopias, five were case studies of human types inimical to the cause of world order, and only one or two can be classed as pure art or entertainment. To these titles must be added three encyclopedic outlines of knowledge slanted to advertise his ideas and promote world-mindedness, more than a dozen collections of articles on world affairs, eight prophetic books arguing his schemes and projects for world reconstruction, and a series of five long short stories and three film scripts—all published as separate volumes and all devoted to the world crisis. Much of this work had been anticipated by prewar volumes, especially by the later prewar novels and romances. But whereas before the war nearly two-thirds of his books were fairly innocent of social philosophy, practically every title he published after 1914 carried a heavy freight of ideas on world reorganization. Again to quote Sir Arthur Salter, "No one will understand Wells, or his place in history, who does not place this dominant and enduring passion in the place it merits."[32] If Wells is measured by his own yardstick, the prophetic passion furnishes in itself a sufficient explanation for his whole career—at any rate, after 1914.

31. Mencken, "The Late Mr. Wells," *Prejudices,* First Series (New York, Knopf, 1919), pp. 28–29.
32. Salter, *Personality in Politics,* p. 121.

From the first, Wells treated the war as a supreme opportunity to achieve a world state, in line with his prophecy in
Anticipations that the old order would collapse from the
sheer weight and complexity of its military establishments
in time of war. Unlike Shaw and Russell, however, he mis-
judged the intentions of the Western Allies. For the first
year or two of the conflict he took up the popular cry that
the Western Allies represented the peace-loving cosmopolitan forces in Europe, whereas the Central Powers stood for
militarism, rampant nationalism, and authoritarianism. His
early wartime journalism broadcast confidence that Western opinion would insist on some kind of world government
as a prime war aim. The Allies would win the war, and they
would make it, in his own phrase, "the war that will end
war."[33]

Little by little, as the war dragged on long beyond his
expectations and the moral issue between Germany and the
West grew more and more uncertain, Wells withdrew his
confidence in Western intentions and his truculent attitude
toward Germany. But the moral issues behind the war itself
remained clear, and he hammered away at these with a
tireless tenacity in one book after another. The World War
was "a time of incalculable plasticity," in which constructive liberal thought had an unprecedented opportunity to
redraw the map of Europe, secure world peace, and plan
a sane collective economic world order to replace warmon-
gering private capitalism. Yet it was also "the end of an
age; the slow, murderous testing and condemnation of
whole systems of ideas that had bound men uneasily in

33. Wells entitled his first volume of wartime journalism *The War
That Will End War:* New York, 1914; cf. Bernard Shaw's *Common
Sense about the War* (1914). But Wells and Shaw did agree, from the
start, on the need for some kind of postwar League of Nations. For
Wells at his worst on the question of war guilt see "The Reckoning
for the War," *London Magazine, 33* (1914), 407–17.

communities for all our lives."[34] The old order had de-
faulted and gone into bankruptcy. A great concentration
of will and moral energy was needed to replace it with
something fundamentally better.

Under the stress and excitement of the war—Wells even
spent part of the summer of 1916 on the French and Italian
fronts as a correspondent—he shocked his rationalist friends
and raised a small storm in theological circles by announc-
ing his conversion to a species of theism of his own invention in a book published in 1917, *God the Invisible King*.
Wells' God was a finite, emergent deity, the evolving will
and mind of humanity, a direct translation of his humanism
into the language of theology. God the Invisible King had
the appearance of a *volte-face;* but it was only another effort
to enlist recruits for the world state. Followers of the finite
Invisible King were bound by their faith to work for the
transfiguration of the world into a "theocracy," into a
"world kingdom of God": in short, into a universal state.
After the war he recanted, blaming his resort to theological
language at least in part on nervous strain caused by the
war, though not until he had written a theological novel
along the general lines of Mrs. Humphry Ward's *Robert
Elsmere* and a dialogue novel based on the Book of Job.[35]

The war also brought Wells into the League of Nations
movement in 1917–19. But his work in the League of Free
Nations Association and later the League of Nations Union

34. *Boon* (New York, 1915), p. 272.
35. *The Soul of a Bishop* (New York, 1917) and *The Undying Fire,*
(New York, 1919). Dozens of articles, pamphlets, and books were published pro and con the "Invisible King" between 1917 and 1919. Two
of the more substantial attacks came from opposing camps: William
Archer's pungent *God and Mr. Wells* (London, 1917) for the Rationalist Press Association, and L. E. Binns' *Mr. Wells's Invisible King*
(London, 1919) for the S.P.C.K. See Wells' account of his "resort to
God" in *Experiment in Autobiography,* pp. 573–78.

proved just as futile as his misadventures with theism. From
the first he insisted on the setting up of world councils to
replace national military establishments and foreign offices
with a world security system strong enough to keep the
peace. With Leonard Woolf he organized a "research committee" drawn from members of the League of Nations
Union to work out practical proposals for the peace conference. The committee existed primarily on paper, and its
only publications, two pamphlets, were written almost entirely by Wells himself.[36] They had little impact on opinion
or events in 1919. And the deliberations at Versailles produced a settlement as un-Wellsian as any settlement could
likely have been.

The year 1919 was decisive in Wells' life, perhaps as decisive as 1914. Unlike nearly all his colleagues in the League
of Nations Union, Wells washed his hands immediately of
the League created at Versailles and became almost over-
night one of its most implacable hecklers. The failure of
the Powers to surrender one iota of their sovereignty or
even dispense with the apparatus of prewar diplomacy convinced him of the essential uselessness of the League. He

36. The two pamphlets were "The Idea of the League of Nations:
Prolegomena to the Study of World-Organisation" and "The Way to
the League of Nations: A Brief Sketch of the Practical Steps Needed
for the Formation of a League," both London, 1919. The members
of the Research Committee of the League of Nations Union at the
time of publication of the first pamphlet were Viscount Grey, Gilbert
Murray, J. A. Spender, A. E. Zimmern, H. Wickham Steed, Lionel
Curtis, William Archer, Viscount Bryce, and Wells. Viscount Bryce's
name was omitted in the second pamphlet, and Ernest Barker, G.
Lowes Dickinson, John Hilton, and Leonard Woolf were added.
Wells served as the committee's chairman. See *Fate of Man*, p. 72, for
Wells' inability to weld the committee into a team. See also Henry R.
Winkler, *The League of Nations Movement in Great Britain, 1914–
1919*, New Brunswick, N.J., 1952. Wells' contribution to the move-
ment is studied briefly on pp. 41–46 and passim.

also criticized the absence of Russia and Germany, after which he was almost pleased at the American decision to remain outside. He attacked the veto provision in the Council and the League's impotence to enforce disarmament. He attacked the terms of peace in the Treaty of Versailles as the vindictive, short-sighted work of a congress of imperialistic conquerors who had divided the spoils of victory among themselves in the worst traditions of "Great Power" diplomacy, sowing the seeds of fresh conflict. At a dozen points—in China, in the Tyrol, in the Polish Corridor, in the Saar, in the prohibition of Austrian *Anschluss*—the peace treaties were perilously unfair. And the League, "that homunculus in a bottle," that "little corner of Balfourian jobs and gentility,"[37] would be powerless to prevent war when, at one of these danger points, friction was fanned to flame.

Wells came to the decision in 1919 that the war—which had seemed at first an almost splendid adventure, a chance to destroy militarism and the nation-state system, a crusade on the plains of Europe for the peace of the world—had accomplished nothing after all. The excitement of the autumn of 1914, the fresh hopes raised by the entrance of the United States, the Russian Revolution, and the dream of an authentic League of Free Nations had all changed to ashes. The opportunity had been kicked away, not out of malice but out of ignorance and narrow-mindedness. The statesmen of the Western world did not see the gravity or the dimensions of the crisis they had to solve, because their minds had been formed in another and suddenly remote age.

If some of his wartime books had misled or confused readers, Wells left no room for doubt after 1919. The world crisis was no longer a subject to be imagined in scientific

37. *The Outline of History* (2 vols. New York, 1920), 2, 558; *The Salvaging of Civilization* (New York, 1921), p. 43.

romances or welcomed as a chance for easy heroism. At just
the time when Oswald Spengler was challenging German
readers with a more esoteric interpretation of the maladies
of Western man, Wells was telling the English-speaking
world in one of his first postwar books, *The Salvaging of
Civilization,* that civilization had shipwrecked. The world
had arrived at the point reached by the Roman and Han
empires in their first years of decay. "This civilization in
which we are living," he wrote, "is tumbling down, and I
think tumbling down very fast . . . I think rapid enormous
efforts will be needed to save it; and . . . I see no such efforts
being made at the present time."[38] Salvaging civilization
turned out to be a vaster job than he would have dreamed
possible only a few years before. The Edwardian Wells had
put his faith in the emergence of a "New Republican"
movement, a movement materializing from out of nowhere,
or at best from groups like the Fabian Society. The Wells
of the war years had hoped for bold initiatives from the Allied governments. Now Wells was convinced there could
be no new world order unless sweeping reforms in Western
education, and a massive campaign of re-education and
propaganda at the adult level, worked a real revolution in
men's minds. He had never been indifferent to the importance of education and propaganda: far from it. But he had
never assigned education so prominent a place in his program. Now the world was involved in "a race between education and catastrophe" to decide the destiny of civilization.[39] If the race was lost, the West would continue its
headlong rush to ruin, and no better world would rise in
its place.

Wells did not merely go on rumbling threats and invent-
ing slogans and glib formulas for world reconstruction. In
the years after the first World War, he made a systematic

38. *Salvaging of Civilization,* p. 45.
39. *Outline of History,* 2, 594.

attempt to re-educate the public mind through the writing of a trilogy of encyclopedic surveys of knowledge that have served ever since as models of dignified and yet thoroughly readable *vulgarisation*. At the same time they were intensely partisan books, written to adjust the thinking of their readers to the world perspectives of the postwar era and make the idea of a planned world order seem to grow naturally and necessarily out of the facts of biology, history, and the social sciences.

The first volume in the trilogy, *The Outline of History,* actually germinated in a project suggested to Wells in 1918 by his experiences with his colleagues—most of them old public school boys and university graduates—in the League of Nations Union. It had been intended as a guide for history teachers, to replace the old national history which Wells supposed had done so much to warp the minds of the reluctant world-planners at Versailles in their formative years. To write it, Wells had to give up producing novels for a few seasons, and although he went back again in 1922 to turning out an annual novel, the missed years reflected his determination to subordinate all his energies to what he now considered his true calling. "I set to work," as he recalled in his autobiography some years later, "undeterred by my burning boats, with the *Encyclopaedia Britannica* at my elbow, to get the general shape of history sketched out."[40] The results had more the quality of fiction than of fact, with all the merits and defects of all Wells' work: scamped, thin, and shallow in detail and method, but projected with penetrating imagination on a scale no professional historian had ever dared to write history before, and brimming over with scores of perceptive suggestions.

As it happened, there was a ready market in 1920 for the kind of book Wells had written, especially in the United

40. *Experiment in Autobiography,* p. 614.

States. Some historians, the protagonists of the "New History," for example, who insisted on making the professional historian responsible for intellectual, social, and economic history as well as "past politics," found *The Outline of History* an intriguing experiment. Authentic world history was just then coming into vogue. The *Outline* appeared at roughly the same time as Spengler's *Decline of the West* in Germany, the first volumes of Henri Berr's *L'Evolution de l'humanité* in France, and James Harvey Robinson's *Mind in the Making* in the United States. But it was the general reading public, perplexed by the gigantic dimensions of the first World War, who appreciated the *Outline* most, above all perplexed Americans struggling to make some sort of mental adjustment to their new role in world affairs. The book ran through several editions, outsold every book save the Bible during one publishing year in the United States, and earned more money than most of Wells' other books put together. In its first twelve years, one and a half million copies were sold in the United States, one hundred thousand in Britain, and thousands more in translation.[41]

The success of the *Outline* prompted him to write two other surveys: *The Science of Life,* an outline of biology done in collaboration with Julian Huxley and Wells' son, G. P. Wells (1929–30), and *The Work, Wealth and Happiness of Mankind,* a skillfully integrated study of the social, economic, and political life of contemporary Western man (1931). Both books sold well, and like the *Outline* both were written to a thesis. *The Science of Life* closed with a study of the highest form of life, *Homo sapiens,* in process of attempting to create a still higher level of life: a collective human mind and will that would find political self-expression in a world commonwealth. And *The Work, Wealth and Happiness of Mankind* offered unlimited possibilities

41. From Wells' own figures in chapter 12 of "Exasperations."

for world state propaganda, all of which Wells exploited fully. Armed with as much basic information as the three volumes of the trilogy supplied, the citizen of the modern state would be able, Wells thought, to respond intelligently to the imperatives of twentieth-century life. Later in the 1930's, during his term of office as president of the Educational Science Section of the British Association for the Advancement of Science, he also published a series of papers recommending reforms in the "informative content" of school curricula in line with the educational philosophy of the trilogy and elaborating on suggestions already made in *The Work, Wealth and Happiness of Mankind* for the writing of a new type of encyclopedia to integrate all human knowledge.[42]

The trilogy of educational books reshaped Wells' public reputation even more than his wartime work. Although many intellectuals continued to admire him, he failed to capture the younger generation in the 1920's. Literary critics deserted him en masse. But he succeeded in multiplying his points of contact with the general literate public. He missed no chances. However incongruous their setting, articles by Wells on world affairs or history or education made their way into newspapers like the *Star, The Daily Mail,* and *Sunday Pictorial* and magazines on the order of *John o'London's Weekly* and *Picture Post.* In the United States the same articles reached a similar audience in the *American Magazine, Liberty,* and *Collier's.* Wells' voice was familiar to B.B.C. listeners from the early days of broadcasting. He wrote several film plays, of which two—*Things to Come* and *Man Who Could Work Miracles*—were made into motion pictures, with much fanfare, in the mid-1930's. He undertook several long lecture tours in the United States and Australia. Everywhere and in every me-

42. *World Brain,* Garden City, N.Y., 1938.

dium he taught the same lessons, preached the same gospel, and delivered the same warnings. Much of it soared well over the heads of his public; they were more interested by now in the celebrity than the prophet. But he persevered. For Wells the widening gap between the intellectuals and the masses, in practice at least, hardly existed. Somehow he managed to go on writing in a vein and style that had the rare faculty of pleasing both, or of failing to please either.

Yet at the same time that Wells was extending and probably overextending himself in a Sisyphean attempt to make world citizens of the new literate masses, he had returned after about 1925 to his old conviction that no world revolution could be successfully planned and executed without the leadership of a revolutionary elite of what he liked to call "functional" people—in effect, scientists, engineers, educators, industrial managers, and public administrators. This return to the thoroughgoing elitism of his Edwardian days marked the last major turning point in his prophetic career. He did not repudiate his early postwar position on the all-importance of education: he continued to insist that a revolutionary conspiracy against the old order had no chance of success without the fullest possible use of all the media of communication and education, and that much of its day-to-day work would be educational work. But enlightenment alone would not overthrow the nation-state system. Enlightened opinion had to be mobilized and guided, and by 1925 he was no longer able to believe even faintly in the possibility of revolutionary initiatives from any existing political institutions. Leadership would have to be sought in a conspiratorial movement outside the law. The Western governments had failed at Versailles, and they had done nothing to redeem themselves since. The Labour party, in office in Britain for the first time in 1924, had behaved like any of the so-called capitalist parties; and democratic France had handled the Ruhr crisis in Germany in

1923–24 with a reckless contempt for human decency. Everywhere democratic politicians were showing the same disconcerting disposition to drift and play politics as usual, as if there had never been a World War. Only in Soviet Russia, ruled by a revolutionary elite, had the war led to anything like a new social order, although Soviet policy suffered from the intrinsic narrowness and meanness of Marxism.[43] In 1922 and again in 1923 he had even run for Parliament as a Labour candidate, in hopes of being able to influence the Labour position on education; and for many years he had been lending his full support to the proportional representation movement in Britain. Now he swung abruptly around. "A phase of great restlessness and discontent," he wrote, "came upon me in 1923–24."[44]

The first fruits of that restlessness were a long, mostly autobiographical novel of ideas, *The World of William Clissold* (1926) and an address, "Democracy under Revision," given at the Sorbonne in 1927 and issued as a short book in the same year. But not until *The Open Conspiracy: Blue Prints for a World Revolution,* published in 1928, was Wells able to offer his public a compact, clear, and detailed statement of his thinking on the strategy of world revolution. *The Open Conspiracy* reflected his final disillusionment with democracy in the special context of the 1920's, but it also fulfilled the leading tendencies in his social thought over a span of thirty years. It gathered all the threads together. It outlined in plausible detail a world conspiracy of "functional" men with interests and responsibilities transcending national frontiers, pledged to work

43. See *Russia in the Shadows* (New York, 1921), an account of Wells' trip to Russia in 1920. He took a position in some ways parallel to Bertrand Russell's. Russell visited Russia in the same year and like Wells was granted an interview with Lenin; see Russell's *Practice and Theory of Bolshevism*, 1920.

44. *Experiment in Autobiography*, p. 631.

for the supersedure of the established political order by a
unified system of scientifically managed world controls; to
this program for world revolution he remained loyal the
rest of his life, down to 1944. Wells may never have produced one really outstanding, carefully reasoned, powerfully written prophetic manifesto, a *Reflections on Violence*
or a *Decline of the West* or a *Revolt of the Masses*. But in
The Open Conspiracy he struck nearer than ever before or
after to the dramatic tension of a Great Book. It was as
close as he could come.

Wells harped on the idea of an "open conspiracy," by
one name or another, in nearly all his writing after 1928.
It appeared prominently in the closing pages of *The Work,
Wealth and Happiness of Mankind,* it figured under one
metamorphosis or another in many of his later novels, and
The Open Conspiracy itself passed through several editions
and reprintings before it disappeared at last, never very
enthusiastically received, under the cumbersome title *What
Are We to Do with Our Lives?*[45]

The Open Conspiracy had been written when Wells was
already past sixty, but the advance of old age had no effect
on his productivity. He brought out novels and stories that
were parables of the world crisis, like *Mr. Blettsworthy on
Rampole Island* (1928), and *The Croquet Player* (1936);
novels that were scathing satires of opponents of world reconstruction, like *The Autocracy of Mr. Parham* (1930)
and *The Bulpington of Blup* (1933); and novels about a
second World War that paved the way for a Utopia created
by a militant party of "open conspirators," like *The Shape
of Things to Come* (1933) and *The Holy Terror* (1939). He
repeated his message over and over again, ringing, it seemed,

45. *The Open Conspiracy* first appeared in 1928 with a slightly
revised second edition in 1930, published only in Britain. *What Are
We to Do with Our Lives?* followed in 1931, in effect a third edition.
There was also a Thinker's Library edition of the latter, London,
1935.

all the possible changes, and when the second World War arrived—just a few months earlier than he had predicted in *The Shape of Things to Come* six years before—he plunged into the business of writing books and articles about it with more energy at first than he had mustered during the early years of the first World War.

But this time his mood was much darker. Although he never seriously entertained the possibility of an Axis victory and gauged accurately at the time the military significance of the Battle of Britain and Hitler's invasion of Russia, he had from the start a gnawing fear founded on past disappointments that the war would end in another inconclusive peace settlement *à la* Versailles. "Hitler," he said, "like the Hohenzollerns, is a mere offensive pustule on the face of a deeply ailing world. To get rid of him and his Nazis will be no more a cure for the world's ills than scraping will heal measles."[46] Even before the war actually began, he had predicted that a second World War would turn out to be a second aimless world holocaust. "We are at present rapidly experiencing," he had written a few months before the invasion of Poland, "a repetition of 1914–1919 on a vastly more disastrous scale." The losers would be blamed for the war and made to pay all over again. "Another insincere attempt to organize 'collective security' on the lines of the League of Nations, another unstable League of victors, will simply accumulate the necessary resentments for another collapse into still more violent conflict."[47]

46. *The New World Order* (New York, 1940), p. 9.

47. *Fate of Man*, pp. 62, 63. "The spectacle of evil in the world during the past half-dozen years—the wanton destruction of homes, the ruthless hounding of decent folk into exile, the bombings of open cities, the cold-blooded massacres and mutilations of children and defenseless gentle people, the rapes and filthy humiliations and, above all, the return of deliberate and organized torture, mental torment and fear to a world from which such things had seemed wellnigh banished—has come near to breaking my spirit altogether": ibid., pp. 85–86.

For the first three years he wore as brave a face as he could. With the help of a hand-picked committee of friends presided over by Lord Sankey, he devoted much of his time to the drafting of a declaration of human rights, which he submitted to national leaders and eminent liberals and socialists all over the world in hopes of launching a world-wide debate on war aims. The declaration was a carefully worded amalgam of cosmopolitanism, liberalism, and socialism. It envisaged a world state and a collectivized world economy; it guaranteed to the world citizen adequate food, shelter, and clothing for the realization of all his mental and physical capacities, complete legal equality, due process of law, the right to education, the right to work, the right to own personal property, the right of privacy, freedom of movement, and freedom of speech and conscience.[48] Wells kept working on the "Sankey Declaration," as he called it, for several years after the Sankey Committee had finished with it in 1940. He simplified the language of the original draft, struck out or amended a few clauses too narrowly Western in conception, published one or another version in nearly all his wartime books, had it translated into Basic English and several foreign languages, and tried to get copies distributed as widely as possible. Although it fed into the stream of ideas that eventuated in the Atlantic

48. The first draft was published in a letter to the London *Times* (October 25, 1939), p. 6. It may also be studied in *The Rights of Man* (Harmondsworth, Middlesex, 1940), pp. 14–17. The original text of the Sankey Declaration based on this draft appeared in *The Common Sense of War and Peace* (Harmondsworth, Middlesex, 1940), pp. 81–89. Wells' final version of the Declaration is available in *'42 to '44: A Contemporary Memoir upon Human Behaviour during the Crisis of the World Revolution* (London, 1944), pp. 45–48. Both in the first and in the last versions of the Declaration he did not include a democratic form of government among the "Rights of Man." Its inclusion in all the other versions was obviously a politic concession to the feelings of other members of the Sankey Committee.

Charter and the Universal Declaration of Human Rights approved by the U.N. General Assembly in 1948, his Declaration had an essentially unsuccessful career. No government, no national leader ever endorsed it.

There was other work to be done: a tour of the United States in 1940, during which Wells flew 24,000 miles to dozens of audiences in major cities from Los Angeles to New York, delivering a lecture, "Two Hemispheres or One World," which may have helped to prepare American opinion for Wendell Willkie's *One World*. And more books: he published nine new books between 1940 and 1942 alone, including two large novels and another revolutionary manifesto, entitled *Phoenix: A Summary of the Inescapable Conditions of World Reorganisation* (1942), which added only a little to the program spelled out in *The Open Conspiracy*.

But not even Wells could go on forever. The Sankey Declaration fell on deaf ears, the Allied governments showed no promise of planning to convert the second World War into a Wellsian world revolution, no Open Conspirators appeared, *Phoenix* sold poorly in Britain, and no American publisher—except Haldeman-Julius of Girard, Kansas—was found to publish it at all. To these omens of prophetic failure was added a serious physical collapse in 1942, during the writing of *Phoenix,* from which Wells never fully recovered. He had kept his youthful vigor and bounce down through his seventy-fifth year. Now, at 76, the last characteristic traces of youthfulness vanished, leaving him suddenly old, angry, ailing, and tired.

After his illness in 1942, his literary output began, at last, to fall off sharply. What little he did write suffered from an almost incoherent bitterness. *Crux Ansata* (1943) was little more than a tantrum, a feeble tirade against the Roman Catholic Church. In 1944 followed *'42 to '44: A Contemporary Memoir* and, if Wells had lived to see it through

the press, a still unpublished "Exasperations: The Last
Testament of H. G. Wells"—two collections of essays and
newspaper articles heavily charged with recrimination and
abuse. Generals, priests, his old colleagues on the Sankey
Committee, Churchill, the royal family, Dean Inge, Sir
Richard Acland, and the world in general fell under the old
man's irascible axe. He had been a fool, he thought, to expect anything of anyone. Nor would there be peace when
the fighting stopped: "The occupation and disarmament of
Germany will end nothing; it will only inaugurate a scram-
ble of such egocentric 'liberators' as de Gaulle and his like,
of the Roman Catholic Church, of the Communist Party,
of the patriotic Polish nationalists in exile, of every silly
little intractable patriotism, and of the Big Business and
banking systems, with their immense stupid cunning, to
gain control of our exhausted world."[49]

Then his spirit crumbled altogether. *Mind at the End of
Its Tether,* with its sentence of unconditional doom, appeared early in 1945, and on August 13, 1946, Wells died
in the aristocratic Nash Terrace house facing Regent's
Park in London, where he had survived all the air raids of
the war years. He had lived just long enough to hear the
news from Hiroshima and observe the first signs of a serious
rift between Soviet Russia and the West. According to Sir
Ernest Barker, who saw him at a reception at Cambridge
University during the war, he wanted his epitaph to read:
"God damn you all: I told you so."[50]

THE DIAGNOSIS

Especially in those last two years, but to a certain indefin-
able degree through all his adult life, Wells was a victim

49. *'42 to '44,* p. 77.
50. Barker, *Age and Youth* (London, Oxford University Press,
1953), p. 108.

of what his Harley Street nerve specialist Dr. Martineau in *The Secret Places of the Heart* described as a new mental disease, the " 'sense of a coming smash . . . a loss of confidence in the general background. So that we seem to float over abysses.' " It was, said Dr. Martineau, a new state of mind, " 'almost the normal state with whole classes of intelligent people' " since 1914.[51] The sense of a coming smash, of a crisis in civilization, overwhelmed Wells' congenital optimism and ruined him as a literary artist. If the account of his career given above seems to make too much of one side of a many-sided personality, it is only because Wells himself chose to let his prophetic instincts rule, and warp, his public life. And, as Dr. Martineau insisted, the fear of a world disaster has shot to epidemic proportions in Western society since the first World War. Wells was carried along on an intellectual tidal wave. Diagnosticians of the sickness of Western civilization have created a whole new species of literature, which by now must have a bibliography running into thousands of volumes. Before studying at closer range in the chapters ahead Wells' formula for world reorganization and his vision of Utopia, it may be useful to review briefly his diagnosis of the twentieth-century crisis in civilization. Like Wells himself, his interpretation of the world's ills was rooted in nineteenth-century anxieties and resentments, but it also anticipated much of the thinking of the newer prophets.

No thinker as impatient or undisciplined as Wells could have settled on one single consistent set of explanations for the twentieth-century world crisis, and there is no use looking for one in his writings. He took full advantage of his license as a prophet to exaggerate first one dilemma and then another, and then still another, and for the sake of rhetorical effect make each bear the whole responsibility.

51. *The Secret Places of the Heart* (New York, 1922), p. 6; cf. Wells' Dr. Norbert in *The Croquet Player* (New York, 1937), pp. 85–86.

At times he stressed fundamental limiting factors in the external universe and in human nature.[52] In his own way he was just as capable of an Augustinian outlook on predestination and original sin as the glummest disciples of Karl Barth. But these were perennial problems rather than specific causes of a specific social collapse; consideration of Wells' ideas on nature and man must be deferred until the next chapter. At other times he confined himself to calling attention to the immediate symptoms of the crisis, to war and business depressions and the failure of social morale in the twentieth century itself. Often he gave his diagnosis a historical dimension, stepping back a few centuries to survey the impact of the mechanization of industry on the scale of modern life. At least once, in several provocative passages in *The Outline of History,* he sketched a whole philosophy of history that has much the same sweep and scope as Spengler's or Toynbee's, though inevitably it lacks the depth.[53]

Since it incorporates all the levels of Wells' social diagnosis, this embryonic philosophy of history in the *Outline* is perhaps the best place to begin; and in the *Outline,* although he is conventionally tagged as an exponent of the linear theory of history,[54] he began with the proposition that human communities pass through cycles of growth and

52. E.g. in *Mr. Blettsworthy on Rampole Island* and *The Croquet Player.*

53. For Wells' rather sour opinion of Spengler and Toynbee see *The New America, the New World* (New York, 1935), pp. 1–2, and *Apropos of Dolores* (New York, 1938), pp. 168–69. Toynbee refers several times, and as a rule favorably, to *The Outline of History* and some of Wells' other books in his *A Study of History,* 11 vols. London, 1934–59. See especially Toynbee's appraisal of the *Outline* in *1,* 4–5.

54. See below, p. 81, for misconceptions of Wells' thinking on the problem of human progress. Of course, Wells *wanted* history to be "linear," just as Toynbee holds no brief for the "vain repetitions of the heathen."

decline repeated, though never exactly, again and again throughout history. Every civilized community owed its existence to the work of a creative elite, a small ruling class of inventive personalities who were capable of sustained imaginative response to challenges and opportunities in the natural and social environment. The society growing under their leadership Wells defined as a "community of will." But in time the community of will settled down. The institutions it had created, or expropriated from conquered peoples, hardened. Vested interests in now traditional ways of life prevented the more creative minds from continuing to exercise leadership, and a new sort of ruling class took their place, a class of priests, office-holders, and great propertied families, whose objective was the maintenance of the social status quo and who lacked the will or elasticity of mind to adapt to changing conditions. The "community of will" became a "community of faith and obedience." The more or less free citizens of the community of will found themselves reduced to enslaved and exploited masses, working at the pleasure of prosperous landowners or religious orders of the state. Treated as property, they ceased to be spiritually committed to the community in which they lived. In due time the community was powerfully threatened from without by "barbarians," by still creative and flexible communities of will on the outside, and inevitably it disintegrated and collapsed. Its masses lacked the will to resist; its institutions were weighed down by outmoded conventions; its whole way of life was weakened fatally by the dry rot of inertia.[55]

This reading of history, based obviously on the cyclical

55. *Outline of History*, 2, 140–48. Wells made the identical distinction between societies ruled by "poietic" types and societies ruled by "kinetic" types in *A Modern Utopia* (New York, 1905), pp. 271–73. Cf. Toynbee's idea of a "creative minority" and of "proletarianization," and see below, p. 167, n. 4.

pattern of interaction between nomadic peoples or city-states and river valley civilizations in ancient history, harmonized with Wells' inclination as a trained biologist to look on history, like Spencer before him and Toynbee after him, in terms of the biological concept of challenge and response. The crucial fact about history for Wells was its infinite capacity for change. "We are, as a species," he once wrote, "caught in an irreversible process."[56] Every change brought a challenge, and every challenge demanded an adaptive response. The community of will succeeded because it could adjust its institutions and habits of thought to changing conditions dynamically; it was willing to learn and able to invent. The community of faith and obedience tried to stay put, to cling for dear life to old familiar landmarks and established procedures: sooner or later, despite its accumulated wealth and power and knowledge, it failed.

Against this general background of ideas, Wells suggested that since the breakdown of medieval society in the West in the sixteenth century, and the parallel breakdown of the medieval empires of the Near and Far East, civilization had been stumbling through an interregnum, "an age of confusion." The sustaining moral and political ideas of the old medieval community of faith and obedience—the dream of a resuscitated Roman Empire and its universal Church—had been smashed beyond recovery by the reformations, revolutions, and wars of the sixteenth and early seventeenth centuries.[57] Now, especially since the mid-eighteenth century, the disunited but still chaotically dynamic fragments of the medieval world were confronted with the greatest challenge and the greatest opportunity in human history. Now—and from this point on, the diagnosis may be followed in dozens of Wells' books—revolutions in science and industrial technics had produced a "wild rush of change in

56. *Experiment in Autobiography*, p. 197.
57. *Outline of History*, 2, 215–16.

the pace, scope, materials, scale, and possibilities of human life."[58] The change of scale had "an effect as though upon the customary succession of day and night there were to dawn an unfamiliar illumination from some strange new star, a light altering all visible values, dispelling accepted shadows, revealing things hitherto unknown."[59] In the grip of that new reorienting force, symbolized by the uncontrollable "Boomfood" in Wells' scientific romance *The Food of the Gods,* nothing in the old social order could remain secure from violent change. The machine age had multiplied man's power over nature and his fellow man immensely, bringing peoples once relatively remote from one another into jarring contact. "Applied to warfare," the new mechanized industry "meant that the power to inflict a blow, the power to destroy, was continually increasing" without any corresponding increase in defensive power.[60]

From *Anticipations* and *The Food of the Gods* in his Edwardian days to his last prophetic books, Wells insisted on holding this "change of scale" in human life immediately responsible for the twentieth-century world crisis—not because the new knowledge and the new power were in themselves evil, but because the mechanical revolution had occurred in a civilization divided against itself, spiritually inchoate, unable or unwilling to make the necessary adjustments in its institutions and ways of life and systems of value. The old religion could not adapt itself. The old ruling classes had failed to bring the new energies under control. And, most important of all, the nation-state, the form of political organization that had emerged as a useful makeshift for the mobilizing of local resources after the break-

58. *War in the Air,* p. 97.
59. *The World of William Clissold* (2 vols. New York, 1926), *1, 212.* See ibid., pp. 212–19, for a conveniently compact statement of Wells' interpretation of the Industrial Revolution.
60. *World Set Free,* p. 118.

down of the Roman and medieval syntheses, had become ludicrously obsolete in the new unlimited world economy created by modern mechanical science. As Wells summed up his case in *Washington and the Riddle of Peace* in 1921:

> Disproportionate development of energy and over-strain are the immediate causes of our present troubles; the scale of modern economic enterprise has outgrown the little boundaries of the European States; science and invention have made war so monstrously destructive and disintegrative that victory is swallowed up in disaster; we are in a world of little nations wielding world-wide powers to the general destruction.[61]

The institutions of the old European order were like the sacred megatheria of Rampole Island, in *Mr. Blettsworthy on Rampole Island,* too old to breed but stubborn and noxious enough to prevent the growth of new life and resist natural death indefinitely.[62] In the same way, the rheumatic traditional life, with its moribund institutions and its out-worn habits of mind, lingered on in the twentieth century, unable to regain its own health and vigor, poisoning every effort to construct a new world order. Yet it could not linger for long. The revolution in transport alone had made "communication . . . so swift, far-reaching, universal and intimate, that a community of destiny is dictated inexorably to mankind, either the unity of a common purpose or the unity of a common débâcle."[63] Either the world, unified for the first time in history by Western machinery, would learn to live as one integrated civilization, or it would commit collective suicide.

Failure, then, to adapt to the new scale of material life

61. *Washington and the Riddle of Peace,* p. 297.
62. *Mr. Blettsworthy on Rampole Island* (Garden City, N.Y., 1928), especially pp. 193–211.
63. *New America,* p. 2.

had toppled civilization in the twentieth century. But when Wells examined at closer range the behavior of institutions and their supporting ideologies, as he did especially after 1920, he discovered that what was, generally speaking, a civilization-wide "collapse" might also and perhaps more accurately be represented as a disastrous disruption of social equilibrium. More than simply failing to adapt, some institutions and ideologies had hypertrophied, whereas others had atrophied or grown much too slowly, so that civilization was no longer in balance, like a body suffering from cancer or acromegaly.[64]

The change of scale itself, of course, had been produced by the hypertrophy of experimental science, the mechanical arts, and the organization of business and finance. Scientists, engineers, and capitalist entrepreneurs had combined their peculiar talents to create, though not by design, a world economy capable in a material way of supplying either the arms for Armageddon or goods and services enough for a planetary Utopia. Other parts of the social organism had swollen immensely under the impact of technological change. Vast fortunes had been piled up by unscrupulous speculators like Edward Ponderevo in *Tono-Bungay,* at incalculable cost to economic stability and social harmony. The Ponderevos of the world had wasted its natural resources. They had caused ruinous inflations and depressions. "The patient, nibbling, enterprising profit-seeker of the past," as Wells wrote in 1940, "magnified and equipped now with the huge claws and teeth the change of scale has

64. See, e.g., *The Shape of Things to Come* (New York, 1933), pp. 31–32. But in all fairness to Wells it should be pointed out that some of his best Edwardian books, like *Tono-Bungay,* made exactly the same dramatic contrast between social hypertrophy and atrophy. What distinguishes the later diagnoses is a more apprehensive and rounded and explicit discussion of the danger of atrophy in social controls, especially the atrophy of religion.

provided for him, has torn the old economic order to rags."[65] But even more dangerous than millionaires were the demagogic politicians and lunatic dictators who used all the instruments of coercion and persuasion provided by modern technics to strengthen and perpetuate the antiquated nation-states of the old order in Europe. At precisely the time when it should have given way to forms of political organization better suited to the new dimensions of life, the nation-state was growing cancerously out of all possibility of control, arming itself with the super-weapons of the new science and competing with its fellows for the subjugation and plunder of Africa and Asia. The cult of nationalism had never before enjoyed so many blind worshipers as in the late nineteenth and twentieth centuries. It was the worship of the "tribal gods" of nationality, of "Britannia" and "Germania" and "La France," which had in the final analysis caused the first World War. Wells even pressed this interpretation in a private audience with Lenin during his visit to Russia in 1920. Wars, Wells insisted, sprang "from nationalist imperialism and not from a Capitalist organisation of society." Lenin—need it be said?— disagreed.[66]

On the other hand, certain features of the old European order had been mortally weakened by the new technics. They had been attacked by critics like Wells himself, they could not survive under the conditions of twentieth-century life: but they had been indispensable to the equipoise of the old order. The traditions of political leadership furnished one salient example. The machine had increased the amount of real wealth in the world, leading not only to a general rise in the standard of living, but also to an immense increase in the world's population. The human race "spent

65. *New World Order*, p. 23.
66. *Russia in the Shadows*, p. 164; and see also *Outline of History*, 2, 244, 434.

the great gifts of science as rapidly as it got them in a mere insensate multiplication of the common life."[67] The power of the "masses" grew steadily, and the old ruling classes, in the changing balance of political power, began to lose their grip, yielding to a new race of vote-catching democratic politicians and bosses. Change occurred so rapidly that it was impossible, even with the best of wills, to assimilate the new masses into the old social structure. They could not be educated fast or well enough. Industrial tycoons and politicians exploited them, pandering to some of their half-formed aspirations. Intellectuals either deserted them in disgust, creating a new self-consciously esoteric literature and art, or catered to their lowest instincts.[68] A new aristocracy assuming the initiatives and responsibilities of creative leadership had never emerged to replace the old ruling class.

The integrality of the old order had also depended on the services of religious bodies: in the West, of the Christian Church. Christianity had provided a fixed code of moral behavior and oriented the individual life to self-surpassing purposes. Now, with Christianity and its Asian counterparts dead or dying, their systems of belief undermined by the revelations of physics, biology, and psychology, the whole structure of civilization had begun to disintegrate, "like a building whose mortar has been changed to sand."[69] The failure of the positive religions, Wells said, had perilously devitalized that indispensable minority of spiritually enlightened souls whose faith normally sustains the rest of

67. *Men Like Gods* (New York, 1923), p. 68; cf. *World of William Clissold, 1,* 218–19.

68. On the treason of the intellectuals see the acute analysis in *The Dream* (New York, 1924), pp. 201–2; also *Boon,* pp. 201–3, and *The Research Magnificent* (New York, 1915), pp. 109–10.

69. *The Open Conspiracy: Blue Prints for a World Revolution* (Garden City, N.Y., 1928), p. 4.

society. It had also knocked the props from under the traditional system of morality. Again, no new faith and no new
moral code—except fratricidal cults like nationalism and
Marxism—had evolved to replace the discredited faiths of
the positive religions.[70]

In *The Shape of Things to Come* Wells also called attention to the failure of family life in the twentieth century,
under the stress of competition from the school, the state,
the giant corporation, and the mass media of communication. The forces disorganizing home life "had not, in their
turn, been converted into 'organic forces.' In default of
these, minds were lapsing towards crude and base self-seek-
ing and entirely individualistic aims."[71] Nor had there yet
been a concerted effort on the part of the educational and
social sciences even to work out comprehensive plans, in a
systematic, scientific way, for the reintegration of human
society at the new level demanded by twentieth-century
conditions. In short, stimulated to irregular growth by the
mechanization of industry and the new science, society had
"achieved . . . a hypertrophy of bone, muscle and stomach,
without any corresponding enlargement of its nervous controls." Modern man was "a monkey alone in a moving
motor car, terrified and imperilled by the disproportion of
his opportunity."[72]

Wells' formula for world salvation has already been suggested in the outline of his prophetic career sketched
above; it follows naturally from his diagnosis of the world
crisis: man could achieve salvation only by planning and
building an organically integrated and functionally articulated world society. New institutions and new faiths in
harmony with the new science and the new technology had

70. See especially ibid., pp. 1–19.
71. *Shape of Things to Come*, p. 253.
72. Ibid., p. 32, and *New America*, p. 3.

to replace the chaos of the discredited past. Instead of competing nation-states, the world commonwealth. Instead of rival disintegrating religions, a world religion of humanity. Instead of economic and class warfare, a planned world economy and a classless society. And when the new world order was firmly established, it would find at its command the same infinite material resources of modern science that had thrown the old order out of balance. It could enlarge and enrich human life beyond all measuring. Nearly all of Wells' prophetic books close—and here Wells' debt to the Enlightenment and nineteenth-century Utopism is most clearly revealed—with a ritual invocation of the possible future. In his favorite phrase, men might one day "stand upon this earth as one stands upon a footstool, and laugh, and reach out their hands amidst the stars."[73] The earth was bright with endless promise; once in control of himself, man might conquer the universe. Only in 1944, after nearly a half-century of warning and planning and dreaming, could Wells bring himself to admit that he had dreamed in vain.

73. *The Discovery of the Future* (London, 1902), p. 95. Wells used the same phrases in *Marriage* (New York, 1912), p. 480, and *Outline of History*, 2, 595.

Chapter Two:

FUNDAMENTAL ASSUMPTIONS

PHILOSOPHICAL CARPETBAGGER

"Wells as a thinker," says Vincent Brome, "is a dubious quantity. In the sense that Newton was a thinker he does not qualify. In his terms he broke no new ground."[1] Except for one patient French doctoral student writing in the mid-1920's,[2] none of Wells' critics has shown much interest in Wells' answers to the problems of philosophy. No professional philosopher ever will. But although he was never a subtle or systematic thinker, or even a thinker at all in the most solemn sense, he did not lead an unexamined life. He arrived in his early years at a world-view—jerry-built though it may have been—that deserves at least a chapter in any study of his prophetic career, for two urgent reasons: Wells' ground assumptions about nature and man explain the general form and direction of his response to the twentieth-century world crisis; they explain what sustained his faith in that response; and they also represent the kind of thinking on fundamental questions which he assumed, with all the exuberant vanity of an eighteenth-century *philosophe,* was becoming general, and would have to become general, before the world could be saved. As with Shaw's fabu-

1. Brome, *H. G. Wells,* p. 179.
2. Georges Connes, *Etude sur la pensée de Wells.* See above, pp. 7–8.

lous quadruped, the "Chesterbelloc," Wells' favorite conceit was to pose as the *Zeitgeist*.[3] The obituary notice he wrote for himself in 1936 accused him as nothing else could: he would be remembered, he hoped, as a "scientific man," and as "a reef-building coral polyp," most of his books forgotten, but one of the builders of "the reef of common ideas on which our civilization stands today."[4]

The role Wells assigned to education as a way of indoctrinating young minds with "the scientific vision of life in the universe,"[5] will be studied in Chapter 3; it is enough to say here that he was always acutely conscious of the importance of the answers young people chose to give in their formative years to the basic problems of philosophy and religion. The world society could not cohere without a world mind. As he insisted in an editorial aside in his last novel, *You Can't Be Too Careful,* the "sane world community" for the sake of social solidarity could tolerate only one world-philosophy and one world-religion. To permit more would result in the same sort of collective schizophrenia that had helped to drive Western civilization to the brink of suicide.[6] Whatever else may be said of his own world-view, and by his own admission he was only a kind of "philosophical carpet-bagger,"[7] it did lead him logically and unavoidably to his vision of world order.

Wells drew his fundamental assumptions about man and nature from a variety of sources. The articles of his personal credo must be analyzed, one by one, each on its own merits,

3. Shaw, "The Chesterbelloc," *Pen Portraits and Reviews* (London, 1932), pp. 71–81.

4. "H. G. Wells Writes His Own Obituary," *Living Age, 351* (1936), 130.

5. *Fate of Man*, p. 64.

6. *You Can't Be Too Careful* (New York, 1942), pp. 271–73; cf. below, p. 221.

7. *Future in America*, p. 231.

for whatever each is worth. But from at least one perspective, all his basic assumptions do hang together. They make
a coherent system in the sense that they are all projected on
the same macrocosmic scale and measured against the same
fixed standard: the picture of the material universe Wells
constructed during his years as a science student in London
in the mid-1880's. Although he was deeply influenced by
many other currents in late nineteenth-century thought,
fundamentally he looked at life through the eyes of a trained
biologist. For him the universe was the enigmatic cosmos
of late nineteenth-century physics; animate nature was the
slaughter and struggle for existence described by Darwin
and Huxley; man was a species of animal, *Homo sapiens,* of
the order *Primates,* thrown up by an accident of evolution
and forced to adapt to its environment or degenerate or
perish. A good many modern thinkers have subscribed to
these ideas, but for Wells they formed the point of departure and the frame of reference for every other idea. The
propositions of physics and biology were his philosophical
meat and drink.

It takes no psychoanalytic training nor any of the laby-
rinthine techniques of contemporary literary criticism to
explain the priority of late Victorian science in Wells'
thought; his personal history makes it abundantly clear.
Until 1884, when he came to London on a scholarship to
study under T. H. Huxley at the Normal School of Science
in South Kensington, he had lived at much the same level
in society as the hero of his novel *Kipps.* His contact with
the world of ideas had been by any reckoning pitifully
slight. Six years of elementary schooling in a one-room village "academy," a year of grammar school, conversations
with second-rate preachers and schoolmasters, dozens of
half-digested cram-books, and a miscellany of good books,
from Plato's *Republic* to Henry George's *Progress and Poverty,* which he read on his own initiative without fully understanding, could hardly have more than awakened his

curiosity. By his own account, Plato and George did help to crystallize his later attitude toward the social order;[8] but essentially he came to Huxley an intellectual *tabula rasa,* a boy of eighteen with a powerful, but still unformed mind.

What happened explains itself. After eighteen years in provincial backwaters, he was suddenly thrust into the presence of genius. Huxley's lucid exposition of the nature and history of life on earth, integrated by the still fresh and simple idea of natural selection, captured him completely. It gave him a picture of the how, when, and where of human life; and it gave him insight into an intellectual method, a forceful example of how human brains could arrive at persuasive truths by clear, orderly, disciplined processes of thought. He had already taken a lively interest in science as a grammar school pupil-teacher. But he still might have turned in some other direction had it not been for the overwhelming impression left by Huxley's teaching. Two later years of work at South Kensington in physics and geology were not, in fact, nearly so satisfying. The first year had been decisive. Around Huxley's course "as a nucleus I arranged a spacious digest of facts," he told the Oxford Philosophical Society in 1903, and acquired "a fairly clear, and complete and ordered view of the ostensibly real universe."[9] Much later, in 1939, he was still able to describe his South Kensington experiences as the most exciting in his life:

> For me these years remain in my memory as if all the time I was putting together an immense jig-saw puzzle in a mood of inspiration. These were the most exciting years in my life. I had been blind and I was learning to see. The world opened out before me. By '88 I saw the world, not precisely as I see it today, but much more as

8. *Experiment in Autobiography,* pp. 140–49.

9. "Scepticism of the Instrument," appendix to *Modern Utopia,* p. 376. It was read to the Oxford Philosophical Society on November 8, 1903, and first published in *Mind,* new ser. *13* (1904), 379–93.

I see it today than as I saw it in 1880. There has been a
lot of expansion and supplementing since, but nothing
like a fundamental reconstruction.[10]

Of course this acceptance of the revelations of Victorian
science did not automatically equip Wells with a complete
world-view in and of itself. The careers, for example, of
Herbert Spencer, Ernst Haeckel, J. S. Haldane, and
John Dewey demonstrate that the "scientific outlook" can
lead a creative thinker in almost any direction he chooses to
take. The facts of physics and biology are susceptible of any
number of interpretations. In Wells' case, the "scientific
outlook" led, first of all, to the kind of interpretation put
upon Darwinian biology by T. H. Huxley himself, and up
to a certain point Wells' fundamental propositions, especially his ideas on nature and progress, mark him as a faithful disciple of both Huxley's philosophy and his biology.
But Wells let science take him much further than it took
Huxley. To see human life consistently from the macrocosmic angle of approach of the evolutionary biologist
meant—for Wells in any event—to grow intellectually indifferent to life at the level of the individual: the individual
nation, the individual community, the individual man. In
spite of his sensuous good humor in everyday life and his
artistic gifts, he tended as a thinker to look upon individuals
only as specimens of a larger reality. In the words of his
alter ego Stephen Stratton in *The Passionate Friends,* "We
are like little figures, dots ascendant upon a vast hillside."
Stratton's romance with Lady Mary had been, he wrote, an
episode of intimacy which he took up for an instant and held
"under a lens,"[11] as a biologist might train his magnifying

---

10. *Fate of Man,* p. 8. See *Experiment in Autobiography,* pp. 159–
96, for a much fuller appreciation of the years at South Kensington.

11. *The Passionate Friends* (New York, 1913), p. 152.

glass upon the courtship of two beetles. The sense of looking at the world from some colossal height, of seeing the
world—in a phrase he often used in his later years—as a
human anthill,[12] goes far to explain his orientation as a
prophet of world order, his talent for projecting problems
on a planetary scale, and his inability to project them on
any other.

The sections which follow discuss, in order, Wells' concept of nature, his idea of man and human nature and the
conditions governing human progress, his thoughts on the
meaning and uses of science, and his idea of an emergent
"racial mind." Whatever other currents of thought influenced his fundamental assumptions, they all reflect his
inveterate disposition to see life in the largest possible
terms, at the level of genus and species.

NATURE ON TRIAL

One of the ironic accidents of the progress of natural science
in the nineteenth and twentieth centuries has been the
growth in the minds of many sensitive thinking men, including Wells, of an authentic horror of nature. Equated
with reason by the *philosophes* of the Enlightenment, worshiped as a goddess by many Romantics, "nature" had enjoyed the best possible reputation for over a century. Except
in the protests of a few eccentrics, like the Marquis de
Sade[13] and the closely related idea of nature as a murderess
of surplus populations given currency by Malthus early in

12. For a time Wells was thinking of giving the title, *The Human
Ant-Hill*, to the book he finally called *The Work, Wealth and Happiness of Mankind* (2 vols. Garden City, N.Y., 1931); see the footnote to
Vol. 1, p. 24. The phrase is used a number of times throughout the
book, and again in later works. Cf. *Mind at the End of Its Tether*, p.
17.

13. See especially Mario Praz, *The Romantic Agony*, trans. Angus
Davidson (2d ed. London, 1951), pp. 93–186 and passim.

the nineteenth century, "nature" remained a good word in Western vocabularies down to the second half of the nineteenth century. The change since then can be blamed—if not entirely, still principally—on Darwin's mechanical and amoral explanation of the origin of species. Darwin stripped nature of benevolence and malevolence alike, but the effect of his demonstration on the popular imagination was to convert nature into a battleground, an arena of wolves and lambs, where every creature competed to keep alive, preferably at the expense of its fellow creatures. "When its whole significance dawns on you," Shaw once said of the Darwinian hypothesis, "your heart sinks into a heap of sand within you. There is a hideous fatalism about it, a ghastly and damnable reduction of beauty and intelligence, of strength and purpose, of honour and aspiration, to such casually picturesque changes as an avalanche may make in a mountain landscape, or a railway accident in a human figure."[14] Following closely the revolution in biology, another in physics has probed beyond the margins of Newton's orderly cosmos to discover a universe infinitely more complex, vast, and alien to human purposes than the men of the Enlightenment could have conceived. In many twentieth-century minds "nature" is a jungle full of sound and fury suspended in a black and inscrutable void.

Emergent evolutionists, vitalists like Shaw himself, and penitent Christians have managed to get around or through the implications of science to reaffirm the meaningfulness of nature. But for others no such triumphant reaffirmation has been possible. The heroes of the novels of Thomas Hardy strive in vain to fulfill their capacity for happiness in a universe ruled by titanic forces indifferent to man. Bertrand Russell has pitted lonely humanity against the juggernaut of "omnipotent matter"; and the ablest exponent of Dar-

14. Shaw, preface to *Back to Methuselah* in *The Works of Bernard Shaw* (31 vols. London, Constable, 1930–31), *16*, xlii.

win's theory of natural selection, T. H. Huxley, drew the easy conclusion from the evolutionary record that nature could not tell good from evil. Herbivore or carnivore, he pointed out, were all the same in nature; between the laws of evolution and human values an impassable gulf would always yawn.

From his first published writings Wells took up Huxley's position. He had probably studied Huxley's idea of nature in his teacher's essays,[15] but it could have reached him just as readily in the ordinary course of his biological work at South Kensington. In any event, Wells always explicitly refused to see anything remotely like human feeling or benevolence or friendliness in the operations of lower nature. Several of his early scientific romances and short stories, for example, were transparent parables of the hostility between man and nature. *The Island of Dr. Moreau* chronicled the failure of a brilliant surgeon to span the gap between man and beast. Little by little Dr. Moreau's Beast-People reverted to their animal natures. The carnivores regained their taste for fresh blood; they all lost, by degrees, their capacity for speech, their sense of shame, the half-human expression in their eyes. In the closing pages of the novel, with the Beast-People in rebellion and Moreau himself dead, Wells' hero was left alone to face nature horribly reduced to its original state: he symbolized mankind stranded in the wilderness of an amoral universe.[16] In *The War of the Worlds* the inhabitants of Mars engaged humanity in mortal

15. See Wells' article, "Huxley," in *Royal College of Science Magazine* (April, 1901), quoted in part by Geoffrey West in his *H. G. Wells,* pp. 49–50.

16. Wells later described the book as "an exercise in youthful blasphemy. Now and then, though I rarely admit it, the universe projects itself towards me in a hideous grimace. It grimaced that time, and I did my best to express my vision of the aimless torture in creation": preface to *Seven Famous Novels* (New York, 1934), p. ix.

combat and were themselves wiped out by terrestrial bac-
teria. The early short stories, too, swarmed with monsters:
a vampire orchid, a giant flying bat, a mad Malay running
amok, a huge prehistoric bird, an unknown species of deep-
sea cephalopod, a race of intelligent ants, giant floating
spiders—all intent on slaughter.[17]

A familiar character in many of Wells' novels is the champion of a sentimentalized view of nature, defeated in debate
with one of Wells' spokesmen, or made to appear ridiculous,
like the wandering lecturer who went about the world san-
dal-shod preaching a return to the "simple natural life" in
A Modern Utopia.[18] Arthur Stubland, in *Joan and Peter*,
served a similar purpose, and came out second best in an argument with Wells' mouthpiece, Oswald Sydenham. "If
Arthur was Ruskinite and Morrisite, Oswald was as completely Huxleyite." Demolishing the illusion that nature
provided for all her children, Oswald described her as a
"half-wit":

> She's distraught. You overrate the jade. She's thinking
> of everything at once. All her affairs got into a hopeless
> mess from the very start. Most of her world is desert
> with water running to waste. A tropical forest is three-
> quarters death and decay, and what is alive is either
> murdering or being murdered. It's only when you come
> to artificial things, such as a ploughed field, for ex-
> ample, that you get space and health and every blade
> doing its best.

Arthur objected that a ploughed field belonged to the

17. "The Flowering of the Strange Orchid," "In the Avu Observa-
tory," "Through a Window," "Aepyornis Island," "The Sea-raiders,"
"The Empire of the Ants," and "The Valley of the Spiders." All of
Wells' short stories through 1926 are available in one volume, *The
Short Stories of H. G. Wells*, Garden City, N.Y., 1929.
18. *Modern Utopia,* chapter 4, "The Voice of Nature," pp. 113–34.

"natural" life of man, but Oswald wanted to know where the "natural" life leaves off and the "artificial" begins. " 'If a plough belongs a foundry belongs—and a coal mine.' "[19]

Wells' most careful statement of the case against nature appeared in his dialogue novel *The Undying Fire* in 1919. Here the straw man to be knocked down was Sir Eliphaz Burrows, who reproached Wells' hero, Job Huss, for vilifying providence. The world was one vast intention, said Sir Eliphaz, and all that happened in nature went according to God's plan. Job challenged Sir Eliphaz to explain parasites, flies, gnats, beasts of prey, accidental death, the ruthless struggle for existence in the plant world, the precarious life of nesting penguins, the aimless rage of elephants, the chaos in an Indian jungle after a rain. Sir Eliphaz pointed to the loveliness of nature, and Job replied,

> There is no beauty one may not balance by an equal ugliness. The wart-hog and the hyaena, the tapeworm and the stinkhorn, are equally God's creations. Nothing you have said points to anything but a cold indifference towards us of this order in which we live. Beauty happens; it is not given. Pain, suffering, happiness; there is no heed. Only in the heart of man burns the fire of righteousness.[20]

Even the alleged mechanical marvels of nature were matched by less celebrated mechanical failures; many of nature's contrivances were absurd, futile, or abortive. Job cited the example of the migratory instinct in some species of European birds, evolved before the appearance of the Mediterranean Sea, which leads thousands of bird to die in the sea every year because they have no place to rest on their autumn journey to Africa. As the patrician in Wells' utopia *Men Like Gods* told his terrestrial visitors, nature " 'except

19. *Joan and Peter* (New York, 1918), pp. 22–23.
20. *Undying Fire*, p. 114.

for our eyes and wills . . . is purposeless and blind. . . . She
made us by accident; all her children are bastards—unde-
sired; she will cherish or expose them, pet or starve or torment without rhyme or reason. She does not heed, she does
not care.' "21

Wells indicted the physical universe in much the same
language as he used against the biological. As early as 1891
in his first published article, "The Rediscovery of the
Unique," he admitted that science had failed after all to
make the universe rational. The history of science, he said,
was like the striking of a match. In the first bright eruption
of the light of science, man imagined he could see the whole
orderly cosmos spread out before him. "It is a curious sensation, now that the preliminary splutter is over and the flame
burns up clear, to see his hands lit and just a glimpse of himself and the patch he stands on visible, and around him, in
place of all that human comfort and beauty he anticipated—
darkness still."22 Even during his flirtation in 1918–19 with
theology, Wells was careful to absolve his "God" of any responsibility for the affairs of inanimate, as well as animate,
nature. The universe external to man he dismissed as the
"Veiled Being," cut off from man by an impenetrable curtain, beyond human good and evil. "There is no reason,"
he wrote in *God the Invisible King,* "to suppose the Veiled
Being either benevolent or malignant towards men."23 In
short, it did not care. Yet in a sense it commanded absolute
obedience of man. "There is order in the universe," Wells'
hero admitted in *The World of William Clissold;* "there
is law, essential and inexorable law. It is law outside of and
independent of our wills, and perhaps irrelevant to our
wills. But it is there." But Clissold, like Wells, had grown

21. *Men Like Gods,* pp. 106–7.
22. "The Rediscovery of the Unique," *Fortnightly Review, 50*
(1891), 111.
23. *God the Invisible King* (New York, 1917), p. xiv.

weary of trying to unravel the mysteries of the cosmos. The universe of the physicists made no appeal whatever to the human heart or mind. For all practical purposes it could be forgotten, as one forgets nightmares and insoluble riddles.[24]

The universe of the biologists, on the other hand, could not be forgotten. Although a great gulf separated human values from animal and plant "values," man, as a product of evolution, was himself intimately related to all other living things. Man, the biological species, remained subject to the basic laws of life: *"Homo sapiens* is no privileged exception to the general conditions that determine the destinies of other living species. It prospers or suffers under the same laws. . . . There is no reason whatever to believe that nature has any greater bias in favor of man than it had in favor of the icthyosaur or the pterodactyl."[25] And among "the general conditions that determine the destinies" of species, two above all could not be altered or ignored by mankind: the law of change and the law of adaptation.

Like Huxley, who once described the state of nature at any given moment as "a temporary phase of a process of incessant change,"[26] Wells found a disposition in all living things to undergo continuous change. The universe was kinetic; without change, life became impossible. French critics have linked Wells with the transformism of Diderot and Bergson,[27] and a similar comparison could be made

24. *World of William Clissold, 1,* 48; and see ibid., pp. 48–54, for Clissold's reactions to Einsteinian physics. Cf. *Experiment in Autobiography,* pp. 182–83.

25. *Fate of Man,* pp. 20, 247.

26. Huxley, *Collected Essays* (9 vols. London, Appleton, 1893–94), *9,* 5.

27. René Seguy, "H.-G. Wells et la pensée contemporaine," *Mercure de France, 95* (1912), 673–99; and Arnaud Dandieu, "Wells et Diderot," ibid., *194* (1927), 513–36.

between Wells and the leaders of the pragmatist movement in British and American philosophy, who—unlike Diderot and Bergson—did exert some direct influence on Wells' thinking. But Wells, Bergson, and the pragmatists alike drew their inspiration ultimately from the lessons of evolutionary biology. Darwin had exploded the Linnaean myth of fixed types; and the laws of natural selection could not possibly operate unless nature supplied herself with a steady flow of mutations. For Wells, inevitable change did not necessarily imply inevitable progress, but change alone was "the law of life."[28] Nature let nothing, human or nonhuman, stand still. By the very nature of things, resistance to change was absurdly futile. "Modern science has made clear to us," Wells wrote in *The Outline of History,* "that . . . no generation repeats the previous generation precisely . . . change, we realize now, is inexhaustible; all things are eternally new."[29]

This nervous interpretation of history, this sense so familiar in recent generations of being borne along irresistibly, culminated in Wells in a kind of hypnotic fascination for change as a thing in itself. For Richard Remington, his hero in *The New Machiavelli,* the world "was all alive, I felt, and changing every day; how it was changing and the changes men might bring about, fascinated my mind beyond measure."[30] In *The World of William Clissold* Heraclitus' maxim Παντα ρει—"All things flow"—was Clissold's favorite expression, the epitaph his brother chose for his grave, and the subtitle of the novel itself: that Heraclitus appealed to Wells should come as no surprise. Far from re-

28. *Modern Utopia,* p. 272.

29. *Outline of History, 1,* 425. Wells' ideas on change as a law of nature may be traced in print as far back as an article he wrote for *The Saturday Review* in 1894. See "The 'Cyclic' Delusion," *Saturday Review, 78* (1894), 506.

30. *New Machiavelli,* p. 107.

senting man's inability as a creature of nature to stand still, Wells saw in constant and violent change the salvation of the species from degeneration. If man succeeded somehow, by making the world weedless and germless and painless, in achieving relative security from old enemies without immediately plunging into new trials and dangers, he would meet exactly the same fate that overtook the decadent world of A.D. 802,701 in *The Time Machine.* " 'We are kept keen on the grindstone of pain and necessity,' " warned the Time Traveller. " 'It is a law of nature we overlook, that intellectual versatility is the compensation for change, danger, and trouble.' "[31]

But it was a logical corollary of the law of change that man could not let change carry him along like a log on a stream. Every challenge thrown up by life, from plagues and floods to the twentieth-century world crisis itself, had to be met by a successful adaptive response. "Adapt or perish," Wells wrote in 1939, "that is and always has been the implacable law of life for all its children."[32] At the biological level, the contemporary crisis in civilization was no more sinister, and no less, than any life-and-death crisis in the history of any species. Adaptation would be rewarded by survival and perhaps an increment in human power. Failure could result in extinction.

Nature had still one more claim on the fortunes of *Homo sapiens:* the fact that every human being was only partly human, that every human being carried in his brain and body the indelible marks of his animal origins. Again following Huxley, Wells rejected the implication in Darwinian biology that the laws of nature decreed fratricidal competition among races and nations and civilizations. Man

31. *The Time Machine* (New York, 1895), pp. 76, 186–87. Cf. the same ideas, forty years later, in *Things to Come* (New York, 1935), pp. 115–17.
32. *Fate of Man,* p. 247.

could choose his own way, following his own lights, of meeting challenges. But there was always the risk that the blind greed and sloth and fear he had inherited from his animal past would betray human interests and values. Although Wells' Samurai in *A Modern Utopia* held as their cardinal belief "the repudiation of the doctrine of original sin,"[33] Wells in effect preached a biological doctrine of original sin, which turned the Christian teaching inside out but amounted to much the same thing. Man himself, quintessential man, was good. By definition, whatever he chose to call good was good; external nature offered no moral guidance. At the same time, because man was not purely and simply man, because he was alloyed with baser stuff, individual human beings were all capable, by nature, of infinite evil. The animals on the Island of Dr. Moreau were brutes carved into men by an insane surgeon, but men themselves had come fresh from the mindless surgery of evolution. "Humanity is but animal rough-hewn to a reasonable shape and in perpetual internal conflict between instinct and injunction."[34]

Wells' analysis of human evil, at least in its bare essentials, also corresponded to the explanations of Freudian psychoanalysis. After becoming acquainted with the literature of psychoanalysis in the 1920's, he often drew on the evidence of psychology and psychiatry as well as on biology to support his idea of the animal content in human nature. Many of his mouthpieces in the later novels, who developed his rapidly darkening view of the human dilemma after 1914, were nerve specialists or psychiatrists or psychologists: Dr. Martineau in *The Secret Places of the Heart,* Dr. Devizes in *Christina Alberta's Father,* Dr. Norbert in *The Croquet*

---

33. *Modern Utopia,* p. 299.
34. Preface to *The Works of H. G. Wells: Atlantic Edition* (28 vols. New York, 1924–27), *2,* ix. Cf. *Outline of History, 1,* 377.

Player, Professor Keppel in *Star-Begotten,* Dr. Kentlake in *Babes in the Darkling Wood.* In *The Croquet Player* especially, he returned to the theme of *The Island of Dr. Moreau* on an even grander scale. As Dr. Moreau's island had been haunted by the Beast-People, now the whole world, symbolized by the village of Cainsmarsh, was haunted by the homicidal ghosts of prehistoric ape-men, and Dr. Norbert lectured the Croquet Player:

> Man is still what he was. Invincibly bestial, envious, malicious, greedy. Man, Sir, unmasked and disillusioned, is the same fearing, snarling, fighting beast he was a hundred thousand years ago. These are no metaphors, Sir. What I tell you is the monstrous reality. The brute has been marking time and dreaming of a progress it has failed to make. Any archaeologist will tell you as much; modern man has no better skull, no better brain. Just a cave man, more or less trained. There has been no real change, no real escape.[35]

A few hundred generations had not been time enough to root out the deeply embedded instincts of the ape. The tension between man and nature was most acute in the human soul itself, and there man fought his ancient enemy in agonizingly close quarters.

From all the foregoing it is clear that Wells' idea of nature was not so much an exercise in metaphysics as a description from the vantage point of a trained biologist of the setting of the human drama. The universe offered itself to Wells as a wasteland, indifferent to human suffering or aspiration

35. *Croquet Player,* p. 89. Cf. *Secret Places of the Heart,* pp. 19–20, in which Dr. Martineau compared the human mind to a house with cellars and attics haunted by "the souls of apes, monkeys, reptiles and creeping things." See also *Star-Begotten* (New York, 1937), pp. 174–76.

and beyond human understanding.[36] But nature for all her neglect of human values imposed her laws upon man. In common with all products of evolution he was obliged to adapt continuously to a continuously changing environment, or accept degeneration and extinction; and yet to remain man—self-governing, reasoning, moral man—he was also forced to fight an exhausting perennial war against the brute instincts in his own nature.

MAN AS PROMETHEUS

From this assessment of nature, *Homo sapiens* emerged in Wells' world-view as a being not unlike the Prometheus of mythology, a rebellious hero whose "business is to defeat Nature and reverse history."[37] No other view of man could have matched Wells' own temperament so closely. "He is a first-class fighting man," wrote Sidney Dark of Wells in

36. Wells was willing at times to admit that there might be a deeper relationship between human life and the cosmos. Speculative intervals punctuate his writings, in which he tried to puzzle out the paradox that moral man could issue from an amoral universe. In *First and Last Things* he even took as his "fundamental act of faith" the assumption that he lived in an orderly universe in which all things were invested with meaning and connected to some vast purpose. *First and Last Things,* p. 66. Uncle Robert Kentlake had similar thoughts in *Babes in the Darkling Wood* (New York, 1940), pp. 242–46. But in both cases Wells insisted that the purpose was inscrutable, beyond human understanding, to be taken on faith. It had no practical meaning at the human level of observation. At the human level "nature" signified "lower nature," the forms of matter and life which had preceded man in the stream of cosmic evolution. What might come later, what the whole evolutionary process was up to, Wells refused to guess. See Sidney Spencer, "H. G. Wells, Materialist and Mystic," *Hibbert Journal, 46* (1948), 358–61; and also Wells' description of himself as neither a materialist nor a mystic, but a "monist," in a letter to the London *Times* (September 29, 1939), p. 4.

37. *The Anatomy of Frustration* (New York, 1936), p. 199.

1922, "and life is a good thing because it gives the first-class fighting man continual opportunity for exciting struggle and insistent battle."[38] Wells belonged to a whole generation of "fighting men": Rudyard Kipling, Hilaire Belloc, G. K. Chesterton, and Bertrand Russell, who each earned a comparable reputation for rugged candor in defense of a militant faith; and Wells' own intellectual heroes of the generation before him, his scientist-hero Huxley, his ideal philosopher William James, and his favorite poet, William Ernest Henley,[39] were all fighting men of the same caliber, whose conceptions of man's place in the universe deeply influenced his own. The more confident intellectual atmosphere of the nineteenth century bred such fighting men in nearly unlimited quantities. Wells' keenness for battle, which faltered but never failed until 1944, identified him as much as anything in the minds of younger, warier generations with the thought-world of the nineteenth century.

In any case, man was a rebel against the whole order of evolved nature. "To rebel against instinct, to rebel against limitation, to evade, to trip up, and at last to close with and grapple and conquer the forces that dominate him," Wells wrote in 1903, "is the fundamental being of man." In another place, mankind was the "Ishmael of the Universe, against everything, and with everything against it." Again, as William Clissold saw the human condition, men were "conscripted in the army of the Titans against the old Jove

38. Dark, *The Outline of H. G. Wells* (London, Parsons, 1922), p. 25.

39. See Jerome Hamilton Buckley, *William Ernest Henley,* Princeton, N.J., 1945. Wells often quoted lines from Henley's "Invictus," which should be enough to suggest his tastes in poetry. "Invictus" was included in the Canon of the Samurai, in *Modern Utopia,* p. 284; it was recommended for the "Bible of Civilization" in *Salvaging of Civilization,* pp. 128–29; it cropped up again in *Mind at the End of Its Tether,* pp. 6–7.

of chance and matter."[40] Wells used the same imagery during the first World War, in his "theological" tract, *God the Invisible King.* The racial being personified as "God" appeared to Wells in the form of an armed warrior, calling men to battle, a figure of courage and youth, not unlike the armed angel in Botticelli's "Tobit," which years before had impressed Wells in Florence and drawn from him the significant confession that if he had to have a savior it would be such a creature and not that "terrible and incomprehensible Galilean with his crown of thorns, his blood-stained hands and feet."[41]

In biological terms man owed his power to play Prometheus to his emancipation from the blind mechanism of natural selection. Unlike any other animal, man, if he chose, could attempt to control the direction of his own evolution. In an early article in *The Fortnightly Review,* cited above,[42] Wells defined human evolution as an "artificial process." Man, he argued, had made no progress through natural selection since becoming recognizably human. The forces of natural selection worked too slowly; there had not been enough time. Civilization could be explained entirely as the fruit of human ingenuity, beginning with the invention of speech and continuing to the present day with the achievements of modern science. Through education, the transmission of the wisdom of social experience, man might have the power to create the world of his choice. In all but a few particulars, Wells' article could have been an adaptation of the Romanes Lecture Huxley

40. *Mankind in the Making* (New York, 1904), p. 73; *New Worlds for Old* (New York, 1908), p. 203; *World of William Clissold, 1,* 92.

41. *God the Invisible King,* pp. 55–68; and *First and Last Things,* p. 116. William Clissold later dismissed Wells' wartime God as a kind of "Prometheus; it was a titanic and not a divine being": *World of William Clissold, 1,* 87.

42. "Human Evolution, an Artificial Process." See p. 22, n. 15.

had given in 1894. Borrowed or not, its ideas framed all his later thought. Nature might force man to fight for survival, but he fought on his own terms. The biological age of dumb obedience was over. "At last comes man and seizes the creative wrist."[43]

Seizing the creative wrist meant for Wells that man had the possibility of literally making the world over again. Whatever nature had done, man might undo and reshape according to his will. Whatever was chaotic or accidental about the external world, whatever in history was only mindlessly copied from the natural life, could be improved upon or replaced by deliberate planning.[44] As the Utopian patrician in *Men Like Gods* explained, " 'With Man came Logos, the Word and the Will into our universe . . . to know it and comprehend it and master it. So that we of Utopia are no longer the beaten and starved children of Nature, but her free and adolescent sons. We have taken over the Old Lady's Estate.' "[45] Of all nature's children man alone had pride, "the Pride that stands up against the whole universe and says, 'in my place and moment, I am Man, militant and ascendant, Man who decides, Man the master of his fate.' "[46]

But the key word was "will." Strongly influenced by William James' *The Will to Believe* and brought up with a generation that doted on Nietzsche, Bergson, and Shaw, Wells found in "will," well informed and properly consecrated, the cure for all man's maladies. "Will is stronger than Fact," he insisted in *A Modern Utopia*, "it can mould and overcome Fact." All that held twentieth-century man from the achievement of world unity was the lack of will.

43. *Social Forces in England and America,* p. 409.
44. This was exactly the definition Wells gave to socialism in 1908 in his *New Worlds for Old,* pp. 21–26.
45. *Men Like Gods,* p. 107.
46. *Anatomy of Frustration,* p. 164.

"Were the will of the mass of men lit and conscious I am firmly convinced it would now burn steadily for synthesis and peace."[47] Even in Wells' least Promethean book, *The History of Mr. Polly,* which endeared him to thousands of readers and critics who had not the slightest sympathy for his social philosophy, the transforming power of human will was dramatized, on a modest scale. Mr. Polly did not aspire to greatness; he willed for no more than the humble Utopia of Potwell Inn; but the theme was there just the same:

> If the world does not please you *you can change it.* Determine to alter it at any price, and you can change it altogether. You may change it to something sinister and angry, to something appalling, but it may be you will change it to something brighter, something more agreeable, and at the worst something much more interesting. . . . There are no circumstances in the world that determined action cannot alter.[48]

As Signor Vinciguerra, the refugee from Mussolini in Wells' postwar novel *Meanwhile,* warned his English hosts, " 'If you have things that you desire it is because you willed well enough to have it so. . . . Nothing comes of itself except weeds and confusion.' "[49]

It should go almost without saying that Wells' confidence in the power of human will did not lead him to a faith in inevitable progress. The moral of *Mr. Polly,* to cite only the example above, was not that man could automatically shape the world after his heart's desire by sheer will-power but rather that, for all he knew, he might succeed; and that, in any event, he could certainly alter the existing state of things in some direction, for good or for evil. The human

47. *Modern Utopia,* pp. 368, 350.
48. *The History of Mr. Polly* (New York, 1910), p. 243.
49. *Meanwhile* (New York, 1927), pp. 286–87.

condition was neither hopeless nor helpless.

But just because Wells was able to fix himself in the public mind, especially in the years before 1914, as a social prophet who believed in the possibility and even the imminent possibility of a world Utopia, who used the word "progress" freely in his books, he has come to be associated more than any other writer of his generation with the nineteenth-century dream of inevitable progress. Critics have been making that association for more than thirty years. From Mark Rampion's satirical cartoon of Wells' idea of history as "a simple crescendo" spiraling "towards Utopian infinity" in Aldous Huxley's *Point Counter Point* in 1928, to the recent assertion by Geoffrey Barraclough that both Shaw and Wells believed in the inevitable amelioration of society through the working of "the inexorable laws of natural selection," Wells has been used by scores of responsible writers as a symbol of Victorian optimism in its fullest flower.[50]

Anyone who takes the trouble to read what Wells wrote about progress must dismiss these interpretations as the purest and sheerest nonsense. Wells' thoughts on progress

50. Aldous Huxley, *Point Counter Point* (London, Chatto and Windus, 1928), pp. 290–91; and Geoffrey Barraclough, *History in a Changing World* (Norman, Okla., University of Oklahoma Press, 1955), p. 225. See also, i.a., Lewis Mumford, *Values for Survival* (New York, 1946), p. 87; Reinhold Niebuhr, *Faith and History* (New York, 1949), pp. 162–63; Joseph Wood Krutch, *The Measure of Man* (Indianapolis, 1953), pp. 15–33; and St. John Ervine, *Bernard Shaw* (New York, 1956), p. 471. Not only is it unfair and inaccurate to scold Wells for a faith he never had; the great Victorians themselves were not the unabashed optimists they are sometimes accused of being nowadays. Helpful correctives of this cliché may be read in Humphry House, "The Mood of Doubt," British Broadcasting Company, *Ideas and Beliefs of the Victorians* (London, 1949), pp. 71–77; and Walter E. Houghton, *The Victorian Frame of Mind, 1830–1870* (New Haven, 1957), pp. 54–89.

never changed, from his first scientific romances down to
his final confession of despair in 1944. They can be reduced
to three simple points, which he repeated over and over
again: first, that *Homo sapiens* had made substantial progress in social organization and in controlling his physical
environment since prehistoric times; second, that it might
lie within his power to make still more progress along the
same lines; and third, that nothing guaranteed man's ultimate success or failure. In one or two of his pre-1914 books,
when the world seemed especially busy and bright, he very
nearly joined the ranks of the believers in inevitable progress. His hopes ran highest in *Anticipations* and *The Discovery of the Future,* both published in 1902. But with these
few doubtful exceptions,[51] and an occasional rhetorical exaggeration in his later work, he was entirely consistent.
Progress was not inevitable. If man's will failed, or if fate
turned against him, he could be wiped out in a wink.

The recent outbreak of interest in science-fiction has
created a fresh market for Wells' early scientific romances,
and from these alone a powerful case could be constructed
against the notion that Wells "believed" in progress. His
son Anthony West published a valuable study in 1957 of
Wells as a pessimist, which leans heavily upon illustrations
chosen from the scientific romances.[52] Too much can be
made of them. They were written primarily as entertainment, to shock and excite and amuse. But each was a perfectly sincere indictment of Victorian complacency. *The
Time Machine,* for example, can be read on almost any
level as a direct assault on the gospel of inevitable progress,
as "a glimpse of the future," in Wells' own description,
"that ran counter to the placid assumption of that time that

51. See especially *Discovery of the Future,* pp. 90–95.
52. West, "H. G. Wells," *Encounter, 8* (1957), 52–59; slightly altered
and abridged as "The Dark World of H. G. Wells," *Harper's, 214*
(1957), 68–73.

Evolution was a pro-human force making things better and better for mankind."[53] The Time Traveller as he flickered through time did see a sort of technological utopia in the near future, but in the more remote future mankind had split into two degenerate species, the dwarfed descendants of the old idle rich and the old proletariat, Carlyle's Dandies and Drudges; and still later, as the Time Traveller approached the end of the world, man became extinct, life slowly disappeared, and the cooling sun stained the silent seas blood red. The Time Traveller "thought but cheerlessly of the Advancement of Mankind, and saw in the growing pile of civilisation only a foolish heaping that must inevitably fall back upon and destroy its makers in the end."[54]

The Time Machine is the most obvious illustration from Wells' earliest work of his disbelief in inevitable progress, but most of the scientific romances were conceived in the same spirit. Mankind narrowly escaped annihilation in *The War of the Worlds,* and again in stories like "The Star." *When the Sleeper Wakes* depicted a totalitarian superstate, in which almost the whole gamut of horrors run by Aldous Huxley in *Brave New World* and George Orwell in *1984* was anticipated in graphic detail. *The First Men in the Moon* described a nightmare civilization of intelligent insects still closer, in some respects, to *Brave New World* than *When the Sleeper Wakes.*[55]

Even without the scientific romances, there is no lack of evidence that Wells failed to share the popular nineteenth-century faith in progress. As he wrote in 1906, commenting

53. Preface to *Seven Famous Novels,* p. ix.

54. *Time Machine,* in an "Epilogue" added for the Atlantic Edition of the collected *Works, 1,* 117. Cf. "Of a Book Unwritten," originally published in 1893, in *Certain Personal Matters* (London, 1897), chapter 23.

55. Cf., e.g., the Selenite practice of rearing their young in machines to Huxley's "Bokanovsky Process."

on the prevalence of that faith in the United States in *The Future in America,*

> One is led unawares to believe that this something called Progress is a natural and necessary and secular process, going on without the definite will of man, carrying us on quite independently of us; one is led unawares to forget that it is after all . . . only a sudden universal jolting forward in history, an affair of two centuries at most, a process for the continuance of which we have no sort of guarantee. Most western Europeans have this delusion of automatic progress in things badly enough, but with Americans it seems to be almost fundamental.[56]

After 1914, as Wells devoted more and more of his time to his prophetic career, the idea of inevitable progress began to seem not only unsound and unacceptable but positively dangerous. It encouraged people to imagine that the twentieth-century world crisis would solve itself, that there was nothing, in the long run, worth worrying about. Job Huss denounced it in a blistering speech in *The Undying Fire,* William Clissold railed against it in *The World of William Clissold,* Arnold Blettsworthy ridiculed it in *Mr. Blettsworthy on Rampole Island.*[57] The historian of the twenty-second century in *The Shape of Things to Come* characterized blind faith in an "underlying benevolence" as the great common error in nineteenth-century schools of thought, Marxist, Spencerian, and Christian alike.[58] Answering his critics in 1940, Wells expressly absolved himself

56. *Future in America,* p. 30. *The War in the Air* and *The World Set Free* are also full of warnings against trusting blindly in "Progress." See above, pp. 27–28.

57. *Undying Fire,* pp. 150–54; *World of William Clissold, 1,* 62, and *2,* 553; *Mr. Blettsworthy on Rampole Island,* pp. 13–26.

58. *Shape of Things to Come,* p. 30.

of any connection at any time in his life with the idea of
automatic progress:

> I have never thought, much less have I asserted, that
> progress was inevitable, though numerous people chose
> to fancy that about me. I have always maintained that
> by a strenuous effort mankind *might* defeat the impar-
> tial destructiveness of nature, but I have always in-
> sisted that only by incessant hard thinking and a better
> co-ordination of man's immense but dispersed powers
> of self-sacrifice and heroism was such a victory possi-
> ble.[59]

To press matters still further, Wells did not even believe,
in the final analysis, that man's will was literally free. Prometheus could rebel against nature, reject the laws of the
jungle, match his will against the chaotic universe, conquer
his animal lower instincts—and still fail miserably. Against
one force he was helpless. He could not fight Fate: the pattern imposed since the beginning of time on all inanimate
and animate matter alike by the rigid sequence of cosmic
cause and effect. Like John Tyndal and T. H. Huxley before him, Wells was a disciple of what J. B. S. Haldane has
labeled "scientific Calvinism."[60] "Take life at the level of
common sensation and common experience," Wells told
the Oxford Philosophical Society in 1903, "and there is no
more indisputable fact than man's freedom of will, unless
it is his complete moral responsibility. But make only the
least penetrating of analyses and you perceive a world of
inevitable consequences, a rigid succession of cause and

59. *Common Sense of War and Peace,* p. 7. Cf. *Anatomy of Frustration,* p. 150; *Apropos of Dolores,* p. 286; and *Babes in the Darkling
Wood,* p. 379.
60. J. B. S. Haldane, "Scientific Calvinism," *The Inequality of Man*
(London, 1932), pp. 27–42. For T. H. Huxley on the impossibility of
free will, see his *Collected Essays, 9,* 141–42.

effect. Insist upon a flat agreement between the two, and there you are! The [mental] Instrument fails."[61] The universe was a rigid four-dimensional system of space and time. Past and future, like sound and color, were subjective illusions. The whole cosmic system existed always and everywhere, and not one jot or tittle had been, could be, or would be altered. "There is no conflict," Wells added in 1942, "between fate and free will; they are major and minor aspects of existence. The major aspect of life is Destiny; the minor is that we do not know our destiny. We struggle because we must; and that struggle is life; but the parts of the drama we enact belong to a system that has neither beginning nor end."[62]

Still, this awareness of cosmic predestination, like the revelations of modern physics,[63] had no practical meaning for moral man. "In this world of men and women, in this world where the grass is green and desire beckons," human will was entirely free.[64] Only after 1944 and *Mind at the End of Its Tether* did Wells bring himself to decide that fate had, after all, turned irrevocably against man, that the cosmic "Antagonist"—the rigid sequence of cause and effect behind all things—had never meant man to win. According to Anthony West, Wells knew all his life that "all human effort was futile and that man was base," although he flinched from telling the hard truth in most of his books.[65] But valuable as West's essay may be as an antidote against the legend of Wells' inexhaustible optimism, it goes too far

61. "Scepticism of the Instrument," *Modern Utopia*, p. 390.

62. *The Conquest of Time* (London, 1942), pp. 83–84.

63. See above, pp. 70–71, for Wells and physics.

64. *Anticipations,* p. 309.

65. West, "Dark World of H. G. Wells," p. 71. Colin Wilson thinks that Wells became an "outsider" in his last book, that he experienced "a moment of supreme *detachment,* an Existentialist revelation of the *unconnectedness* of external nature and the internal 'ego.' " Wilson, *The Outsider* (Boston, Houghton Mifflin, 1956), p. 134 n.

in the opposite direction. Unless Wells was a consummate hypocrite, *Mind at the End of Its Tether* contradicted all he had ever believed about the rules of the game between man and destiny. Fate might turn against man, but man could never know, until the last blow had been delivered. As if fearing an approaching failure of nerve, Wells insisted in a number of his later books that he could never admit defeat, whatever happened. "While there is still life in a species," he wrote in 1939, "no biological defeat is complete."[66] For nearly the whole course of his career as a prophet of world order, Wells believed no more in inevitable disaster than in inevitable progress. Prometheus had no choice but to go on fighting. "I am neither a pessimist nor an optimist at bottom," Wells wrote in 1933. "This is an entirely indifferent world in which wilful wisdom seems to have a perfectly fair chance."[67]

A Spirit of Light and Order

The phrase "wilful wisdom" suggests that Promethean man needed more than will alone to have a fair chance at victory. There was also "wisdom"—knowledge, clear-headedness, objectivity, in short, Wells' omnibus word for systematic straight thinking, "Science."

Merely having identified himself in some inextricable way with "Science" cost Wells thousands of partisans in the last half of his prophetic career. Like "progress," "science" is nowadays a word in ill repute with a significantly large number of Western thinking people. The recent revival of interest in Bernard Shaw probably owes a great deal to his skeptical bias against science and scientists. But in Wells' formative years science enjoyed a prestige among the

66. *Fate of Man*, p. 90. See also *After Democracy*, p. 219; *Apropos of Dolores*, p. 40; *All Aboard for Ararat* (New York, 1941), p. 102.
67. Preface to *Seven Famous Novels*, p. ix.

intellectual avant-garde that nothing venerated by mid-twentieth-century thinkers can even begin to match. Its fascination for Wells, and its importance in providing the framework within which he arrived at his fundamental assumptions, have been discussed in the first section of this chapter. It need hardly be added that Wells did not look on science as merely a personal answer to a personal need; science was an integral part of his program for world salvation. Science cut right and left at old and antiquated ways of life, replaced the authority of the Christian faith with a new and ampler authority, respected no social distinctions, played no favorites, and knew no national or cultural frontiers. "Science was coming," Richard Remington learned from his father in *The New Machiavelli*, "a spirit of light and order, to the rescue of a world groaning and travailing in muddle for the want of it."[68]

Wells' enthusiasm for science sprang out of a deep respect for the virtues of the scientific life. Quite apart from his hero-worship of Huxley, Wells had a close life-long friendship with Sir Richard Gregory, and he recorded a similar admiration for Sir Ray Lankester in the character of Sir Rupert York in *The World of William Clissold*. Darwin, Metchnikov, Soddy, Jung, Freud, Einstein, and Pavlov, among others, were repeatedly singled out in his books for accolades. Rudely irreverent as Wells may have been toward genius in other fields, he had a measureless affection for scientists and scientific work. Science alone, in a world of increasing uncertainty and moral confusion, could offer a young man something solid and convincing. George Ponderevo's deliverance in *Tono-Bungay* was typical. With a divorce pending from his wife and disgusted by his uncle's patent medicine empire, he turned to science, and "Science, with her order, her inhuman distance, yet steely cer-

68. *New Machiavelli*, p. 33.

tainties, saved me from despair. . . . Scientific truth is the remotest of mistresses; she hides in strange places, she is attained by tortuous and laborious roads, but *she is always there!* Win to her and she will not fail you; she is yours and mankind's for ever. She is reality, the one reality I have found in this strange disorder of existence."[69] In *Marriage* Wells suggested that when the intellectual history of his time came to be written,

> Nothing I think will stand out more strikingly than the empty gulf in quality between the superb and richly fruitful scientific investigations that are going on and the general thought of other educated sections of the community. . . . [In scientific work] the human mind has achieved a new and higher quality of attitude and gesture, a veracity, self-detachment and self-abnegating vigour of criticism that tend to spread out and must ultimately spread out to every other human affair. In these uncontroversial issues at least mankind has learnt the rich rewards that ensue from patience and infinite pains.[70]

Just what Wells meant by "Science" was not always clear. But he certainly understood it in a looser sense than it was understood by the Positivists in his own time or by such contemporary spokesmen of the philosophy of science as Philipp Frank or F. S. C. Northrop. Science with a capital "S" was rather Remington's "spirit of light and order." It was clear, hard, systematic, disciplined thought, fueled with the data of sensory experience: illustrated by, but not entirely confined to, the methods of modern natural science. As Professor Ernest Keppel explained in *Star-Begotten*, " 'a new sort of mind' " was coming into the world, " 'with a new, simpler, clearer, and more powerful way of thinking.' "

69. *Tono-Bungay,* pp. 236, 324.
70. *Marriage,* p. 251.

This new sort of mind had so far been most successful in the exact sciences, and it had greatly accelerated the collapse of the existing social order without contributing much to the building of a new order; but the only hope of salvation lay in the willful and coordinated application of the scientific spirit to human problems on every level.[71] Wells had almost a Frenchman's passion for the ideal of clarity, and another passion that may have owed something to his Protestant origins for honesty. Together they represent most of what seems to have crossed his mind when he thought of the scientific spirit.

"Half the difference between Utopia and our world," said Mr. Barnstaple in *Men Like Gods*, ". . . lay in this, that our atmosphere was dense and poisonous with lies and shams." The Utopians even made the principle "that Lying is the Blackest Crime" a fundamental article of their code of liberties, on the theory that freedom is impossible where deliberate deception of any kind is tolerated.[72] Wells was always fond of contrasting the truthful atheist-scientist with the compromising or dishonest mind untouched by scientific training. A religious shame burned the cheeks of most of his young heroes in the early short stories and novels at the very thought of dishonesty. The science student in "A Slip under the Microscope" confessed that he had accidentally let a preparation slip under the microscope during an examination, which cost him his scholarship and forced him to quit his studies. Another science student, Mr. Lewisham, of *Love and Mr. Lewisham,* stuck to his stubborn moral bias against lying and cheating in spite of a brilliant intellectual defense of deceit offered by the medium Chaffery, and sobbed with remorse when he had to exaggerate his academic qualifications and list himself a member of the Church of England in order to get a teaching job. George

71. *Star-Begotten,* pp. 155–56.
72. *Men Like Gods,* p. 273.

Ponderevo later took the same stand against his uncle in *Tono-Bungay,* and in *The Bulpington of Blup* Wells devoted a whole novel to the contrast between the truth-telling scientist, personified by the Broxted family, and the habitually lying aesthete, personified by Theodore Bulpington. In short, as Wells wrote during the second World War, truth was the scientific man's God.[73]

Scientists were obliged not only to keep rigidly to the truth if they expected results: they had also to think clearly and coherently. " 'The real villain in the piece—in the whole human drama—is . . . muddle-headedness,' " Richard Remington told his wife, " 'and it matters very little if it's virtuous-minded or wicked.' " Muddle was for Wells the natural mental state. "Savagery with its numerous taboos, its occultism, and fetish, its complex ritualism is mentally more intricate than civilization. The minds of savages are even more tortuous than they are confused; they are misdirected by crazy classification and encumbered with symbolism, metaphor, metonymy and elaborate falsifications; it is the civilized man who thinks simply and clearly."[74]

Muddle-headedness was not itself a cause of human ills so much as a complex of more basic flaws in human nature and the social environment, from apathy, laziness, and irascibility to inadequate diet and poor education. But whatever the explanation for it, muddle-headedness ruled almost everywhere in the normal prescientific society. People

73. "The scientific worker . . . does in fact believe in Truth—which is his God." *Guide to the New World* (London, 1941), p. 103. In another wartime book Wells compared truth to holy water, which he could sprinkle at will over any menace in his dreams that threatened mankind; and the menace exploded harmlessly. *The Happy Turning* (New York, 1946), p. 9. *The Happy Turning* was a "dream-book" written in 1942, originally for circulation among Wells' friends; the English edition was published in 1945.

74. *New Machiavelli,* p. 349; *Mr. Blettsworthy on Rampole Island,* pp. 174–75.

would not for a variety of reasons state their problems
clearly and set about to solve them coolly and methodically.
The comet that visited the earth in one of Wells' scientific
romances transformed humanity by adding a new ingredient to the atmosphere, which literally eliminated muddle-
headedness. As the utopian narrator recalled,

> In that time of muddle and obscurity people were
> overtaken by needs and toil and hot passions before
> they had the chance of even a year or so of clear think-
> ing. . . . We were angry and hasty because we stifled
> in the darkness, in a poisoned and vitiated air. That
> deliberate animation of the intelligence which is now
> the universal quality, that vigor with consideration,
> that judgment with confident enterprise which shine
> through all our world, were things disintegrated and
> unknown in the corrupting atmosphere of our former
> state.[75]

In the real world, obviously, the role of the comet was being
played, less spectacularly, by the scientific spirit.

Wells attempted a formal definition of the scientific
method in several books, and he usually began by explaining that historically the scientific method had grown out
of the nominalism of late medieval philosophy. It was a
systematic effort "to find the *true,* the most significant and
fruitful, classification of things and substances."[76] The scientist remained always faithful to the "facts," and realizing
that classification was only an intellectual convenience and
not fundamentally true to nature, he fit his system of classification to the "facts" as he observed them, changing where
necessary to account for new "facts."

But even this somewhat lame definition, almost tailor-

75. *In the Days of the Comet* (New York, 1906), pp. 49–50.
76. *Outline of History,* 2, 170–71.

made for comparative anatomy (Wells' first love among the sciences), did not always suit him. William Burroughs Steele preferred a simpler definition, which recalls the elements of the scientific "spirit" discussed above. Essentially, said Steele, science was "candour. What is the scientific method? Bare, cold, clear, sceptical observation, and then the utmost precision of statement. Continual re-examination of the statement. Incessant search and testing."[77] So long as knowledge was sought systematically with a candid, open, inquiring mind, almost any modification of the scientific method made necessary by the peculiar properties of the object under study could yield a "scientific" result. Darwin, for example, was more a historian than a scientist in the usual sense. He measured nothing; he painstakingly reconstructed significant episodes in natural history. The sociologist, too, was in a unique position. He had only one unit of observation, all human society. It followed that sociologists could not operate after the example of physical scientists, but had somehow to combine the objective study of the behavior of society with subjective methods of interpretation, criticism, and social anticipation.[78] Wells cheerfully agreed with critics of science that it still left immense territories unexplored. In *You Can't Be Too Careful* he described modern science as only the first wave, the first fruits of an underlying mental process of sustained free reasoning, which might in time bring man well beyond the attitudes and procedures of what he now called science. He detected the tell-tale signs of a possible intellectual hardening of the arteries in the scientific world. By the 1940's science was becoming too highly specialized and institutionalized. It might be losing some of that youthful resilience that enabled creative scientific minds in the past to produce

77. *Anatomy of Frustration,* p. 205.
78. "The So-called Science of Sociology," *Social Forces in England and America,* especially pp. 231, 235.

great unifying generalizations and pioneer the opening of new frontiers in research.[79]

But science in the happier, broader sense, this new spirit in man's search for truth which Wells defined by stringing together adjectives like "hard" and "clear" and "orderly" and "candid," was the only possible instrument of man's deliverance from the confusion and animal drift of the world crisis. Although Wells had no faith in the benevolence or providential goodness of science, he did insist that without the weapons only science could provide, without material means and knowledge, *Homo sapiens* would topple back helplessly into the crucibles of the indifferent universe from which he had evolved. Science in the broadest sense was man's uniquely human way of arming himself against nature, of enlisting his brain power in the service of survival and conquest. And in each new era of history, fresh advances in science simultaneously solved old problems and raised new ones that could be solved only by further refinement and improvement in scientific method. " 'Science,' " King Egbert told the statesmen assembled at the Conference of Brissago after the great atomic world war in *The World Set Free*, " 'is the new king of the world' "—because science was the universal method of truth-seeking evolved by the mind of the race, the "way of thinking" of the emergent racial being, the "knowledge" in the racial mind.[80] Sir Richmond Hardy, a spokesman for Wells of a type familiar in the later novels, argued in *The Secret Places of the Heart* for the hammering out of sane scientific methods of developing the resources of the world and governing men " 'in the place of our present methods of snatch and wrangle. . . . We may not live to see even the beginnings of success, but

79. *You Can't Be Too Careful*, pp. 280–81.
80. *World Set Free*, p. 178. See also *Research Magnificent*, p. 117, and the general introduction to the Atlantic Edition of the *Works*, 1, xvii.

the spirit of order, the spirit that has already produced organized science, if only there are a few faithful, persistent people to stick to the job, will in the long run certainly save mankind and make human life—clean and splendid.' "[81]

The same writers and critics who have seized on Wells as a typical exponent of the doctrine of inevitable progress also like to belabor him for his "faith" in science. Here again a plea must be entered in his defense.[82] To a considerable extent Wells won his spurs as a literary man by his very success in demolishing the popular myth of science as a morally benevolent force. Science offered man unlimited power; without science Prometheus was almost helpless against nature. But in and of itself, science could do neither good nor evil. If used to advance human welfare, it could supply the means for a world Utopia. If misused, it might wreck civilization. Wells' scientific romances recorded invention after invention put to catastrophic use. In his two pre-1914 prophecies of world war, *The War in the Air* and *The World Set Free,* for example, he twice blew the world to bits with the help of advances in military technology. A familiar figure in the romances was the absent-minded scientist who had no idea of the social implications of his work:

81. *Secret Places of the Heart,* p. 200.
82. A perfectly good one has already been made by Esmé Wingfield-Stratford in his penetrating notebook of Edwardian impressions, *The Victorian Aftermath:* "Science, to Mr. Wells, was no beneficent fairy, but a djinn of unlimited power, which, if it were not controlled, would be capable of destroying those who had been rash enough to call him up, and laying waste their whole world. . . . It was his constant preoccupation throughout his subsequent career to save mankind from the fate of the mechanic who is caught up and crushed in his own machinery." Wingfield-Stratford's argument is based principally on the early scientific romances and short stories. See *The Victorian Aftermath,* in *The Victorian Cycle* (New York, Morrow, 1935), pp. 147–49.

Professor Gibberne, the inventor of "The New Accelerator," which would enable a man to live hundreds or thousands of times faster than normal; Cavor, who compounded the antigravity substance in *The First Men in the Moon;* and Bensington, who gave the world *The Food of the Gods.* Taken unawares by the effects of the Food on his colleague's infant son, Bensington summarized the dilemma of the scientific age:

> "It is another instance," he generalised, "of the thing that is continually happening. We—if indeed I may presume to the adjective—*scientific* men—we work of course always for a theoretical result—a purely theoretical result. But, incidentally, we do set forces in operation—*new* forces. We mustn't control them— and nobody else *can.*"[83]

After the first World War, Wells grew even more conscious of the amorality of scientific work. His old-fashioned rationalist in *The Undying Fire,* Dr. Elihu Barrack, insisted on the sovereignty of fact, but Job Huss could not agree. Science was easy, he said. A mere handful of scientists could supply the race with all it wanted and needed in no time at all, but what men lacked was the will and the common allegiance to humanity to use the free gifts of science for human welfare. " 'They solve the problems of material science in vain until they have solved their social and political problems.' "[84] No writer did more than Wells to disseminate the now almost tiresome idea that man's material progress has dangerously outstripped his moral and social development. As Wells pointed out in *The Open Conspiracy,* however exemplary the lives of scientific men may be, scientists as such should not be expected to lead humanity to the scientifically organized world community. "The

83. *The Food of the Gods* (New York, 1904), p. 68.
84. *Undying Fire,* p. 185.

world of science," he wrote, is essentially "a miscellany of specialists." Scientists had to be incorporated into the greater scheme of social advance by "the man of more general intelligence and wider purpose. The company of scientific men is less like a host of guiding angels than like a swarm of marvellous bees—endowed with stings—which must be hived and cherished and multiplied by the Open Conspiracy."[85]

The Wells J. M. Keynes once fondly called the "stinks master" of his generation[86] did not, then, nourish any illusions about the innate beneficence of the exact sciences. He respected scientists as men of exceptional dedication and creative power. He saw in the scientific method a great step forward in the organization of human mental effort. He found in the world of science the "origin of nearly all the great initiatives that characterise our times."[87] In the extension to social problems of the scientific spirit, the spirit of experiment, clear-headedness, intellectual honesty, and orderly thinking he placed his deepest hopes for the salvation of the species. In this sense he was a generation's "stinks master," and in no other. "Science stands, a too competent servant," he wrote in 1905, "behind her wrangling underbred masters, holding out resources, devices, and remedies they are too stupid to use."[88] The elimination of human stupidity was in itself a task larger than science could undertake. The world-view suggested by modern physics and biology would help to enlarge the perspectives of the thinking man; but in the most important of the sciences, the social sciences, where techniques for the engineering of human happiness and enlightenment had to be de-

85. *Open Conspiracy*, pp. 147–48.
86. Keynes' letter in *Stalin-Wells Talk* (London, 1934), p. 36. American translation: "science teacher."
87. *Open Conspiracy*, p. 146.
88. *Modern Utopia*, p. 102.

vised, the initiative remained with the wills of unique and incalculable men. More than thirty years after he had vigorously criticized Comte and Spencer and the whole positivist tradition in sociology before a gathering of the Sociological Society, he reiterated his convictiton in *World Brain* that in the organization of society, in what he called "constructive sociology," analysis and observation had to be creatively joined with the free exercise of imagination, moral feeling, and the aesthetic sense.[89] Science could tell men the best way to achieve certain specified purposes, and it could give men a common background of ideas from which to arrive at those purposes. But it was only Prometheus' fire, not Prometheus himself.

THE MIND OF THE RACE

The articles in Wells' credo discussed up to this point have been ideas or value judgments or attitudes about the nature of things—about the universe, evolution, human nature, the condition of man's will, the resources of man's intellect. Taken all together, they make a fairly coherent and consistent faith, a kind of scientific humanism not too unlike the humanistic world-view of T. H. Huxley. But Wells felt the need of something more, a synthetic idea sweeping enough to bind all his fundamental assumptions into a meaningful unity with the emotive appeal of religion.

For many of Wells' contemporaries who shared his general outlook on life, and for many who did not, the search for a religion ended in the discovery of socialism. Wells himself discovered socialism in early adolescence, through Henry George's *Progress and Poverty,* and by his second year at the Normal School of Science in South Kensington he and some of his fellow students had broken out in red

89. *World Brain,* pp. x–xi. "We have to assume certain desiderata before we can get down to effective, applicable work" (ibid., p. xi).

ties.[90] During his years in the Fabian Society, 1903–08, he was in touch with the keenest minds in British socialism. He wrote a Fabian tract, one of the best, entitled "This Misery of Boots," and one major book on socialist doctrine, *New Worlds for Old* (1908), which, in the judgment of a latter-day Fabian, G. D. H. Cole, "was certainly the most influential piece of Socialist propaganda in Great Britain since Blatchford's *Merrie England.*"[91] From his first books to his last Wells called himself a socialist, accepted the socialist position on property, and believed wholeheartedly in social planning. Yet, although many of the propositions of socialism found their way into his program for world reconstruction, socialism itself was not the kind of religion Wells was looking for.

Except perhaps in *New Worlds for Old,* where he stretched socialism to take in nearly his whole social philosophy, Wells always complained that socialism, while good enough as far as it went,[92] failed to penetrate deeply enough into the needs and problems of men. It was a one-track philosophy. It answered only one kind of question. He made the criticism often enough before the first World War,[93] but after 1914 he broke with the socialist movement, as a movement, altogether. The same thing happened to his fellow Fabian Graham Wallas, for much the same reason. Socialism could not explain the "Great War"; the war opened up to clear view dimensions of the crisis in civiliza-

90. *Experiment in Autobiography,* pp. 140–43, 193.

91. Cole, *A History of Socialist Thought, 1789–1939* (5 vols. London, Macmillan, 1953–60), *3,* Pt. I, 204–5. *Merrie England* was first published in 1894.

92. But by "socialism" Wells did not mean Marxism. For his low opinion of Marxism see *Russia in the Shadows,* chapter 3, "The Quintessence of Bolshevism," and *World of William Clissold, 1,* 166–80.

93. See *Mankind in the Making,* p. 267; *Socialism and the Family* (London, 1906), pp. 7–9; *Marriage,* p. 286.

tion that the Fabian Society had always conspicuously ignored.[94] After 1914 Wells consistently took the position
that socialism had exhausted its creative possibilities. What
was useful in the socialist movement to the cause of world
order and reconstruction had expanded into the general
intellectual atmosphere and become part of the thinking of
all right-minded people. Whatever parties and organized
groups still existed to preach one or another brand of doctrinaire socialism had shriveled into narrow, lifeless sects.
According to William Clissold, socialism had "gone—gone
like Chartism, like Puritanism, like the naturalism of Rousseau or the civic virtue of Robespierre. . . . It is not that I
have left Socialism, but that Socialism has passed away from
my world."[95]

Instead, Wells turned to another kind of religion altogether, a more comprehensive creed, more in harmony with
his fundamental assumptions, and especially with his habitual inclination to look on life from the perspectives of biology. It was at once the capstone and the mortar of his faith:
a belief in the emergence in human evolution of a collective racial being with a collective racial mind, which gathered the results of individual mental effort into a single
fund of racial wisdom and grew gradually toward organic
consciousness of itself. Individuals could escape the frustrations inherent in the fact of their individuality and mortal-

94. In 1916 Wallas wrote that socialism appeared to him doomed
"to go the way of 'natural rights' and the 'greatest happiness principle,' and in our new need we may find a new name for our hopes."
Wallas, *Men and Ideas*, ed. May Wallas (London, Allen and Unwin,
1940), p. 107. Wallas left the Fabian Society in 1904, after twenty
years with the "Old Gang."

95. *World of William Clissold, 1,* 157; cf. *The Elements of Reconstruction* (London, 1916), p. 45, and *Men Like Gods*, p. 313. Wells
viewed the British Labour party and other labor movements in Europe
and the United States as political expressions of trade unionism,
rather than socialism. See, e.g., *World Brain*, p. 164.

ity only by consecrating their lives to the service of the Mind of the Race.

At times Wells seemed to be using the "Mind of the Race" as no more than a convenient figure of speech, equivalent to "mankind" or "humanity" or *Homo sapiens*. At one point in his career he went to the other extreme of equating it with God. But the idea persisted for all its permutations of meaning through the whole course of his work. Humanity conceived merely as a Promethean rebel left unclear the relationship between individual lives and the racial life. Personifying and endowing the species with an organic intellect rendered the relationship, at any rate for Wells, forcefully clear. It also made more dramatic the cleavage between quintessential humanity and man's animal lower nature. The individual life could be warped and cheapened by yielding to destructive or debilitating or brutal instincts: the racial life, accumulating wisdom and truth in the racial mind, was man's highest self.

The gospel of the racial mind invaded almost every novel Wells ever wrote. It appeared time and again in his sociological books. In the end it took on the proportions of a religion. What *Humanité* was to Auguste Comte and the "Life Force" to Bernard Shaw, the "Mind of the Race" was to H. G. Wells. The world civilization he urged on humanity in his career as a prophet of world order would have been in effect the temporal embodiment of the racial mind, grown at last to mature consciousness of itself.

No article of faith better illustrates Wells' debt to the thought-world of the nineteenth century and to the influence especially of evolutionary biology than his organic concept of humanity; but to do him full justice it should be pointed out that very early in his career he analyzed his humanistic religious faith in terms of a set of answers he gave with an appealing amateurishness to the classical philosophical problem of "the one and the many." He did not come to his religion quite as naively as he might have, nor was his intelligence ever wholly and uncritically absorbed in it. Part of him always stood a little outside and peered— just a little skeptically—in.

The philosophical carpetbagger in Wells took a certain unprofessional pride in his handling of the problem of "the one and the many," of essence and existence. His attention had been called in that direction by the evidence in Huxley's course in comparative anatomy, and also by his geological studies at South Kensington[96]—evidence that species and classes of things had no real existence in themselves but were only convenient inventions of the human mind to reduce the sensed world to manageable proportions. Darwin had conclusively demonstrated the illusiveness of the old idea of fixed types in biology, and under Huxley's spell Wells arrived at a nominalism that dogmatically asserted the absolute uniqueness of objects, from atoms to individual members of a biological species, and so on up the scale of the organization of matter. "The Rediscovery of the Unique" presented his thesis to the readers of *The Fortnightly Review* in 1891. Formal elaborations and amendments followed in his Oxford speech, "Scepticism of the Instrument," published as an appendix in *A Modern Utopia,* and in *First and Last Things.* The "rediscovery of the unique" amounted to little more than a brew of Heraclitus and William of Ockham; but as he originally conceived it, Wells thought it would shatter the idea of natural law, the atomic theory, pure logic, the bases of common morality, and the validity of mathematics. Mankind was to be thrown back on something very like pragmatism. The line of thought developed in "The Rediscovery of the Unique" might even have ended in existentialism. But its

96. *Experiment in Autobiography,* pp. 179–81.

real significance was rather that it involved Wells deeply
in the problem of essence and existence. His thinking led
him around in the end to an approach which stood just as
far as possible from the existentialist's.

Wells expounded his nominalism in its fullest terms in
Book I of *First and Last Things*. He maintained that since
all objects were unique, classification was, strictly speaking,
impossible; that all objects in any event were endlessly becoming other objects; that negative and absolute terms had
no correspondents in objective reality; and that the mental
instrument was prone to commit the fallacy of reasoning on
different planes simultaneously. It was the last point that
enabled Wells to square his nominalism with his habitual
reference to the object "humanity"—or *Homo sapiens* or
"mankind" or "the mind of the race." All things were
unique, but at different levels or planes of reality. It all
depended on the plane in which objects were observed. At
the atomic level ethical values did not exist, but for living
human beings faced with the necessity of choosing courses
of action, beliefs and preferences were pragmatically indispensable. To confuse moral decisions with the evidence
of physics was to reason on different planes simultaneously,
which was invalid. By the same reasoning, belief in some
sort of emergent deity could be justified. "It is possible to
regard God as a Being synthetic in relation to men and societies, just as the idea of a universe of atoms and molecules
and inorganic relationships is analytical in relation to human life." In other words, all objects save the smallest were
unique amalgams of uniques, and an emergent divine being
could be just as "real" as an individual human being, since
both would owe their existence to the existence of lower
constituent orders in nature.[97]

97. "Scepticism of the Instrument," *Modern Utopia*, p. 392. Wells
emphasized the point even more strongly in a revised edition of *First
and Last Things* which he issued in 1917. "As we pass up the scale to

But the transcendent reality Wells actually professed to see emerging here and now was the collective being of humanity, rather than any "God." At the level of the individual the species *Homo sapiens* might be nothing more than a swarm of unique individuals descended in an unbroken sequence from remote protozoan ancestors; yet *Homo sapiens* was more than a name. At this moment in cosmic time it also denoted a class of similar if not identical individuals, evolving in ceaseless interaction with one another, and through the unique gift of speech able to pool their experiences and so give birth to a higher order of being entirely: a racial memory, a collective mind, the emergent intelligence of an emergent racial being.[98] As Wells grew older, he tended to look at life more and more from the synthetic level of the racial being and less and less from the analytical level of the individual. At the end of his spiritual pilgrimage he virtually accepted the realist argument that the whole is real and the individual an illusion. In the symbolic prologue to *The Undying Fire* he even likened the opposition of essence and existence to the interplay of good and evil. God was here represented as the inscrutable creator, who created things perfect and exact, only to allow the intrusion of a marginal inexactness in things through the intervention of Satan. God corrected the marginal uniqueness by creation at a higher level, and Satan upset the equilibrium all over again. Satan's intervention permit-

---

biological species," he wrote, "we begin to realise that there is a reality transcending the individual and we begin to apprehend the justice of the Realist's arguments so far as classifications by kind is concerned" (pp. 46–47).

98. It was the habit of the "modern" student of biology, said Wells, to "think of a living species as a single whole, as a synthetic being, unique, conducting a unique struggle against the universe, made up of practically similar but still unique individuals, beings of a less complex grade" (ibid., p. 49).

ted evolution, but the ultimate purpose of God was by implication a perfect and finished and evolved absolute unity.
Essence, then, was finally to overwhelm existence. And at
the moment, God's highest creation, whom He had filled
with His own spirit, was Man. The dialectic of good and
evil was the method of evolution, from absolute and perfect
nonbeing to absolute and perfect all-being. Whatever was
good in individual men was distilled in Man, the momentary vehicle of the evolving divine essence. If it had been
in Wells' nature to settle down and work out ideas in carefully elaborate detail, in the manner of system-spinning
philosophers and theologians, he might have made something of a splash in twentieth-century religious thought.

In philosophy the line of thinking he pursued in "The
Rediscovery of the Unique" and *First and Last Things* fed
into the same intellectual currents that produced the assault
on absolute terms and metaphysical inquiry generally by
pragmatism and logical positivism, the criticisms of formal
logic undertaken by John Dewey and Henri Bergson, and
the blossoming interest in recent years in semantics. Wells'
direct influence has been negligible, except on the level of
transmission. *First and Last Things,* for example, probably
helped to give wider currency to pragmatism during the
heyday of William James and F. C. S. Schiller. It is worth
recalling that William James himself deeply admired Wells'
work. Of *First and Last Things* he wrote to Wells that "the
first two 'books' should be entitled 'philosophy without
humbug' and used as a textbook in all the colleges of the
world. . . . I have been 35 years on the way to similar con-
clusions."[99] Wells also helped to stimulate the interest of
the book-reading public in semantics. His work has been
widely quoted in popular expositions of semantics, and

99. James to Wells, November 28, 1908, *The Letters of William
James,* ed. Henry James (2 vols. Boston, Atlantic Monthly Press, 1920),
2, 316.

Stuart Chase acknowledges that his own interest in semantics owes something to Wells' "Scepticism of the Instrument."[100]

But for a study of Wells' social philosophy, the religious implications of his hybrid nominalism matter most. Exploiting the metaphysical notion of higher and lower planes of being and the "scale of observation,"[101] he was able to justify without ceasing to be a nominalist altogether his faith in an emergent racial being, and to insist that in dedication to this synthetic racial being lay mankind's hopes for spiritual reorientation in the wake of the collapse of the positive religions.

Wells' "racial being" was by no stretch of the imagination a rare and lonely god. Nineteenth- and early twentieth-century thought teems with time-bound emergent deities. Scores of thinkers preached some sort of faith in what is potential in time, in place of the traditional Christian and mystical faith in a power outside of time. Hegel's *Weltgeist,* Comte's *Humanité,* Spencer's organismic humanity inevitably improving itself by the laws of evolution, Nietzsche's doctrine of superhumanity, the conception of a finite God given currency by J. S. Mill, Hastings Rashdall, and William James, the vitalism of Bergson and Shaw, the emergent evolutionism of Samuel Alexander and Lloyd Morgan, the theories of divine immanence in the liberal movement in Protestant theology, and du Noüy's telefinalism—all are exhibits in evidence of the influence chiefly of evolutionary thinking, both before and after Darwin, in Western intellectual history. The faith of progress itself—especially the idea of progress as built into the evolutionary scheme of

100. Chase, *The Tyranny of Words* (New York, 1938), p. 4.
101. Quite independently, Pierre Lecomte du Noüy used some of the same methods and arguments to reach a not entirely dissimilar world-view in his *Human Destiny,* 1947.

things—is in every way the psychological equivalent of religion.

Wells' own insistence on the collective quality of the racial being and the racial mind had still another source, apart from evolutionary biology. As Ernest Barker long ago made clear in his *Political Thought in England from Herbert Spencer to the Present Day,* the English intellectual avant-garde after 1870 or 1880 found itself in a mood of violent reaction against Benthamite individualism, which had become almost the official economic and political philosophy of the comfortably prosperous mid-Victorian bourgeoisie. The collectivist temper of the age produced socialism; but it was also felt in the new imperialism, in integral nationalism, and in the idealism of Green, Bradley, and Bosanquet, all of which emphasized the collective and corporate nature of the state or of society and refuted the utilitarian conception of the state as a mere instrument for promoting the happiness of the individual. Borrowing from Hegel,[102] Bosanquet's books in particular brimmed with references to the "collective mind" of the state. The sociologists of the period, from Bagehot and Durkheim to Graham Wallas, developed a social psychology for the study of collective mental phenomena which made abundant use of terms like "group consciousness." The international Positivist movement centered in Paris and, represented in England during the last third of the nineteenth century by Richard Congreve and Frederic Harrison, largely followed its master, Comte, in subordinating individual welfare and referring human religious feeling to the service of the col-

---

102. Ironically, Wells always considered Hegel a humbug and Hegelianism a pastime for wool-gathering dons. See the satirical portraits of Hegelians in *New Machiavelli,* pp. 102–4, and *Bealby* (New York, 1915), pp. 25–26, 36–38. Lord Moggeridge in *Bealby* is, of course, R. B. Haldane.

lective being of *Humanité*.[103] Wells never named his sources. Perhaps he was never conscious of having any.[104] But his idea of an emergent racial mind was an entirely typical product of the mental climate in which he worked.

The racial mind made its debut in that germinal book of prophecies, *Anticipations,* rendered vaguely as "a greater will," a sort of secular process working through individual lives to the spacious future of humanity and beyond.[105] Wells' next sociological treatise, *Mankind in the Making,* urged its readers to see

> our wills only as temporary manifestations of an am-
> pler will, our lives as passing phases of a greater Life,
> and to accept these facts even joyfully, to take our
> places in that larger scheme with a sense of relief and
> discovery, to go with that larger being, to serve that
> larger being, as a soldier marches, a mere unit in the
> larger being of his army, and serving his army, joy-
> fully into battle.[106]

103. See Ernest Barker, *Political Thought in England from Herbert Spencer to the Present Day* (London, 1915), and John Edwin McGee, *A Crusade for Humanity: The History of Organized Positivism in England* (London, 1931). A typical Positivist tract is F. S. Marvin's *The Living Past,* one of the English precursors of *The Outline of History*. Marvin studded his text with references to the being of humanity, and to "that collective mind by which [Western man] is surrounded and controlled as his body is by the air": *Living Past* (Oxford, Clarendon Press, 1913), p. 267.

104. He did acknowledge William James' idea of a finite God in *God the Invisible King,* p. 172. For Comte see *Experiment in Autobiography,* p. 562.

105. *Anticipations,* pp. 268, 316, 343. In his introduction to a new edition (London, Chapman and Hall) in 1914, Wells identified the "greater will" with the "Collective Mind" and defined it as "a racial purpose to which our reason in the measure of its strength, submits us" (p. xii). The 1914 edition contained the same text as the 1902 edition.

106. *Mankind in the Making,* p. 15.

The Epilogue of *A Modern Utopia* used the classical organic analogy:

> Ever and again . . . come glimpses of a comprehensive scheme . . . the scheme of a synthetic wider being, the great State, mankind, in which we all move and go, like blood corpuscles, like nerve cells, it may be at times like brain cells, in the body of a man. . . . Even for me, upon occasion, the little lures of the immediate life are seen small and vain, and the soul goes out to that mighty Being, to apprehend it and serve it and possess.[107]

By the time he was ready to make a first formal statement of his fundamental beliefs, in *First and Last Things* (1908), he had fully committed himself to a religious faith in the emergent collective mind of the species: "religious" in the sense that Wells professed to find salvation in the willful subordination of his individual will to the service of the transcendental racial will. As he explained in *First and Last Things*, "In this persuasion I find the ruling idea of which I stand in need, the ruling idea that reconciles and adjudicates among my warring motives. In it I find both concentration of myself and escape from myself, in a word, I find *Salvation*." The doctrine of racial mind, with its corollary of a world city of mankind, satisfied fully Wells' craving for spiritual synthesis. It bound idea to idea, fact to fact, desire to desire. With a solemnity much more believable in print than it might have been in the irreverent squeak of his own voice, he concluded:

> I am a temporary enclosure for a temporary purpose; that served, and my skull and teeth, my idiosyncrasy

107. *Modern Utopia*, pp. 372–73; see also *In the Days of the Comet*, p. 334; *Future in America*, pp. 207–8; *New Worlds for Old*, p. 267.

and desire, will disperse, I believe, like the timbers of a booth after a fair. . . . I shall serve my purpose and pass under the wheel and end. That distresses me not at all. Immortality would distress and perplex me. . . . I believe in the great and growing Being of the Species from which I rise, to which I return, and which, it may be, will ultimately even transcend the limitation of the Species and grow into the Conscious Being, the eternally conscious Being of all things. Believing that I cannot also believe that my peculiar little thread will not undergo synthesis and vanish as a separate thing.[108]

Once Wells had firmly settled his own mind, he managed easily enough to convert all his fictional heroes to the same faith. Richard Remington in *The New Machiavelli* compared men to the cells and corpuscles in "some great brain beyond our understanding." Richard Trafford, lying in his hut in Labrador in the closing pages of *Marriage*, managed in spite of a high fever and delirium to tell his wife Marjorie that "all good men with brains, all books, all art, all religions" were attempts on the part of an immortal being to achieve organic self-consciousness. And Stephen Stratton, the protagonist of *The Passionate Friends*, called it "a collective mind, a collective will towards achievement," which struggled out of the accidents of the individual life, linked nation to nation, and strove toward cosmopolis.[109] The honor roll of Wellsian heroes who preached the racial mind reads straight through to his last novels. They nearly all shared the same faith.

Wells first used the actual expression "mind of the race" in a queer farrago of farce and wistful sarcasm published in

108. *First and Last Things,* pp. 95, 110–11.
109. *New Machiavelli,* p. 304; *Marriage,* pp. 477–81; *Passionate Friends,* p. 235.

1915 under the title *Boon*.[110] One year later, in *Mr. Britling Sees It Through,* and at greater length in 1917, in *God the Invisible King,* he set out to translate his idea of a racial being and a racial mind into Christian terms, in order—as he explained later—to appeal to well-meaning souls who could not dispense with at least the simulacrum of a personal God.[111] Something of that brief adventure in theologizing has already been told,[112] and although it has a certain intrinsic interest of its own, it lies too far off the main course of Wells' thought to be worth treating at length here. "God the Invisible King" was on the surface of things a muscular Saviour, a militant God who led humanity into battle. But under closer examination he proved to be a finite god, who had begun when *Homo sapiens* had begun, who had no power apart from human power. In short, he was the immortal evolving part of man, in one of Wells' own phrases, "the undying human memory, the increasing human will." William Clissold later described Wells' wartime God as "Prometheus; it was a titanic and not a divine being."[113]

Titanic or divine, the Invisible King reigned for only a short time. After one last theological novel published in 1919, *The Undying Fire,* Wells returned resiliently to his

110. Most of the chapters were written in 1911. *Boon* is remembered nowadays for its ragging of Henry James. But most of the book is a tenderly witty and sensitive debate on the idea of a racial mind.

111. In addition to the confession in his *Experiment in Autobiography,* pp. 573–78, Wells offered an even franker apology for *God the Invisible King* in "Exasperations." He had been, he wrote, a "theological Quisling" and he wanted to purge his conscience by "full confession and repentance." "Exasperations," pp. 17a, 22. In the same chapter, "Heart Searchings of a Successful Radical," he also credited most of his theological ideas to talks he had had before the first World War with people like Stewart Headlam and G. K. Chesterton.

112. See above, p. 35.

113. *God the Invisible King,* p. 61; *World of William Clissold, 1,* 87.

prewar faith—if it is fair to say he had ever really deserted it.[114]

The mind of the race survived Wells' theological experiments without injury. Dr. Martineau in *The Secret Places of the Heart* (1922) was working out a psychology of self-transcendence to help bring individuals into union with the larger racial life. Dr. Devizes in *Christina Alberta's Father* (1925) and William Clissold both expressly avowed themselves disciples of the mind of the race.[115] In *The Science of Life* (1929–30) Wells was able to define the social and political life of man entirely in terms of "super-minds." All through history, he wrote, man had been striving toward some higher collective consciousness, which was reflected in such incomplete syntheses as the ideas of "class," "nation," "church." The next step was the unification of the whole mental effort of the race in a single world mind and world state: classes, nations, churches

---

114. Even in 1917 Wells did admit, in effect, that the Invisible King was only a personification of the mind of the race, in a passage from the 1917 edition of *First and Last Things*, p. vi. "To-day we seem nearer both hell and heaven than then," he wrote, comparing his state of mind at the time of writing, 1917, to his state of mind in 1908, "things are more personal and more personified; and while in 1908 I wrote about 'that collective mind' which must 'ultimately direct the evolution of our specific being,' I write now boldly to-day in 'God the Invisible King' of God, the ruling mind of the race, and of the Kingdom of God unifying mankind. The shape of the idea remains the same, but the clay has become alive. We have all lived greatly in these last years; we are no longer suspicious of strong phrases for mighty things."

115. *Christina Alberta's Father* (New York, 1925), pp. 289–91; *World of William Clissold*, *1*, 82–91. The passage from *Clissold* recorded parts of a conversation which had actually taken place between Wells and Carl Jung. Wells imagined, via Clissold, that there was a close affinity between the "mind of the race" and Jung on the collective psyche.

seem to have now under current conditions a ruling disposition to coalesce. They seem to be heading towards an ultimate unification into a collective human organism, whose knowledge and memory will be all science and all history, which will synthesize the pervading will to live and reproduce into a collective purpose of continuation and growth. Upon that creative organization of thought and will the continuing succession of conscious individual lives, drawing upon and adding to its resources, will go on. At the end of our vista of the progressive mental development of mankind stands the promise of Man, consciously controlling his own destinies and the destinies of all life upon this planet.[116]

Although Wells' racial mind existed only through the minds of individual men and could not intervene between man and his fate, it had for Wells a profound religious significance all the same. Individuals groping for some clue to their purpose in the scheme of things could identify themselves with a process almost infinitely larger than their own lives. The racial mind followed a flow of direction in time. Through literature, art, and science it offered each new generation of men increasingly greater knowledge and mastery of their environment. The individual who contributed to the growth of the mind of the race transcended his own imperfect, mortal, narrow self and found salvation in allegiance and surrender to purposes higher than his own. He fell into place in history. At Wells' scale of observation "the race is the drama and we are the incidents." Individuals were merely episodes in a performance, who

116. *The Science of Life*, with Julian Huxley and G. P. Wells (2 vols. Garden City, N.Y., 1931), 2, 1473. The chapter from which this passage was taken was written by H. G. Wells. See the original MS in the Wells Archive.

could escape their own mortality and insignificance only by giving themselves wholly to the demands of that larger drama in which, for a brief time, they had their existence.[117]

It was the very briefness of the individual life that contrasted most vividly with the life of the race and made the need for religion so humanly urgent. "In physical as in mental fact," Wells wrote, "we separate persons . . . are but fragments, set apart for a little while in order that we may return to the general life again with fresh experiences and fresh acquirements, as bees return with pollen and nourishment to the fellowship of the hive."[118] The idiosyncrasies of personality disappeared at death, and only the essence of mankind remained imperishable. The race went on, gathering strength and knowledge where it could, but the individual entirely disintegrated, leaving behind him only the consequences of his life. " 'We live and then we die,' " said Trafford in *Marriage,* " 'and the threads run, dispersing this way and that. To make other people again.' "[119]

So much greater was the racial adventure than any mortal participant in the adventure that, for Wells, no individuals among the billions ever born deserved to be singled out for the kind of apotheosis so dear to nineteenth-century historians. Like the garrulous uncle in his *Select Conversations,* Wells "had a low opinion of eminent people."[120] The best examples of this low opinion may be read in *The Outline of History,* which owed some of its phenomenal success to its iconoclasm. But Wells had always argued against the Great Man thesis. "There are those who believe entirely in

117. *First and Last Things,* p. 102; cf. *God the Invisible King,* pp. 71–73.

118. "The Human Adventure," *Social Forces in England and America,* p. 414.

119. *Marriage,* p. 477.

120. *Select Conversations with an Uncle* (New York, 1895), p. 5.

the individual man," he wrote in 1902, "and those who believe entirely in the forces behind the individual man; and for my own part I must confess myself a rather extreme case of the latter kind. ... I believe that these great men of ours are no more than images and symbols and instruments taken, as it were, haphazard by the incessant and consistent forces behind them; they are the pen-nibs Fate has used for her writing."[121] All individual effort, taken in itself, was feeble; "great men" and "small men" alike could find freedom from their sense of ultimate futility only in selfless service to the racial being.

Especially in his later years, under the influence of Pavlov, Watson, and the behaviorist movement in psychology, Wells came to insist that individuals were not only mortal but also discontinuous and illusory. They did not exist at all in the objective universe, save as partially integrated bundles of material stuff. They lacked continuity in space, and they underwent drastic changes in time. Individuality, Wells told a radio audience in 1929, was "a convenient biological illusion." He was nowadays hardly any more like the H. G. Wells of 1866 or 1886 or 1896 than he was like his grandfather. His moods and thoughts changed, his body changed from hour to hour. This did not mean, of course, that individuals should try to purge themselves of individuality. "It is a sin," he added, "to bury the talent, the individual gift which we possess for the good of the master being, Man," just as it was a sin to subordinate the self to collectivities less than Man which resisted the coming of world order.[122] But individuals were means to ends, and not ends in themselves. Wells compared the conscious life in *The Conquest of Time* to "the pictures on a cinema screen. They are discontinuous 'Nows,' but they follow one

121. *Discovery of the Future*, pp. 66–68.
122. *After Democracy*, pp. 132, 136; cf. *First and Last Things*, p. 103.

another so rapidly that they seem continuous."[123] He even composed a curious doctoral thesis during the second World War to prove that the apparent integrality of individual life in *Homo sapiens* was sheer illusion. The "self" was "a multitude of loosely linked series of behaviour systems which take control of the body and participate in a common delusion of being one single self." The wise man escaped the frustration of individuality by losing himself "in the discovery . . . of his own idiosyncratic creative possibility" for the service of mankind. "And, at the last throb, a soft dark restful curtain falls for ever upon that personal life and our contribution has been made."[124]

Finally, Wells fully intended his ideal of service to the racial mind to be understood as a religion. "Religion" was for him a good word. Man, he wrote in *A Modern Utopia*, "is religious; religion is as natural to him as lust and anger."[125] The "synthetic motive" discussed in *First and Last Things,* which bound all the warring motives in men into some effect of working unity, was fundamentally religious in nature. Salvation could be won only by recognizing the muddle of conflicting instinctual drives and imposing on them order and synthesis, which was to say, "religion."[126] In *The Open Conspiracy* he introduced his subject with several brief prominent chapters explaining the all-importance of religion in human life. The collapse

123. *Conquest of Time,* p. 85.

124. "Thesis on the Quality of Illusion in the Continuity of the Individual Life in the Higher Metazoa with Particular Reference to the Species *Homo sapiens,*" published in *'42 to '44,* pp. 169, 193; and *Conquest of Time,* p. 86.

125. *Modern Utopia,* p. 300.

126. *First and Last Things,* pp. 87–90. "I write in phrases that the evangelical Christianity of my childhood made familiar to me, because they are the most expressive phrases I have ever met for the psychological facts with which I am dealing" (ibid., p. 125).

of its religion, he pointed out, was the gravest event in the decline of modern civilization. The only route to salvation lay through a new kind of religion, an unorganized, uninstitutionalized religion of commitment to the collective being of humanity, in which, he said, was embedded the quintessence of all the great historic religions. All the positive religions had taught subordination of self to purposes transcending the immediate life. In the coming world civilization,

> the impulse to devotion, to universal service and to a complete escape from self, which has been the common underlying force in all the great religions of the last five and twenty centuries, an impulse which ebbed so perceptibly during the prosperity, laxity, disillusionment and scepticism of the past seventy or eighty years, will reappear again, stripped and plain, as the recognized fundamental structural impulse in human society.[127]

To these fundamental convictions about nature, man, and knowledge, and to this religious faith of service to the emergent mind of the race, Wells' social philosophy was securely anchored. He might have been a successful literary man without his fundamental assumptions: but not a prophet of world order. His idea of nature as blindly hostile to human aspiration, his conception of man as a rebellious Prometheus, and his belief in an emergent racial being evolving toward organic unity led him inevitably to the idea of an integrated world civilization. His indebtedness to

127. *Open Conspiracy,* chapters 1–3; *Outline of History,* 2, 582. The Positivists were fond of defining the "essence" of religion in these terms. In the "capacity of sacrifice regardless of self," J. Cotter Morison wrote in 1888, "we have the purest essence of the best religions": *The Service of Man* (London, Kegan Paul, Trench, 1888), p. 261.

what he understood of science made him stress the importance of indoctrinating young people in schools with the
"scientific" world-view; science itself made the planning
and management of a complex industrialized world society
feasible. Wells' insistence on the sovereignty in human affairs of the collective will and mind of the race, and of
scientific knowledge, which was the knowledge in the racial
"brain," made him impatient with democracy and sympathetic to the idea of government by functional elites of
managers and scientists. Hardly a single feature of his prophetic program cannot be traced directly back to, or was not
at least powerfully strengthened and sustained by, his fundamental assumptions.

But Wells was not primarily a philosopher or a religious
teacher, any more than he was in any conventional sense a
scientist. Stirred to a feeling of terrible urgency by the twentieth-century crisis in civilization, he devoted most of his
time and energy to the formulation of a program for the
achievement of world order. The first steps in his agenda
consisted of doing what he had done for himself, diagnosing
the world's woes, defining basic attitudes and approaches,
and thinking through the human problem in all its dimensions. This had to be followed, as he came to believe, by a
world revolution in education, which in turn would grow
by degrees into an Open Conspiracy against the old order
of society and finally into a revolution culminating in the
establishment of a new world civilization. The chapters
which follow discuss this program step by step, beginning
with his proposals for a renaissance in education.

Chapter Three:

EDUCATION

THE MEANING OF EDUCATION

One of the most characteristic and influential features of H. G. Wells' serious writing was its relentless insistence on the power of ideas in history. Humanity had to think as one, before it could live as one. "All the things that men and nations do," he wrote in *The Outline of History*, "are the outcome of instinctive motives reacting upon the ideas which talk and books and newspapers and schoolmasters and so forth have put into people's heads. . . . All human history is fundamentally a history of ideas."[1] Especially in the years after 1919, he maintained that the achievement of world order depended on a massive educational effort, and at the heart of that effort the propagation of the idea of a planned world society. There was no hope of world revolution without immense changes in the world's habits of mind.

This emphasis on education broadly defined developed from Wells' religious, or at least quasi-religious, concept of an emergent racial mind. Like many contemporary students of intellectual history, social philosophy, and world politics, he was always inclined to see life first of all in terms of men-

1. *Outline of History*, 2, 508.

tal activity, rather than in terms of economics or politics or geography.[2] He was a forerunner of all those commentators who nowadays interpret the world crisis as an "ideologial conflict" and a battle for the "minds of men." If the human race had civilized itself by brain work, only by more brain work could it save itself from catastrophe. "To this day," as he warned socialist readers in *New Worlds for Old* (1908), "the majority of Socialists still fail to grasp completely the . . . fact that every human soul moves within its *circle of ideas*, resisting enlargement, incapable indeed if once it is adult of any extensive enlargement, and that all effectual human progress can be achieved only through such enlargement." As Wells looked on socialism, it was an attempt on the part of the still incoherent collective mind "to pull itself together, to develop and establish a governing idea of itself. . . . The Socialist movement is from this point of view, no less than the development of the collective self-consciousness of humanity."[3]

The first World War and even more the inconclusive peace patched together at Versailles brought home to Wells the awful consequences of defective education. That the war had occurred at all was serious enough. What disturbed him most, however, was the inability of the world's statesmen or the opinion sustaining them to grasp the full dimensions of the world crisis in 1919. Blinkered especially

2. See, e.g., Gemini Twain in *Babes in the Darkling Wood*, pp. 400–1: "The one and sole *reality* in human life is mental. It always has been; it always will be. Our selves are the mental assemblage of our activities. Theology and worship, religion, philosophy, science, imagination, propaganda and teaching, are the essentials upon which all purposive action, all cooperation and material achievement depend. Violence and the forcible prevention of violence are both merely the realisation of ideas. A bomb is a whole complex of thought embodied. . . . To live is to think; to act consciously is merely thinking by action; there is no other living."

3. *New Worlds for Old*, pp. 209, 273–74.

by the low quality of history teaching in the prewar world, the men at Versailles lacked perspective. Their minds were inelastic, closed to new prospects and new problems. They had tried to solve a twentieth-century dilemma along nineteenth-century lines. And world opinion was in no sense ahead of them. A full-scale program of re-education was needed to bring the confused and drifting wills of men up to the level of resolve and knowledge necessary to get civilization under control and ensure it against fresh wars and even extinction. If the world was to be saved, Wells wrote in 1924, a new educational movement had to be launched, comparable in vigor and thrust to the mechanical revolution of the eighteenth and nineteenth centuries. The mechanical revolution had entirely changed the visible aspects of life. It had abolished physical distance. The new revolution would abolish mental distance.[4] Until it did, until the minds of men everywhere were prepared by education for world citizenship, action at any other level was bound to be ineffectual. "Before we can talk politics, finance, business, or morals, we must see that we have got the right mental habits and the right foundation of realized facts. There is nothing much to be done with our lives until we have seen to that."[5] Wells clung to this persuasion all his life. Toward the end, when he felt time running out for humanity, it was because the race he had once prophesied "between education and catastrophe" had turned into a "walk-over" for catastrophe. He could not join in the enthusiasms of the world federalists in the late 1930's:

> I do not believe that a world order can come into existence without a preliminary mental cosmopolis. I may be mistaken in that. Political federation, loose and

4. *A Year of Prophesying* (New York, 1925), p. 301.
5. *What Are We to Do with Our Lives?* (Garden City, N.Y., 1931), p. 21.

confused at first, may precede and impose the necessary mental adaptations. That is too round-about and
slow a process for the limitations of my imagination.
World democracy, I believe, would get lost on the
way.[6]

Wells' use of the word "education" illustrates the best
and the worst qualities of his writing. A logician would find
it deplorable. Spinning out his thoughts in loose, rhapsodic
periods, he could make "education" mean almost anything.
Sometimes it was "literature," sometimes "thought," sometimes the "transmission" of racial experience.[7] Wells in
fact was groping for a functional, organic term that would
comprise all the mental activities of the collective being
of humanity. To draw on all the definitions he attempted,
"education" included the transmission of ideas and knowledge from one mind to another, the integration of knowledge, the development of natural ability, and the learning
process at every level, from simple memorizing to abstruse
research. In the Utopia of *The Shape of Things to Come,*
the word had "come now to cover almost all intellectual activities throughout life except research and artistic creation," but in a later book he insisted that education in the
modern world "broadens out to embrace research and
fresh thought—all research and fresh thought however rec-
ondite. 'I cannot find any point,' says Steele, 'at which I can
draw the line between research however specialized and
poetic expression however precious, and the general educational process of mankind.' The highest springs and the
remotest creeks are all in touch with the ocean."[8] In short,

6. *Fate of Man,* pp. 43, 84.

7. Cf. Hallery's sweeping use of the term "literature" in *Boon,* pp.
166–67.

8. *Shape of Things to Come,* p. 129; *Anatomy of Frustration,* pp.
119–20.

as an instrument for ensuring racial survival and progress, "education" denoted both the dissemination of knowledge and ideas, and creative mental work. In one instance, individual cells in the racial mind were put in closer contact with the general life of the mind. In the other, the mind itself reached out and increased its knowledge of its environment. Both were instances of learning.

Even in the more limited sense of "education," to mean only the dissemination or transmission of knowledge, skills, ideas, and values, Wells was always careful to point out that formal education constituted only the barest fraction of it. "People are too apt," said William Clissold, "to identify schools and education. Never was there a more mischievous error."[9] Schoolmasters taught, but so did parents, preachers, public lecturers, the mass media of communication, books, and plays. So far as the mind of the race was concerned, it made no difference at all whether information reached minds in schoolrooms or through books, magazines, newspapers, films, or radio programs. Under some circumstances the schoolroom and the university lecture hall were the best places in the world to avoid an education.

Nor was it sufficient just to learn. As much as any Roman Catholic educational theorist, Wells argued that education had to be purposive, animated by a social philosophy, dedicated to the service of values transcending individual values. "Essentially the work of the schoolmaster," in the words of Wells' alter ego in *Boon,* was "to prepare the young and naturally overindividualized mind for communion with the Mind of the Race."[10] As Wells indicated in *The Science of Life,* a modern education had to achieve four related objectives: the training of all the individual faculties, the development of a *persona* and the acquisition of enough self-knowledge to ensure personal happiness, the presenta-

9. *World of William Clissold,* 2, 627.
10. *Boon,* p. 192.

tion of knowledge in such a way as to establish in individual minds the modern scientific world-view and a vision of the human adventure in the broadest possible perspective, and the special technical training needed by the individual for the enactment of his own chosen role in the racial drama.[11] In much of his thinking about education, especially after 1919, Wells also assumed that the idea of a planned world commonwealth would have to become the dominant theme in modern education, to the same extent that Marxism informed communist education or the teaching of the Church informed Catholic education. "The idea of a world commonweal," he wrote in 1921, "has to . . . dominate education everywhere in the world. When that end is achieved, then the world state will be achieved, and it can be achieved in no other way."[12] To some extent the task could be accomplished in progressive schools. But much of the responsibility fell upon "teachers" outside the academic profession, and especially upon men of letters. If "education" at one end of Wells' semantic spectrum denoted the imparting and seeking out of knowledge, at the other end it overlapped with, and for Wells' purposes replaced, "propaganda."

Wells' educational proposals and projects fall into three broad divisions. In spite of his customary contempt for most formal schoolmastering, he devoted a large section of his work to constructive criticism of the British educational system, enough to have prompted F. H. Doughty's book about Wells as an educator in 1926.[13] Then, between 1920 and 1932, he produced three outline surveys of general knowledge, the "trilogy" mentioned in Chapter 1 above, as a contribution to adult education. And in the 1930's he campaigned in a number of books for what is now usually defined as "intellectual integration," the synthesis of knowl-

11. *Science of Life*, 2, 1464.
12. *Salvaging of Civilization*, p. 21.
13. Doughty, *H. G. Wells: Educationist*.

edge through a world encyclopedia and the establishment of a world brain center, to serve both as a functionally integrated catalogue of knowledge and ultimately as the headquarters of the service controls of the world state.

THE SCHOOLS, THE UNIVERSITIES, AND WORLD ORDER

Virtually all the critics of the Victorian-Edwardian *ancien régime,* from Shaw and Wells to Bertrand Russell, took a special delight in assailing its system of formal education. From within and without, the schools and universities of the old order were subjected to a merciless fire of criticism over the years, above all during the first quarter of the twentieth century. The result was an impressive array of reforms. Throughout much of the Western world standards of education rose steeply, curricula were modernized, schools were democratized, school-leaving ages were increased, and the universities lost at least some of their medieval patina.

But even when reforming educators followed his proposals, Wells was not satisfied. The technical quality of education and research might have improved during his lifetime, but formal education never lent itself to the propaganda of world order. It never, in any sense, became infused with an ideology, except in totalitarian states, where every available modern educational device was marshaled in the service of causes inimical to world order. For Wells the *sine qua non* of a new departure in education was ideological commitment: no amount of piecemeal reform mattered unless it was guided and coordinated every step of the way by an enlivening social purpose, specifically by the idea of a planned world society.

Wells' novels are crowded with the casualties of formal education, ranging from mentally stunted members of the lower middle class thrown on the labor market by the state with only six or eight grossly inadequate years of schooling to the polished but empty-minded products of the older sort of public school and university. He found British education monstrously class-conscious, insanely obsessed with Greek and Latin, plagued by unimaginative and intellectually second-rate schoolmasters, rotten with puerile athleticism, desperately short of funds for expansion, hopelessly out of touch with the real world—with science, modern languages, modern history, the world political and economic crisis, the reawakening civilizations of the East, all that really mattered to students preparing to live and work and vote in the radically new world of the twentieth century. And he was puzzled, as educational reformers are always puzzled, by the dilemma of how to raise standards without somehow fundamentally altering the quality of the schoolmaster and the don. In Britain especially, all sorts of religious and social pressures prevented creative minds from making or even wanting to make their way into the system. The schoolmaster by the very nature of his trade had to be fairly orthodox, unimaginative, cautious, conservative, polite. He had to please. More than once Wells had to confess himself amazed at his own naiveté, for trying to make revolutionists—of all people—out of schoolmasters.

But he tried. He realized the indispensability of formal schooling. Education had made all the difference in his own experience. Without the advantage of his grammar school and college work, he might have remained all his life, fretful and unused, in the nethermost layer of the English lower middle classes. Simultaneously with his blistering derision of the teaching fraternity in novel after novel, he offered a wide variety of constructive proposals for the transformation of formal education into an instrument for the propaganda of world order. Some of his ideas took hold—so much so that it became fashionable in later years to twit him with his failure to keep informed about educational "progress." Other ideas of his remain untried.

Essentially, Wells pinned his hopes on an educational renaissance in the schools, rather than in the universities. So far as formal education was concerned, he saw the university more as a research center, for the training of specialists and the pursuit of new knowledge. He reserved to primary and secondary schools the responsibility of inculcating the modern scientific world-view, of reaching young people in their most plastic years with a balanced and integrated picture of what he habitually called the "real world," the world as it was, in all its variety and immensity, with all its opportunity for progressive change, and all its susceptibility to breakdown and collapse.

Wells' most carefully worked-out suggestions for educational reform in the schools appeared in a paper he offered the Educational Science Section of the British Association for the Advancement of Science in 1937. The paper dealt only with what Wells called the "informative content" of education, but it was just in this perhaps pedestrian matter of "information" that he saw in his later years the greatest opportunity for serving the cause of world order in the schools. His central idea was the overwhelming importance of building up in young minds a comprehensive view of human civilization and man's place in the universe, so that future generations would get into the habit of thinking and living on a world scale. Prewar generations had grown up thinking and living in terms of classes and nation-states; insofar as they had seen the rest of humanity at all, they had seen it from cramped, warped local perspectives. Understanding among peoples could be won only by rescaling school curricula throughout the world to the new planetary dimensions of human intercourse. Since the scale on which most people did their thinking, the general frames of reference in which they filed information, were formed quite early in life, Wells argued that "the main beams and girders of the mental framework must be laid down . . . before the close of adolescence."[14] Assuming, after the British example, that a child could count on receiving only ten years of public schooling and only six hours a week could be given over to strictly "informative" teaching, Wells estimated that the laying down of these "main beams and girders" had to be done in just 2,400 hours, which made economy in the choice of materials absolutely imperative. Three fields of study, pursued with increasing depth and complexity through the ten-year span of schooling, would have to do: biological science, physical science, and world history and sociology.

At age seven and eight, for example, children might be introduced to the subject matter of each of the three fields by studying things familiar to them in everyday life. Biology could begin as a description of various types of plants and animals, and the presentation of elementary facts about human physiology and health. Another class could be given over to rudimentary physics: states of matter, the composition of matter, the earth's surface. Still a third class could be devoted to a study of elementary ideas about the development of civilization: stone-age culture, the coming of agriculture and the domestication of animals, trade, towns, ships, nomadic cultures, warfare, and the like, without any special attention being paid to names, dates, or places. Children aged nine to twelve would then be ready for much more advanced study, with the use of notebooks, time charts, maps, and so forth. Biology could now be a study of the elements of physiology and anatomy, together with an outline of evolution and paleontology. The physical science class would get into chemistry, the laws of physics, a study of modern industrial technology, geography, geology, and ecol-

14. "The Informative Content of Education," *World Brain,* p. 102.

ogy, all in broad simplified surveys. The historical class would study the outlines of world history, from the earliest civilizations down to the rise of the modern nation-state. In the final four years students would undertake rigorous systematic study, with training and experience in the use of museums, libraries, and laboratories. They would select one of the sciences for intensive advanced work, and the history class would subdivide into as many as four separate classes, one for study of contemporary ideologies and social types, leading to the choice of a personal role in sociey; another for an investigation of the machinery of society—communications and trade, industry, money, property, and the like—stressing themes common to most parts of the world; another for the study of world economic geography and geology; and a fourth for the elements of modern political and economic history.[15]

It was a typically Wellsian proposal, at first glance reasonable, realistic, and promising, but in the last analysis impracticable. It would have meant impossibly drastic changes in almost every school curriculum in Britain, let alone the world. It would have required a perceptible increase in the quality of teachers. A committee of the British Association circularized forty-seven British schools to see how nearly their program of instruction matched Wells'. More than half replied, and the consensus was that Wells expected too much. The subject matter he would teach was "both too wide in scope . . . and too advanced in its demands upon the capacity of the pupils."[16] Training and discipline, techniques and methods, mattered most, and if these were all first-rate, teachers could teach almost anything. F. J. C. Hearnshaw chided Wells for being out of date, in an article

15. See ibid., pp. 95–130, for the whole lecture, and especially the diagram on pp. 106–7.
16. Quoted in W. H. G. Armytage, *Sir Richard Gregory* (London, Macmillan, 1957), p. 156.

in *The Journal of Education*. Wells had lost contact with developments in educational theory. Nowadays the emphasis was on training of the intellect, and not on information. The Germans were the best informed people in the world, but few of them knew how to think for themselves.[17]

Hearnshaw and many other educators completely missed Wells' point. Wells was no more interested in information for its own sake than they. His concern was for the scale of information, for the size of the framework of facts and ideas with which young minds were to be outfitted in their most impressionable years. Make them world-conscious, prepare them to live in the whole world, he maintained, and many of them would be able to grasp the dimensions of the twentieth-century world crisis. Public opinion would be receptive at last to unifying initiatives. Keep them in blinders, teach them only national history and national problems or the antiquated formulas of this or that positive religion, fail to give them a broad, connected picture of man's place in the universe, and world order would be out of reach forever.

Apart from the kind of reforms suggested in the British Association lecture and elsewhere,[18] Wells had something to say about other aspects of schooling, and it was here perhaps that he wielded the greatest immediate influence.[19] His contributions to the campaigns against Greek and Latin, ancient history, and games were especially successful, and together with the efforts of many other men of letters cleared the ground for major curricular reform. He helped

17. F. J. C. Hearnshaw, "Mr. H. G. Wells as an Educationist," *Journal of Education*, 69 (1937), 647–48.

18. Cf. the teaching program suggested in *World Brain* with Job Huss' similar program at Woldingstanton School in *The Undying Fire*.

19. For assessments of Wells' influence in British education see Doughty, *H. G. Wells: Educationist,* and Edward C. Mack, *Public Schools and British Opinion since 1860* (New York, 1941), passim.

interest British and American educators in the early teaching of modern foreign languages, including even Russian and Hindustani, to take the place of Greek and Latin; and in his schemes for reform there usually appeared much practical, common-sense advice on the better teaching of English, on the importance of drawing, and on the need in a scientific age for the laying of a solid foundation in mathematics. One paper published in 1921 aroused a horrified chorus of protests with a proposal that seems today almost trite. There would never be enough schoolmasters of really high caliber to go around, Wells pointed out, which meant that modern education had to be machined. National education departments would have to engage qualified educators to standardize for wholesale manufacture educational materials, school libraries, courses of instruction, textbooks, and so forth, so that even a second-rate teacher could, by following the notes and using the materials suggested by the experts, provide his pupils with a sound education. Wells recommended full exploitation of modern teaching equipment: laboratory demonstrations on film, to save time and money and avoid embarrassment; and gramophone recordings, to teach languages and music. These were bold proposals; they made Wells few friends at the time among British schoolmasters.[20]

At least, he would have let schoolmasters go on being schoolmasters. He dealt with dons on a different basis. The longer he studied universities on both sides of the Atlantic, the more convinced he became that universities had no place in the new world order save as centers of research and

20. See *Salvaging of Civilization*, pp. 157–66. Other important sources for Wells' ideas about primary and secondary education are *Joan and Peter, The Undying Fire,* and *The Story of a Great Schoolmaster.* The last, 1924, is a short biography of F. W. Sanderson, for many years headmaster of Oundle School and a heterodox educator after Wells' own heart. Wells sent his sons to Oundle.

specialized training. The liberal education they pretended
to give could be much more thoroughly assimilated in the
last three or four years of schooling. Even the best of them
were overgrown with tradition, walled off from the rest of
the world like medieval cloisters and hopelessly irrelevant
to contemporary needs. Undergraduate life had become an
unnatural protraction of adolescence. In the bookless world
of the past, universities might have been indispensable. In
the world of the twentieth century, an advanced general
education could be obtained directly from books, from the
press, from alert everyday living. If the proper background
were supplied in school, if interests were stimulated and
captured early in life and students taught how to study and
read independently, the general education courses at the
university could be eliminated altogether. "A time must
come," said William Clissold, "when Oxford and Cambridge will signify no more in the current intellectual life
of the world than the monastery of Mount Athos or the
lamaseries of Tibet do now, when their colleges will stand
empty and clean for the amateur of architecture and the
sight-seeing tourist." The university would be replaced entirely by the research center, where distinguished scholars
and scientists worked in company with selected advanced
students. The results of their investigations would be published internationally, and they would be heard not "in the
lecture theatres of provincial towns" but at conferences re-
ported in the world's press and broadcast by world radio
networks.[21] Wells anticipated an almost sudden collapse of
undergraduate life, in response to the challenge of the twentieth-century world crisis. There would come a general realization of the essential frivolousness of colleges: "The undergraduate body may melt away quite suddenly, dispersing to
forms of work and training of a more specialized and continuous sort, and with that the university properly speaking,

21. *World of William Clissold,* 2, 659, 660.

that immense obsolescent educational gesture, that miscellaneous great gathering of students and teachers, will achieve a culminating gala of sport and splendour—and cease."[22]

Much of the work of the research university would continue along present lines. But after the first World War Wells' attentions were drawn to new developments in the social sciences. He began to see in sociological and economic research a solution for one of the thorniest problems of the would-be revolutionist: the absence of an accepted "right way" of organizing society, in the sense that a certain rough unanimity existed among scientists and engineers as to the right way of building a factory or drilling an oil well or navigating a ship on the high seas.

Before the first World War he had tended to look contemptuously on sociologists, psychologists, and economists. Like Graham Wallas he had accused them of still being, at heart, followers of Comte, weaving highly intellectualized systems out of a few oversimplified propositions. But the work of institutions like the London School of Economics and the New School for Social Research in the United States[23] persuaded him of the possibility of authentic

22. *Work, Wealth and Happiness of Mankind*, 2, 815. And if it did not, after all, cease, it would at least change its character profoundly. Wells restored the undergraduate college to his educational scheme in his B.A.A.S. lecture in 1937, but it was still more a technical or graduate school than an undergraduate college in the current sense. About half the student's time would be devoted to serious work in a special field and the rest given over to detailed study of contemporary ideologies, the economic and political organization of the contemporary world, and major issues in twentieth-century world history and politics: *World Brain*, pp. 106, 125.

23. Wells was deeply impressed by the New School. Its spirit, he wrote in his introduction to the British edition of James Harvey Robinson's *The Mind in the Making*, "liberates something of my private dreams into the world of reality": Robinson, *The Mind in the Making* (London, Cape, 1923), p. 7.

sciences of social behavior. World planning did not have to depend entirely on the triumph of one arbitrary set of values over any number of other sets. If economists, for example, could work out, in conjunction with social psychologists, the best, most expedient way of organizing a sound world banking and currency system, then any movement pledged to the achievement of world order could go before world public opinion, existing governments, and financial experts with a concrete, practicable scheme. World order would not have to be shot and shouted into existence: the necessary revolutionary changes in social organization could be made scientifically. What economists could do with money and banking, other social scientists could do in other spheres. Industrial psychology promised to discover the "right way" of winning industrial peace. Students of administration working in the field could offer effective schemes for linking and expanding world service organizations. The possibilities were endless. But it would take work:

> Escape from economic frustration to universal abundance and social justice depend upon a mighty intellectual effort. It will have to be an effort as extensive as a world war and far more prolonged. Upon the organization and co-ordination of thousands of students and men of experience, discussing and publishing freely, helping and stimulating one another, depends the possibility of an advance into enduring plenty. And at present there is nothing in the wide world to represent the vital science needed but a few scattered professors and specialists working with negligible resources and the disconnectedness of amateurs.[24]

The importance Wells attached to sociological research in his later years may be gauged by its place in the timetable

24. *Anatomy of Frustration*, pp. 115–16.

of world revolution sketched out in his Utopian novel *The Shape of Things to Come.* The first great event in the rise of the "Modern State" movement which founded a world state in the disastrous years after the second World War was the publication of a seminal study of the "psychological laws" underlying the various forms of human association. The book, entitled *Social Nucleation,* was to enjoy a success in the second half of the twentieth century analogous to the success of *Das Kapital* and *The Origin of Species* in the second half of the nineteenth century. It explained the mechanics of human cooperation; it defined the tasks of education; it plotted the future course of the world revolution.[25] Wells was unconsciously harking back to the systematic sociology of his own youth. *Social Nucleation* did not sound much like a twentieth-century book, but it emphasized all the same his hopes for the social sciences. And it recalled his earlier prophecy, in 1924, that most of the great scientific advances of the twentieth and twenty-first centuries would be made by the medical, behavioral, and social sciences, rather than by the exact sciences.[26]

OUTLINES: AN EXPERIMENT IN ADULT EDUCATION

Wells did not wait for any sort of renaissance in the schools and universities. In retrospect, the most remarkable feature about his educational work was his decision, in 1918, to pass directly from theory to practice and take a personal hand in the educating of the world. He assumed at first that his contribution would be negligible, at most an initiative, but it later turned into a full-scale project that brought Wells more readers than he had ever reached in his brightest years of novel-writing before the war. The first step was the com-

25. *Shape of Things to Come,* pp. 250–58.
26. "The Gifts of the New Sciences," *Strand Magazine, 67* (1924), 152–58.

pilation in 1918–19 of *The Outline of History,* originally intended as a guide to the teaching of world history for schoolmasters. Its enormous success with the general reading public prompted Wells to write two more outlines of general knowledge in the late 1920's, *The Science of Life* (in collaboration with his son G. P. Wells and with Julian Huxley) and *The Work, Wealth and Happiness of Mankind.* The trilogy, taken all together, illustrated Wells' conviction that education could continue and had to continue beyond formal schooling, in great measure through books written by popularizers of knowledge like himself. The specific aim of the trilogy was identical with the aim of Wells' proposals for curricular reform in the 1937 British Association lecture: to provide a broad-perspective view of man and society, in order to enlist its readers in the twentieth-century search for world order. Each book was, in part, information selected to give a continuous and integrated picture of the human race or its origins or natural environment; and each book was, in part, undisguised propaganda for the socialist world state.

In time the success of the trilogy convinced him that the educational revolution he prophesied would begin at the adult level, rather than in the schools: "The school teacher cannot outrun public opinion. If he does so, he loses his job, and there is an end to the matter. The first battles for the New Education of our new world must be fought in the adult mind."[27] Even if few adult minds could actually be reconstructed by books like *The Outline of History* or *The Science of Life,* still the public interest in their approach to knowledge might ultimately percolate into the schools, help to alter curricula, and even stir the enthusiasm of the more progressive sort of schoolmaster. In any event, it was easier and quicker to begin influencing world opinion through

27. *Work, Wealth and Happiness of Mankind, 1,* 8.

books than it was to effect a revolution in anything as incorrigibly institutionalized as the world's school systems. Not that Wells wrote his trilogy of educational books quickly. He worked on them as carefully as he knew how, read widely, consulted scores of experts, and emerged with large, accurate, reliable, substantial volumes that have hardly ever been equaled for workmanship in the field of popular educational literature.

Each of the three has its own peculiar merit, but *The Outline of History* was many times over the best-selling volume of the trilogy and the most influential. It was exactly what Wells might have been expected to write: the fresh approach to historiography of a brilliant amateur, shallow and superficial in many ways, brisk and inventive in many others, lively throughout. In one respect, there was nothing new about it; Wells was writing old-fashioned didactic universal history, after the example of Voltaire or Gibbon. Like the *philosophes,* he cared much less for the differences between nations and civilizations than for the qualities and historical experiences they all shared. He was not contrasting East and West, Slav and German, yellow and white. He was writing the history of a biological species in process of civilization in geological time, and he was selecting his materials in such a way as to make them justify a moral judgment. Two American historians in a recent textbook describe the *Outline* as a "widely-read tract for world government,"[28] and in a sense it was. Wells almost said so himself in 1931:

> *The Outline of History* is not a whole history of life. Its main theme is the growth of human intercommunication and human communities and their rulers and con-

28. C. E. Black and E. C. Helmreich, *Twentieth Century Europe* (New York, Knopf, 1950), p. 828.

flicts, the story of how and why the myriads of little tribal systems of ten thousand years ago have fought and coalesced into the sixty- or seventy-odd governments of to-day and are now straining and labouring in the grip of forces that must presently accomplish their final unison.[29]

But *The Outline of History* was also more than a tract. No student of the development of what James Harvey Robinson dubbed the New History can get very far without taking the *Outline* into serious consideration, both as a leading British example of New History and subsequently as the best known general history to popularize the historiographical approach of the New History.

A mere tract for world government using historical arguments could have taken almost any form. What made the *Outline* of interest even to professional historians, and so all the more valuable in the long run as propaganda, was its dynamic sense of the scope and scale of history. For Wells, as for Robinson and the New Historians in the United States and for Henri Berr in France, history was the record of the whole human past: nothing could conceivably lie outside the historian's province. Independently of the New Historians, Wells had long before the publication of the *Outline* attacked the kind of history then being taught in most schools and universities as hopelessly provincial and fatally lopsided. The old history amounted in practice to the polit-

29. *What Are We to Do with Our Lives?*, pp. 16–17; cf. *Experiment in Autobiography*, p. 614. Wells had exactly this view of history long before he went to work on the *Outline*. "*The essential fact in man's history* to my sense," he wrote in 1908, "is the slow unfolding of a sense of community with his kind, of the possibilities of co-operations leading to scarce-dreamt-of collective powers, of a synthesis of the species, of the development of a common general idea, a common general purpose out of a present confusion": *First and Last Things*, p. 92.

ical and military history of single nations, studied *in vacuo,* with scarcely any reference to the development of ideas, to economics, to geography, to cultural patterns. Scientific or unscientific, good, bad, or indifferent, it was incomplete. It was no more history, in the proper sense of the word, than red or blue or green was the spectrum. As he put it much later, in 1931, the old history was

> partly like heavy stale gossip about incredible individ-
> uals, partly like trying to get interested in the litigation
> of unknown people in a remote country, and partly
> like watching a university don playing soldiers on his
> study floor. (How he loves his "Decisive Battles of the
> World"!) The murder or execution of one or another
> of the more tiresome characters in the story comes as
> an all too rare relief.[30]

The Outline of History, just because it did move in one of the main streams of early twentieth-century historio-graphical thought, had forerunners. Scholarly comparisons —perhaps unnecessary comparisons—could be drawn with Voltaire, Condorcet, and especially Kant, and Wells con-fessed to having been strongly influenced by Winwood Reade's *The Martyrdom of Man.*[31] In the twentieth cen-tury itself, in Britain alone, William Archer had written

---

30. *Work, Wealth and Happiness of Mankind, 2,* 818. It is interest-ing to compare Wells' discussion of the inadequacy of national history in his article "History Is One" (1919) with Arnold J. Toynbee's in *A Study of History, 1,* 17–22. Both take English history as their example and both, up to a point, use the same arguments. "History Is One" was first published in Britain in *John o' London's Weekly* (April 12, 19, 1919) and in the United States in the *Saturday Evening Post* (May 3, 1919). It also appeared in the Atlantic Edition of the *Works, 27,* 3–16.

31. *Outline of History, 1,* vii.

a synopsis of human history in a book intended for the enlightenment of schoolmasters in 1905 which bears a close general resemblance to the *Outline;*[32] and in 1913 F. S. Marvin published *The Living Past,* a study under Positivist influences of "universal," actually Western, history, which in some ways anticipated the *Outline.* A few textbooks had also appeared before the first World War in the United States, written by New Historians, treating at least the history of Western civilization synthetically.[33] And in 1920, the year of *The Outline of History,* Henri Berr began the publication in France of his 100-volume universal history *L'Evolution de l'humanité.* Although the latter was planned as and remains to the present day, with over sixty volumes published, a scholarly history done piecemeal by selected experts, it has come perhaps closest to the *Outline* in imaginative sweep.[34]

But *The Outline of History* was unique. Originally conceived as an essay on the sources and vicissitudes of the idea of European unity since the Caesars, it grew by degrees into a universal history of prodigious proportions. There has still not been anything written quite like it. Setting the stage for the entrance of man, Wells devoted the first five chapters to a rapid survey of the history of the earth and the origins of life; in the next seven he traced the development of early man from the first sub-men through flint implements and fire to the invention of language. Most

32. "Kappa" (William Archer), *Let Youth But Know* (London, 1905), pp. 69–116. Wells read and reviewed the book when it was first published. See his article, "The Schoolmaster and the Empire," in *Social Forces in England and America,* pp. 255–67.

33. See, e.g., James Henry Breasted, James Harvey Robinson, and Charles A. Beard, *Outlines of European History,* 2 vols. Boston, 1912–14.

34. Like the *Outline,* it began with a survey of paleontology and anthropology, E. Perrier's *La Terre avant l'histoire.*

critics of the *Outline* liked the prehistoric books best.[35] But Wells was not writing for entertainment's sake. By the time he had reached recorded history, he had accustomed his readers to thinking of the human race as the conquering hero in a cosmic conflict between brute nature and emergent intelligence. Quite as much as the events in Eden controlled the whole course of the Christian epic, the events in Wells' account of prehistoric life supplied him with the plan and meaning of history. Intelligence had succeeded in creating civilized communities at the dawn of recorded history. From that point on, in Wells' imagination, history was essentially the endeavor of intelligence to bring all civilized communities and all their affairs under conscious control.

Setting the stage proved somewhat easier than writing the play. Wells had the great ancient river-valley civilizations of East and West to account for, and Greece and Rome, the Arab and Turkish empires, the Mongolian ascendancy in Asia, medieval and Renaissance Europe, the Western world in the age of imperialism, nationalism, capitalism, and world war. It took him a thousand pages; and many of the later chapters, in spite of lengthy quotations from Herodotus and Gibbon, are not good history by almost any standards. But every chapter is shot through with illuminating insights, and Wells' materials, drawn from a vast variety of sources, make the *Outline* richly synthetic in the best traditions of the New History. Social,

35. Wells himself felt most at home in writing prehistory, as any scientist would, if he tried his hand at an outline of history. William Clissold's confession is a useful clue: "No other part of history so interests me as the opening chapter before the documents begin. There is no excessive presentation of persons and personal names; egoism has left nothing but defaced monuments and disconnected boasts, and we seem to come nearer to the realities of human life than we do in many a later age when kings and princes and their policies monopolise the foreground": *World of William Clissold, 1,* 205.

economic, and intellectual history all figured in the drama, and were often skillfully managed. By and large, Wells had least success in the deadlier branches of the historian's trade, above all in constitutional and diplomatic history. Much of his straight political history amounted to gossip of the same variety he himself deplored—designed, however, not to glorify the "great men" of political history but to make them out as strutting popinjays and clowns much overrated as history-makers, in reality instruments of forces infinitely more powerful than themselves.

The *Outline* might also be seen as a kind of forerunner in its own right of all the interpretative studies of world history which have reached the market in the past three decades, and especially of Arnold J. Toynbee's *A Study of History,* which has come very near to replacing it in the public imagination, at least in the United States. Wells' discussion, for example, of the cyclical pattern in the history of empires, studied in Chapter 1 above,[36] seems to anticipate Toynbee and parallel Spengler at a number of points. But as an educational book, with a mission, *The Outline of History* was only incidentally an exercise in "metahistory." Far more important to Wells' purposes was his discovery in history of cumulative progress in science, learning, and the arts, and a steady growth in the scale of human intercourse. He took special pains to point out the origins and progress of three great "structural ideas" since the sixth century B.C., which had exerted an irresistible fascination over men's minds ever since: the idea of a universal science, crystallized by the ancient Greeks; the idea of universal righteousness, of an ordained world order of peace and brotherhood, developed by the principal world religions; and the idea of a universal state, embodied in the careers of the Caesars and Shih Huang Ti. These three ideas, acting singly or in con-

36. See above, pp. 50–52.

cert, had for thousands of years driven creative geniuses to seek to unify mankind, intellectually, spiritually, and politically.

Yet, in spite of all their efforts, the accumulating wealth of human ingenuity, and the increasing interdependence of peoples, no religious movement or empire had succeeded in becoming literally universal. Each had faded in turn as it exhausted its creative possibilities and as its defenses were wrecked by challenges from outside the pale of its influence. The creative *élan* of its founders rarely recurred in its defenders. In the case of both empires and religions the early years of rapid growth were never followed up by educational programs on a scale vast enough and continuously intelligent enough to keep pace with their sheer physical expansion. Empires could not survive long because they could not assimilate their subject peoples, could not give them a common education, could not keep them interested, informed, and imbued with a sense of moral allegiance to the universal polity. So the universal religions. The great religious initiatives in history were never "accompanied by any understanding of the vast educational task, the vast work of lucid and varied exposition and intellectual organization involved in its propositions. They all present the same history of a rapid spreading, like a little water poured over a great area, and then of superficiality and corruption."[37]

Now, in the twentieth century, Wells concluded, a sudden rapid development of science and the mechanical arts had made the immediate unification of humanity both physically simple and physically imperative. A race was on, between education and catastrophe, between cosmopolis and chaos. Either mankind, confronted with the specter of world war, brought its mind and will into deliberate focus,

37. *Outline of History*, 2, 30.

or it would perish. The closing pages belonged entirely to the prophetic Wells. The *Outline* ended with the usual peroration, the ritual invocation of Utopia, the familiar Wellsian nostalgia for a world yet unborn.

Wells had taken less than two years with the sparingly used editorial assistance of four eminent experts to write the *Outline*.[38] But the repercussions went on for decades. The *Outline* ran through six editions, sold more than two million copies, and produced a large critical literature. Writing outlines of history became a profitable and popular business for historians and literary people generally.[39] Partly as a result of the interest generated by the *Outline*, "World History" grew in favor as a course in schools and colleges, at least in the United States, and a few teachers even used the *Outline* as a textbook.

The book encountered every kind of response, from

38. They were Ernest Barker, Sir H. H. Johnston, Sir E. Ray Lankester, and Gilbert Murray. "On the whole," wrote Sir Ernest Barker, "the advisory editors served as an outwork or bastion, which seemed to suggest an assurance of strength; but the inner keep, and indeed the whole of the bailey, were Wells' own unaided work": Barker, *Age and Youth*, p. 107.

39. Among the world histories written since the *Outline* for popular consumption, two of the better known are Hendrik Willem van Loon, *The Story of Mankind,* New York, 1921; and Joseph Reither, *World History at a Glance,* New York, 1942. Wells himself published another, *A Short History of the World* (1922), which became a bestseller in its own right and later appeared in Penguin, Pocket Book, and Thinker's Library editions. It was based on, but not condensed from, the *Outline.* Since the *Outline,* several historians have put together world histories at the college textbook level. See especially Lynn Thorndike, *A Short History of Civilization,* New York, 1926; Hermann Schneider, *The History of World Civilization* (1927), trans. Margaret M. Green, 2 vols. New York, 1931; George A. Dorsey, *Man's Own Show: Civilization,* New York, 1931; and James Edgar Swain, *A History of World Civilization,* New York, 1938. Histories of Western civilization are still more numerous, but not in the Wellsian tradition.

partisan slander and professorial disdain to outspoken enthusiasm. Graham Wallas and Bernard Shaw liked it, and Harold Laski called it "the greatest public service the universities have been rendered in a generation."[40] Archbishop Richard Downey and Hilaire Belloc published hypercritical antidotes to protect Catholic readers against its influence.[41] In the United States, another Catholic writer, Condé B. Pallen, prepared a "symposium" of mostly unfavorable criticisms, which was published, replete with dire warnings against the use of the *Outline* in schools, by the National Civic Federation.[42] For the most part British historians

40. Harold Laski to Wells, January 7, 1921, in the Wells Archive. For Wallas' views see his *Our Social Heritage* (New Haven, 1921), p. 207. Shaw thought the *Outline* should replace the Book of Genesis. Shaw, *Adventures of the Black Girl in Her Search for God* (London, 1932), p. 68.

41. Richard Downey, *Some Errors of H. G. Wells,* London, 1921; and Hilaire Belloc, "A Few Words with H. G. Wells," *Dublin Review, 166* (1920), 182–202, and "Mr. Wells' 'Outline of History,' " *London Mercury, 3* (1920), 43–62. In 1925 Wells undertook another serial publication of the *Outline,* and Belloc matched its fortnightly parts with twenty-four fortnightly essays of his own in *The Catholic Universe* and *The Catholic Bulletin,* which he published in book form in 1926 as *A Companion to Mr. Wells's "Outline of History."* Wells fired back with a little book, *Mr. Belloc Objects to "The Outline of History"* (1926), and Belloc countered with *Mr. Belloc Still Objects to Mr. Wells's "Outline of History"* (London, 1926), at which point the controversialists finally sputtered into silence. Belloc's biographers are still under the picturesque illusion that Belloc outpointed Wells in their debate in 1925–26. See Eleanor and Reginald Jebb, *Testimony to Hilaire Belloc* (London, 1956), pp. 81–84; and Robert Speaight, *The Life of Hilaire Belloc* (London, 1957), pp. 397–403. Both accounts are marked by deliberate misrepresentation, a fine ignorance of biology, and authentic Bellocian rancor. For a more dispassionate version of the debate see Vincent Brome, *Six Studies in Quarrelling* (London, 1958), pp. 170–89.

42. *Symposium of Opinions upon The Outline of History,* New York, 1921.

were indifferent or inarticulately hostile. One professor of Greek history wrote a pamphlet entitled *Mr. Wells as Historian,* so pathetically bad that its writer played into Wells' hands and furnished him with some striking illustrative material for a pamphlet of his own, *The New Teaching of History.*[43] In the United States most of the more conscientious reviews were written by New Historians, including Carl Becker, J. Salwyn Schapiro, and Carlton J. H. Hayes. They all found serious fault with Wells' methods, sources, and content but applauded his scale of operations and his objectives. Hayes thought Wells was "making the world safe for historians. Henceforth professors will not fear to walk where Mr. Wells has leaped, and eventually one of them or a group of them will produce a history of man in the universe that will be as sound and reliable as the 'Outline' before us is inaccurate and impressionistic."[44]

Unfortunately for Wells' standing among the intellectual avant-garde, the general public for its part had no reservations at all. Like the cinema epics of the late Cecil B. De Mille, the *Outline* became oppressively fashionable in the

43. A. W. Gomme, *Mr. Wells as Historian,* Glasgow, 1921. Wells' pamphlet *The New Teaching of History,* reprinted from the *Fortnightly Review,* was published in London in 1921.

44. Carlton J. H. Hayes, "The Other-worldly Mr. Wells," *Freeman,* 3 (1921), 21. See also J. Salwyn Schapiro, "H. G. Wells's 'Outline of History,' " in B. A. Heydrick, ed., *Types of the Essay* (New York, 1921), pp. 209–33, and Carl Becker, "Mr. Wells and the New History," *Everyman His Own Historian* (New York, 1935), pp. 169–90. Wells always intended that his *Outline* should be replaced by a professionally written history, done on the same scale. He had even tried to interest historians in writing a general world history before deciding in 1918 to write one himself. "Critics [of the *Outline*] may rest assured," he wrote in 1921, "that nothing but a better Outline will put an end to its career": *New Teaching of History,* p. 8.

middle middle class.[45] The more popularity it accumulated
with the lower levels of the reading public, the less it appealed to the upper levels, until in mid-century, although
it still sells fairly well in the United States, *The Outline of
History* is mostly a dust-collector. Every well-stocked private
library started at least twenty years ago, and every history
department bookshelf, has a copy. Few are read.

But Wells did not write the *Outline* for posterity, or to
please historians. It was a book written for its own time, to
educate and warn and guide. It proposed to reconstruct the
minds and realign the loyalties of its readers. There could

45. It got to the point of poetry contests. When Wells' American
publishers, Macmillan, offered a prize of $100 for the best rhymed
review of the *Outline,* the winning contestant's final stanza read:
> If life's a race where education
> Strives with disaster, as he tells,
> Millions will here achieve salvation
> And say with me, "Thank God for Wells!"

The Prize Rhymed Review of H. G. Wells, The Outline of History
(New York, Macmillan, 1921), p. 6. Wells admitted in later years that
the commercial success of the *Outline* in America had been far out
of proportion to its probable influence. "In various formats we sold
over a million at a great pace. I do not think that more than a minute
percentage of that tremendous issue was ever more than glanced at.
I doubt if more than two or three thousand were ever attentively read.
It was bought and stowed away. When the topic of this H. G. Wells,
who was trying to tell the world something, came up, the good Anglo-
Saxon world could say: 'We know all about H. G. W. We've got an
illustrated copy of his *Outline* in the library and the Christmas before
last we made it our gift book to all our friends' ": from the MS of
"Exasperations" in the Wells Archive, pp. 105–6. At the present
writing (1960), the Doubleday Dollar Book Club is offering a two-
volume edition of the *Outline*—along with such items as a cook book,
the *Ladies' Home Journal Book of Interior Decoration,* and novels
by Frank G. Slaughter and Frances Parkinson Keyes—at the "amaz-
ing" price of "any four" for 99¢, together with membership in the
Club. *Satis superque.*

be no world peace, Wells argued in the original introduction, either between peoples or between social classes *"without common historical ideas."* History was perhaps the single most important ingredient in the cement of culture. All the great societies of the world down to the present time had "used some sort of cosmogony and world history as a basis. It may indeed be argued that without such a basis any true binding culture of men is inconceivable. Without it we are a chaos."[46] As he wrote in a lecture delivered shortly before the second World War, much of the blame for the brewing of wars had to be shouldered by the old nationalistic school of history teaching:

> I put it to you that if we want the world to become a consistent whole, we must think of it as a whole. We must not deal with states, nations and empires as primary things which have to be reconciled and welded together, if we want world peace, we must deal with these divisions as secondary things which have appeared and disappeared almost incidentally in the course of a larger and longer biological adventure. Education can wipe them out completely.[47]

Part of that educational thrust against the old local and national order could be achieved by grounding the potential world citizen in world history. But so far as the "informative content" of education was concerned, Wells saw need for two more outlines on the scale of *The Outline of History*. He carried his experiment in adult education through to completion in 1929–31 by publishing *The Science of Life* and *The Work, Wealth and Happiness of Mankind*.

Although the second and third parts of Wells' educational "trilogy" did not equal the first in sales, they both

46. *Outline of History, 1,* vi–vii.
47. *Travels of a Republican Radical in Search of Hot Water* (Harmondsworth, Middlesex, 1939), p. 99.

reached hundreds of thousands of readers. *The Science of Life,* if only because most of it was written by professional biologists, proved more useful as a source of information than *The Outline of History. The Work, Wealth and Happiness of Mankind* fell short of both its predecessors in most respects, but it was also the most original work of the three, and presented by far the greatest intellectual challenge to its author.

First plans for the writing of *The Science of Life* were drafted in 1925 by Wells and Julian Huxley. Wells' eldest son, G. P. Wells, joined the team later, and the work was finished early in 1929. Although Wells wrote several individual sections, was principally responsible for the plan and scale of the book, and taskmastered the whole project from beginning to end, the great bulk of the manuscript originated with the two junior partners.[48]

As in the case of the *Outline,* the most striking feature of *The Science of Life* is its immense range. No general biology before or since has covered quite so much ground. *The Outline of History* took the history of all mankind within its purview; *The Science of Life* was written to explain, somewhat more disinterestedly, the whole nature and history of life on earth, from its mineral origins to the biology of human thought and association. Wells' introduction offers a panoramic view of the modes and types of life, defines life itself, describes its terrestrial setting, and introduces the reader to the science of biology. Books I and II, in effect, are two further introductory sections, surveying the elements of animal anatomy and physiology and reviewing the principal plant and animal phyla. In Book III, Julian Hux-

---

48. From the MS in the Wells Archive, it appears that Wells wrote most of the introduction, a few sections in Bks. III and VIII, and most of Bk. IX. Julian Huxley wrote Bks. III–VI and parts of VIII, G. P. Wells Bks. I, II, and VII. This was confirmed by G. P. Wells in a talk with the present writer.

ley broaches "The Incontrovertible Fact of Evolution," on which the remaining books of *The Science of Life* were securely hinged. Evolution vested life with a historical dimension. For Wells, as for Julian Huxley, it was the key to the understanding of all the rest of biology, and for Julian Huxley if not for Wells, the great universal touchstone of moral values.[49] Book IV discusses in more detail the evolutionary mechanism and its implications for philosophy, following the neo-Darwinian explanation just then in process of winning general acceptance among biologists: a process in which Julian Huxley himself figured prominently.[50] Book V draws on the evolutionary record to outline the history of life on earth. Book VI is an introduction to ecology, Book VII discusses health and disease. In Book VIII the authors tackle psychology, animal and human, dealing on the way with the question of spiritualism and extrasensory perception in a chapter written by Wells himself. *The Science of Life* culminates in a ninth Book, mostly by Wells, entitled "Biology of the Human Race," in which the unique characteristics of the species *Homo sapiens* are catalogued, with special reference to patterns of social life and the prospects of a world civilization. Wells was an old hand at studying human affairs from the perspectives of biology. The transition from science to propaganda was managed smoothly.

Wells' work on *The Science of Life* strengthened his conviction of the essential unity of biology and social science. He had always accepted Comte's hierarchical classification of the sciences. It now became all the more clear to him that history, sociology, political and economic science, psy-

49. See Huxley, *Evolution and Ethics,* London, 1947; published in the United States as *Touchstone for Ethics,* New York, 1947.

50. See especially Huxley, *Evolution, the Modern Synthesis,* London, 1942; and George Gaylord Simpson, *The Meaning of Evolution,* New Haven, 1949.

chology, and anthropology were all branches, shooting off
at one angle or another, from the parent trunk of biology,
just as *Homo sapiens* was a form, modified by evolution, of
life. History was a continuation of paleontology; and the
social sciences, viewed as a whole, were merely human ecology, the science of the way human beings adapt to their environment, what habitats they prefer, how they get their
food, how they amuse themselves, how they regulate their
social relations, and so forth. But the social scientists could
not fit the pieces together. The various social sciences overlapped, contradicted one another, worked at cross purposes.
Wells saw in the vastness of the biological approach a way
to melt them down and pour them into an ampler mould, if
not at first to expedite research, at least for the less exacting
requirements of general education. Out of his reflections
evolved *The Work, Wealth and Happiness of Mankind.*

After an abortive effort to produce the book in collaboration with two assistants, Wells took over the writing himself, and had it ready for publication in 1931. *The Work,
Wealth and Happiness of Mankind* appeared in book stores
at just a time when all three items were coming to be extraordinarily scarce in the world; but the ineffective title
only underscored the novelty of Wells' approach. He had
struggled for months to find the most descriptive possible
title: to define concisely the subject he had surveyed. There
were no words for it, except "human ecology," and he
could not trust the ordinary reader to know the meaning
of "ecology." Nor was he exactly sure what "human" ecology
meant himself. At one point it was "the science of the balance of human life." In another place he described *The
Work, Wealth and Happiness of Mankind* as "a picture of
all mankind to-day, a picture of living mankind active,
working, spending, making and destroying." In still another
it was "a review of all human activities in relation to each
other, the work of people and the needs of people, cultiva-

tion, manufacture, trade, direction, government, and all.
. . . It was, in fact, an outline of economic, social, and political science."[51] The concept eluded precise definition, but
Wells felt he had hit upon something good, and he offered
his book in evidence.

The Work, Wealth and Happiness of Mankind was perhaps a little less substantial than its two predecessors, but
much reading and the criticisms of people like Graham
Wallas, Herman Finer, J. M. Keynes, Harold Laski, Kingsley Martin, and Sir Arthur Salter saved it from elementary
errors. Wells also had the help of several competent research
assistants. If read from cover to cover, the book accomplishes
exactly what Wells' other outlines accomplish: it takes an
almost immeasurably vast subject, shrinks it to scale, and
lays it out in clear, bright, candid English for the layman to
read at his leisure. It allows him to find himself and his work
in the larger life and work of the species. Like the other
outlines, it was intended in the final analysis more to orient
than to inform its readers.

In effect Wells had produced a functional description of
modern industrial civilization, drawing most of his material
from Western sources, and from nearly all the social studies
and sciences. In order, he invaded the territory of the
economic anthropologist, the historian of science, the econo-
mist, the industrial psychologist, the sociologist, the political scientist, and the educationist. He described preindus-
trial economies; traced the development of modern science
and technology; described twentieth-century agriculture,
housing, manufacturing, distribution, and finance; discussed labor relations, penology, class structure under capitalism, the role of women in modern society, and the uses

51. *Work, Wealth and Happiness of Mankind, 1, 3, 35; What Are
We to Do with Our Lives?,* pp. 17–18. A later edition (Garden City,
N.Y., Garden City Publishing Co., 1936) carried the title, *The Outline
of Man's Work and Wealth.*

of leisure; surveyed the governments of the world and assessed Western political life; and reviewed modern systems of education, closing with a plea for thoroughgoing educational reform to prepare world opinion for the gradual displacement of local sovereignty by world controls, and a recapitulation of the program for nonviolent world revolution which he had published in 1928 in *The Open Conspiracy*. *The Work, Wealth and Happiness of Mankind*, like its predecessors, ended in propaganda for world order. It made all the clearer Wells' belief that education, here biologically defined as "the modification and elaboration of instinct, of innate dispositions . . . through experience," would have to begin at least to revolutionize mental habits before any tangible success could be achieved in revolutionizing the political and economic institutions of the established order.[52]

In the chapter on education, as part of his proposals for educational reform, Wells also suggested the compilation of a new kind of integrative "world encyclopaedia" to do in a more responsible and systematic way for all the branches of human knowledge what he had attempted to do for the social sciences in *The Work, Wealth and Happiness of Mankind*. He continued to press the idea of a world encyclopedia, and a world "brain organization," all through the 1930's. The campaign occupies a place all its own in his career as a prophet of world order.

INTELLECTUAL INTEGRATION

Wells' definition of "education" to embrace every kind of learning, especially adaptive learning, and his habitual use of the analogy between individual brains and the mind of the race, explain the importance he came to attach in the later years of his prophetic career to the idea of an encyclo-

52. *Work, Wealth and Happiness of Mankind*, 2, 749, 787–88.

pedic reorganization of human knowledge. The instruments of human salvation—science, social research, schools, adult education—could not be effective, he said, unless knowledge was freely and universally accessible for use; and in order to be fully accessible, it had to be systematized. The relations between the various branches of knowledge had to be clarified, and all fields of research kept in constant contact with one another, to ensure that all the existing information relevant to a given problem under study could be made immediately available on demand. Nor would research alone profit from the synthesis of knowledge. If it resulted in the publication of an integrative world encyclopedia, the synthesis of knowledge would provide the layman with an accurate, correlated picture of man and the universe, of which Wells' own trilogy of educational books was only an early anticipation. It would little by little transfer most of the business of governments from the sphere of the politician into the sphere of the expert and the technical adviser. The policy-making powers of politicians would in time dwindle to insignificance, if knowledge and the pursuit of knowledge could be organized well enough to take most of the guesswork out of the direction of human affairs. Just as the individual cells of the racial brain had to keep in close touch with the mental life of the race, so the racial brain itself had to keep in close touch with the mental life of its component cells. Individual intelligence was determined by the number and efficiency of neural connections in the cerebral hemispheres; the collective intelligence of mankind, its capacity for intelligent collective response to crises in its growth, depended in the same way on how effectively its constituent brains were integrated.[53]

53. Wells himself did not carry the analogy quite this far, but it is clearly implied in his later work. See, e.g., his explanation of the work of the world brain center at Barcelona in *Shape of Things to Come* p. 420.

Some of the accents were uniquely his own, but Wells' encyclopedism grew out of a well-founded tradition in the history of Western thought. What Frank Manuel, in writing about Saint-Simon, calls "the *idée fixe* . . . that scientists and philosophers must collaborate to create a unity out of all knowledge in order to save mankind from chaos"[54] has possessed thinkers from Bacon and Comenius through Leibniz, Diderot, Saint-Simon, and Comte down to Otto Neurath and Lancelot Law Whyte in our own time. Although the problem of the unity of knowledge is immeasurably more acute in the twentieth century than ever before, the arguments for integration have remained fundamentally the same. The integrators complain about the fragmentation of knowledge produced by intellectual specialization, assert the metaphysical unity of being, and insist on the need for the encyclopedic systematizing of knowledge, using some comprehensive scheme or other for reorganizing the specialized disciplines and redividing intellectual labor. Of this encyclopedic tradition, Wells was perhaps the leading representative in his own generation.

Wells never developed an authentic interest in intellectual integration for its own sake. He was accustomed to taking the "metaphysical unity of being" for granted. What concerned him far more was the biological unity of the human race, and he became an encyclopedist because he saw in the solution of the problem of the unity of knowledge an important step toward the solution of the far more vital problem of world order. The human race would never live together in creative harmony, he kept saying, until it learned to think as one. Nor could it learn to think as one unless, among other things, the whole sprawling intellectual apparatus of modern civilization could be dynamically integrated. What the world needed was a brain center, a

54. Frank E. Manuel, *The New World of Henri Saint-Simon* (Cambridge, Mass., Harvard University Press, 1956), p. 81.

superuniversity, a League of Nations Institute of Intellectual Cooperation raised to colossal proportions.

The well-meaning villain in the piece was the specialized brain-worker. Following the lessons of evolution, Wells always insisted on the importance of versatility to adaptive response. Intellectual progress, he said, depended on less, rather than more, specialization.

> Of all the solemn imbecilities one hears, surely the most foolish is this, that we are in "an age of specialisation." The comparative fruitfulness and hopefulness of our social order, in comparison with any other social system, lies in its flat contradiction of that absurdity. Our medical and surgical advances, for example, are almost entirely due to the invasion of medical research by the chemist. . . . Change of function, arrest of specialisation by innovations in method and appliance, progress by the infringement of professional boundaries and the defiance of rule: these are the commonplaces of our time. The trained man, the specialised man, is the most unfortunate of men; the world leaves him behind, and he has lost his power of overtaking it. Versatility, alert adaptability, these are our urgent needs.[55]

At one level, Wells' scientific romance *The First Men in the Moon* could be read as a Swiftian satire on specialization. The brain-workers, like all other kinds of workers, were minutely specialized in the Selenite society. Each one had his own function, which walled him off from all his fellows. "The experts," as Cavor radioed back to earth, "for the most part ignore me completely, even as they ignore each other, or notice me only to begin a clamorous exhibition of their

55. *Social Forces in England and America,* pp. 105–6; cf. another essay in this collection, "An Age of Specialisation," pp. 281–86, first written in 1904—a similar indictment.

distinctive skill. The erudite for the most part are rapt in an impervious and apoplectic complacency from which only a denial of their erudition can rouse them."[56]

The theme recurs a number of times over the years in Wells' books. Specialization, carried to the usual extremes, warped scientific research and retarded the necessary flow of knowledge from the research worker to the general public and to industry and government. The division of labor should not also, he thought, mean the division of laborers. The specialized thinking man had to come out of his profession now and then to see what was going on in related fields, and he had to be equipped with a fairly comprehensive world-view to fulfill his responsibilities as an intelligent human being living in a social situation.

Vulgarisation was one answer. Wells had set new standards for the popularizing of knowledge in the 1920's, and many younger writers followed his example, without necessarily sharing his social philosophy—among them, Will Durant, Hendrik Willem van Loon, C. E. M. Joad, and Lancelot Hogben. But Wells came in later years to suspect that *vulgarisation* could not do the job alone. There was a limit to the capacities of amateurs like himself. Nor would any indiscriminate kind of popularizing necessarily contribute to integration. The important thing was the extent to which the *vulgarisateur* himself conceived and persuaded his readers to conceive of physical, biological, and social processes as wholes. "I dislike isolated events and disconnected details," Wells wrote in *World Brain*. "I really hate statements, views, prejudices and beliefs that jump at you suddenly out of mid-air. I like my world as coherent and consistent as possible."[57] It was the contrast he had drawn in his autobiography between his own mind and Joseph Con-

---

56. *The First Men in the Moon* (Indianapolis, 1901), p. 279.
57. *World Brain*, p. 3.

rad's. The two of them had once debated on the beach near Wells' house at Sandgate how a boat they saw on the water should be described. Conrad wanted to see it as vividly as possible—he would scratch about in his mind until he had dug up *le mot juste*. But Wells had to admit that "in nineteen cases out of twenty I would just let the boat be there in the commonest phrases possible." He would want "to see it and to see it only in relation to something else—a story, a thesis. And I suppose if I had been pressed about it I would have betrayed a disposition to link that story or thesis to something still more extensive and that to something still more extensive and so ultimately to link it up to my philosophy and my world outlook."[58]

The popularizer integrated the materials of the subject he was popularizing, if he did his work well. But after *The Work, Wealth and Happiness of Mankind* Wells directed his attention to the more serious and more far-reaching project of a world encyclopedia. The kind of encyclopedia he envisioned would systematize and outline the whole body of human knowledge in one swoop. Unlike the piecemeal enterprises of the popularizer, the world encyclopedia would take responsibility for all knowledge. It would be a general education in itself. The experience gained by the experts who collaborated in its production would be immeasurably valuable, both for the experts themselves and as an example to the rest of the scientific and scholarly world.

The idea of a synthetic world encyclopedia had been fermenting in Wells' mind for a great many years, before he proposed it in 1931. Stephen Stratton's publishing firm in *The Passionate Friends* had planned to issue an annually revised world encyclopedia, in which an authoritative series of all kinds of reference books, from gazetteers and diction-

---

58. *Experiment in Autobiography*, p. 528. Cf. *Anatomy of Frustration*, pp. 62–63.

aries to textbooks and bibliographies, would be consoli-
dated. In *The Salvaging of Civilization* Wells had ventilated
Comenius' idea of a "common book of history, science and
wisdom, which should form the basis and framework for the
thoughts and imaginations of every citizen in the world,"
and suggested the compilation of a "Bible of Civilization"
based on Comenius' scheme.[59] But the proposals in 1931,
presented in one of the chapters of *The Work, Wealth and
Happiness of Mankind,* were meant to be taken much more
seriously.

Wells began by surveying briefly the history of encyclopedism since Comenius. He was especially struck by the admission of the editor of the current edition of *The Encyclopaedia Britannica* that the *Britannica* no longer pretended
to be a directive synthesis of knowledge. The current edition, Wells wrote, "is a diffusion, not a synthesis. . . . It is an
all too characteristic product of our time. It is multitudinous, defective and discursive in just this present phase of
the world's history when the need for directive general con-
cepts, gripped firmly and held steadfastly, is the supreme
need of our race."[60] An authentic world encyclopedia would
be a far vaster project than the *Britannica.* An endowed organization employing thousands of permanent workers, op-
erating on a much larger scale than any university in the
world, would be charged with preparing it and keeping it
constantly up to date. The encyclopedia staff would, in fact,
serve as a coordinator of the universities. It would become,
if it prospered, the world's archive, the world's bibliographical center, and the world's mental clearing house, directing
the transmission of knowledge from the research worker to
the man on the street. Unlike the *Britannica* or any other
major encyclopedia currently in print, Wells' world encyclo-

59. *Salvaging of Civilization,* p. 97.
60. *Work, Wealth and Happiness of Mankind,* 2, 845.

pedia would be arranged by fields of study, rather than alphabetically by item. Instead of a hodge-podge of miscellaneous articles, it would be a series of integrative essays, textbooks in miniature, edited by a single staff with a single format, in which all the branches of knowledge would be represented. Unlike the *Britannica* or any other encyclopedia, it would be thoroughly and conscientiously edited—planned as a whole and scrupulously reviewed for clarity, coherence, and accuracy by a staff of specialists in integration.

Wells tentatively divided his world encyclopedia into thirteen separate sections, beginning with the basic tools of thought and speech and culminating in the arts. The first section would be devoted to philosophy: with a critical inventory of philosophical systems, a review of the history of philosophy, and essays on logic, philology, symbols, and mathematics. The second section would deal with the languages of the world and their literatures, and the third in somewhat more detail than before with the whole field of mathematics. The fourth section would explore the material sciences from physics and chemistry to astronomy, the fifth biology, the sixth medicine, recreation, and health. In the seventh section the encyclopedists would provide a general review of world history. The eighth section would study national histories, and with these would be included a "political atlas" of the world and a world biographical dictionary. Section nine would be a more or less sociological study of religion, social ethics, education, law, penology, and the like. The tenth and eleventh sections would outline modern industrial organization and the economics of distribution and finance. Section twelve would summarize human artistic achievement, and the thirteenth section would be a dictionary index.

The idea of a world encyclopedia grew on Wells during the next few years. It appeared again in *The Anatomy of*

Frustration and *The Camford Visitation,* and in November 1936 Wells delivered a lecture on the subject at the Royal Institution, which became the first essay in his book *World Brain* and provoked at least a ripple of response.[61] The lecture suggested an encyclopedia of anywhere from twenty to forty volumes. Most of the ideas in *The Work, Wealth and Happiness of Mankind* were recalled, and Wells stressed the possibility that a world encyclopedia would also prove a powerful factor in reducing differences of opinion on issues vital to world order. Wherever important differences existed in a given field of study, as to methodology or interpretation, the reader

> would find, not casual summaries of opinions, but very carefully chosen and correlated statements and arguments. I do not imagine the major subjects as being dealt with in special articles rather hastily written, in what has been the tradition of Encyclopaedias since the days of Diderot's heroic effort. . . . The modern World Encyclopaedia should consist of selections, extracts, quotations, very carefully assembled with the approval of outstanding authorities in each subject, carefully collated and edited and critically presented. It would not be a miscellany, but a concentration, a clarification and a synthesis. . . . It might act not merely as an assembly of fact and statement, but as an organ of adjustment and adjudication, a clearing house of misunderstandings; it would be deliberately a synthesis, and so act as a flux and a filter for a very great quantity of human misapprehension. It would *compel* men to come to terms with one another. I think it

61. See the editorial in *Nature, 138* (1936), 899–900. Wells' lecture was also reprinted in the same issue, pp. 917–24; see also J. D. Bernal, *The Social Function of Science* (London, 1939), pp. 306–7, and Reginald A. Smith, *Towards a Living Encyclopaedia,* London, 1942.

would relegate *"quot homines, tot sententiae"* back to
the Latin comedy from which it emerged.[62]

Wells urged the immediate formation of a world encyclopedia promotional society, to publicize the idea and hire
experts who would prepare a comprehensive bibliography
of the most authoritative general books in each field to be
covered by the encyclopedia. This master bibliography of
key books, which might total as few as ten thousand titles,
would be published separately, not only for the use of the
editors of the encyclopedia, but also as a reference book in
its own right. The world encyclopedia society would then
organize a general editorial board and departmental boards;
authorities in all fields would be invited to contribute; their
work would be carefully edited and integrated by the permanent staff, and the first edition, probably in English,
would appear on the market, with translations, in whole or
in part, into other world languages to follow.

Wells, characteristically, had even bigger ideas. Almost as
soon as he had suggested it, he began to see the project of a
world encyclopedia as only the opening phase in the creation of a world "brain center," a world bureau of reference,
which would in time have the same relation to the mind of
the race that individual brains have to individual minds.
Wells had long been interested in world economic information services as functional steps toward world government.[63]
But the existence of a world encyclopedia society and staff
opened up all sorts of more far-reaching possibilities. The
staff would be employed permanently, to revise the encyclopedia from year to year. With its access to specialized information in unlimited quantities and in unlimited variety, it

62. *World Brain*, pp. 19–20, 23.
63. See, e.g., *Open Conspiracy*, pp. 43–44.

might readily become the nucleus of a much larger organization, a world archive, a keeper of records and statistics, a clearing house for universities, a coordinator of research institutes, a universal bibliographical center: its possibilities were endless.

Wells never, and perhaps deliberately never, allowed the idea of a "world brain" to become anything more than the barest imaginative notion in his later writing. It remained only partly visualized and partly formed in his own mind: a scientist among poets, he was also and always a poet among scientists. But in every sense the project of a world brain represented the culminating point in his theory of education. Education was the mind of the race extending its knowledge and self-control. It was inevitable that Wells should insist that both full knowledge and full self-control ultimately demanded some kind of world organization devoted to thoroughgoing intellectual synthesis. Schools, research centers, informative general literature, and the world encyclopedia itself might all contribute to the intellectual organization of the world; but their contributions would be pointless if they failed to lead in the long run to the creation of a directive world brain.

But the project of a world brain center belonged to the relatively distant future.[64] Long before it could be possible as a going concern, Wells assumed that the movement for educational reform and reorientation would grow by degrees into a much broader movement with tentacles reaching into business and government, an Open Conspiracy of men of wealth and power and learning, to seize, sabotage, or by-pass the political institutions of the old order and organize a world state.

64. See below, p. 222.

Chapter Four:

THE OPEN CONSPIRACY

THE SALT OF THE EARTH

In Wells' prophetic schedule all the ideas and proposals studied up to now were intended to prepare world opinion and enlist true believers for the ultimate campaign to bring the human race under one polity. There would be no world revolution, no salvation from the twentieth-century world crisis, without a massive reorientation of human thought. On the other hand, there would be no world Utopia without a world revolution. The change that began in men's minds had to culminate, sooner or later, in overt acts of subversion and civil disobedience. The kind of world revolution preached in *The Open Conspiracy* would never warm the heart of a proselyte of Karl Marx or Georges Sorel; but it was meant to climax, certainly, in a thoroughgoing reconstruction of society; and its methods, although Wells foresaw only incidental violence, were essentially extralegal. The revolution would not come of its own accord. Nor would existing governments help it along complaisantly. All its battles would have to be fought and won against towering opposition.

The key to an understanding of Wells' theory of world revolution, a key which must be examined carefully before turning to the Open Conspiracy itself, is his thinking on the old problem of leaders and followers. Nothing in his fundamental assumptions inclined Wells to sympathy with the democratic ideal. For Wells, what counted most in life was the emergence of quintessential humanity from the animal chaos of lower nature. All individuals, all institutions, all ideas had to be judged in terms of their value in the racial war against nature. To be true to his faith, Wells was forced to reject doctrinaire democracy, and by the same token doctrinaire liberalism, in favor of some species of elitism. Because not all men shared equally in the quintessentially human qualities—intelligence, Promethean courage, altruism —not all men could share equally in the work of the revolution. Because, in fact, the vast majority of men were dull, lazy, jealous, and self-centered, they leaned too far toward the animal side of human nature to be trusted with an active role either in the revolution or in the governance of mankind after the revolution. From Wells' point of view, letting the "people" rule was equivalent to turning back the clock of evolution. Democracy betrayed *Homo sapiens* to his ancient enemy.

Wells' theory of world revolution by Open Conspiracy rested, then, on a firm belief in the need for a revolutionary elite. In place of democracy, he would have substituted aristocracy: but of a very special kind. From its first appearance in *Anticipations* in 1902 to the last wartime books of the 1940's, Wells' elite consisted exclusively of "functional" men, men of high natural intelligence and professional competence, who performed the creative and managerial work of the world. At first, in *Anticipations,* membership in the elite was limited to scientists, engineers, and physicians, men of scientific training who would become "at last consciously *the* state, controlling and restricting very greatly the . . . non-functional masses."[1] But in later books Wells enlarged his definition of "functional," to include a greater variety of creative and managerial professions; and he took

1. *Anticipations,* p. 167.

increasingly more pains to delineate the inner spiritual resources necessary to members of a revolutionary elite.

It was Wells' attention to the matter of "spiritual resources" that lifted his political philosophy above the level of many of the elitist doctrines preached and practiced after 1918. It would be a gross distortion to brand him a protofascist. Viewed from at least one angle, he was simply in the Platonist tradition, which is to say in the old historic main stream of elitist thought.[2] A grateful admirer of Plato's *Republic*,[3] he remained under its spell all his life. The Samurai in *A Modern Utopia* certainly owed more to Plato than to Japan. Like the ruling class in *The Republic,* they were to be wise, dispassionate, wholly devoted to the welfare of the state.

But much more, the Samurai were animated by Wells' own scientific humanism. The aristocratic spirit for him was not some stiff-necked kind of allegiance to a class ideal: insofar as possible, the Samurai and all the other revolutionary and managing elites imagined or proposed by Wells had their *raison d'être* from biology. Their first loyalty was to the evolving human race, to the emergent racial mind. Hence, they could not be self-consciously a governing class; there was no place in Wells' thought for *Junkerherrschaft* or the *Führerprinzip* or anything remotely similar. The elite consisted wholly of the most capable element in humanity, dedicated with a scientist's dedication to truth, service, and racial progress. They were, fundamentally, a religious order. In his lecture at the Sorbonne in 1927, "Democracy under Revision," and in *The Open Conspiracy* in 1928

2. "All elitists," says Carl J. Friedrich, ". . . resound with Platonism. Indeed the elite is a modern version of Plato's guardian class": Friedrich, *The New Belief in the Common Man* (Boston, Little, Brown, 1942), p. 251. Wells said much the same thing in *Shape of Things to Come*, p. 125.

3. See above, pp. 62–63.

Wells expressly linked his idea of a conspiratorial elite with the history of the great positive religions. There had always been, he wrote, "a profoundly serious minority in the mass of our generally indifferent species," and this minority— "the salt of the earth"—had made possible the growth of the world religions and would, if the world was to be saved, provide the spiritual initiative for the achievement of the world state.[4] Wells could even see an intimation of the coming elite in the Russian Communist party, which also displayed religious fanaticism and selfless dedication to the idea of a new world order.

Still, although the members of the elite had to beware of developing the mentality of an irresponsible privileged ruling class, they could not lose sight of their essential quality. Wells' New Republicans in *Anticipations,* his Samurai in *A Modern Utopia,* and dozens of his fictional heroes from Remington in *The New Machiavelli* (1911) to Gemini Twain in *Babes in the Darkling Wood* (1940) all were unashamedly aristocrats, conscious of a high calling in life, aware of their own importance. Their posture of almost priggish solemnity and dignity was so alien to Wells himself, as a man, that he was unable to infuse them with even the semblance of life. But they indicate just the same how far he was willing to go to yoke his literary talents to the service of his social philosophy.

Of all the aristocratic heroes in Wells' novels, William Porphyry Benham of *The Research Magnificent,* published in 1915, stands out as the most completely developed. The book was in essence a novel about the aristocratic ideal, a sort of Wellsian *Pilgrim's Progress,* with overtones of *Also*

4. Toynbee uses this passage from "Democracy under Revision," reprinted in *The Way the World Is Going,* p. 74, to help define his own concept of the "creative minority" in *A Study of History, 3,* 239. Cf. *Open Conspiracy,* p. 2. All this ties in, of course, with Wells' philosophy of history. See above, pp. 50–51.

sprach Zarathustra. While still at school, Benham conceived the ruling passion of his life: to live nobly. As Benham defined it, the aristocratic spirit moved a man not only to guide his fellow men but also to lead a selfless, self-surpassing life himself, to feel a personal responsibility for human progress, and to extirpate all traces of weakness from his character. The stages in Benham's growth were each illustrations of the barriers human nature sets in the path of the voluntary aristocrat, with the lesson that each could be surmounted, and the harder lesson—in the circumstances of Benham's death—that the "research magnificent," the search for an aristocratic way of life, need not end in happiness or personal success. The first obstacle was fear, which Benham learned to conquer through faith in the immortal spirit of mankind. The second was indulgence, and the third jealousy, both overcome by Benham's rigorous denial of his animal lower nature. The fourth, prejudice, the partisan spirit which divides the nations, races, and classes of men, Benham encountered and conquered last, only to die in defense of his principles, caught in a hail of gunfire trying to prevent a massacre in South Africa.

The principles Benham died to defend were not only values for personal conduct; they involved an explicit renunciation of the democratic form of government. The world, said Benham in his student years, labored in an Age of Confusion. This Age, he wrote, "is Democracy; it is all that Democracy can ever give us. Democracy, if it means anything, means the rule of the planless man, the rule of the unkempt mind." Democracy simply did not work, as Benham's friend Prothero pointed out later. The world state would have to be "an aristocratic republic of all the capable men in the world" because "democracy dies five miles from the parish pump."[5] Modern representative democracy on a

5. *Research Magnificent*, pp. 122, 134.

national scale turned out to be a fraud, a manipulation and exploitation of unintelligent masses by scheming politicians and selfish private interests. The natural democrat was the egotistical common man who chose to lead an everyday life according to his impulses and habits. The natural aristocrat, the man on whose higher ambitions racial progress depended, was the self-abnegating, self-transcending uncommon man, intelligent and imaginative enough to see beyond the routines of the habitual common life of man to a better world. A democratic government could be a government only of whims and wiles, a creature of expediencies and immediate impulses. Its usefulness to mankind in the era of the world crisis had ended.

The antidemocratic sentiments in *The Research Magnificent* stemmed from no temporary loss of faith in democracy. Although Wells tried off and on during the middle years of his life to publicize electoral reform and make some creative use of the labor movement in British domestic politics,[6] he was one of the twentieth century's most confirmed antidemocrats. In a century which listened to the strictures on democracy of Pareto, Ortega y Gasset, Santayana, Babbitt, Mencken, Shaw, Kipling, Belloc, and T. S. Eliot, Wells may not always have been the most audible antidemocrat, but he contributed as much as any of these to the intellectual attack.

The antidemocratic tradition in England had deep roots. Although Wells' fundamental assumptions alone were enough to turn him against democracy, he undoubtedly absorbed much of the antidemocratic feeling in Carlyle and

6. In his autobiography Wells publicly apologized for his compromises with parliamentary politics, admitting that his "theoretical dissent from modern democratic theory" had often been "contradicted very flatly" by some of the causes he had championed. *Experiment in Autobiography,* p. 207.

Ruskin, whose work he had read extensively during his student years in the 1880's; he belonged to a generation much influenced, too, by the criticisms of Matthew Arnold and W. E. H. Lecky, and in the late 1890's and early 1900's by the aristocratic mysticism of Friedrich Nietzsche.[7] Even the Edwardian liberals, with all their radicalism, entertained dark suspicions of the practicability of democracy.[8] M. Ostrogorski published a revealing study of the mechanics of party politics in 1902, *Democracy and the Organization of Political Parties,* which Wells knew, and there were also Gustave le Bon's studies of crowd psychology, often cited by Wells, the new social psychology of Wells' close friend Graham Wallas, and the liberal disillusionment in practical democracy expressed in books like L. T. Hobhouse's *Democracy and Reaction* (1904) and J. A. Hobson's *Imperialism* (1902). The party boss, the popularity of imperialism, the rise of the yellow journalist, and widespread political corruption gave thoughtful liberals on both sides of the Atlantic abundant cause for alarm. Many writers began to wonder if the enfranchisement of the masses had been wise after all. Was the "common man" educable? Was he intelligent enough to be a responsible citizen? Many socialists and liberals, as well as conservatives, thought not.

Wells could not have agreed more emphatically. *Anticipations* included a chapter prophesying "the end of the great Democratic, Wholesale, or Homogeneous phase in the world's history."[9] Two Edwardian novels, *The Sea Lady*

7. But Wells never admitted any fondness for Nietzsche. See his caricature of the Nietzschean strong man, Ostrog, in *When the Sleeper Wakes,* and also his remarks on Nietzsche in *You Can't Be Too Careful,* p. 287.

8. See C. H. Driver, "Social and Political Ideas," in F. J. C. Hearnshaw, ed., *Edwardian England, A.D. 1901–1910* (London, 1933), pp. 234–41.

9. *Anticipations,* p. 62; see ibid., chapter 5, "The Life-History of Democracy."

and *The New Machiavelli,* featured heroes who deserted politics in disgust after promising Parliamentary careers. Attacks on democracy became routine in the postwar novels of ideas, and in 1932 Wells brought out a volume of prophetic esays entitled, significantly, *After Democracy.* The historian of the twenty-second century in *The Shape of Things to Come* summed up the indictment. Democracy, he wrote, had been the natural ideology of industrial capitalism, an early reaction against feudal inequalities, which had made of the so-called common man "a mystical sympathetic being, essentially a God, whose altar was the hustings and whose oracle the ballot box." In practice, the "common man" had become an excuse for capitalistic piracy, war, and irresponsible government. The rulers of the world, said the historian,

> recoiled from any suggestion of definitive or novel action on the plea that their function was purely representative. Behind them all the reader feels the sprawling uneasy presence of that poor invertebrate mass deity of theirs, the Voter, easily roused to panic and frantic action against novel, bold or radical measures, very amenable to patriotic claptrap, very easily scared and maddened into war. ... An entirely irresponsible Press, mercenary or partisan, played upon his baser emotions, which were so easy to play upon, and made no appeal whatever to his intelligence or his conscience.[10]

But in one special sense Wells could accept "democracy": when he took it to mean equality of opportunity. So, in *First and Last Things* (1908), he was able to extract from democracy the idea that every man should be free to contribute what lay in his power to contribute to human

10. *Shape of Things to Come,* pp. 114–15.

welfare: democracy was the fellowship of all men in the racial adventure.[11] Wells' alter ego Steele pointedly removed all chance of confusion in *The Anatomy of Frustration.* " 'When I write of democracy in a favourable sense,' he says, 'I intend no more and no less than this, that every human being shall have the right and shall be given all the opportunity that can be given, to contribute to human achievement just as far as his or her will and power go. Privileges of birth, advantages of wealth, race barriers, are sins against this democratic reality.' "[12] In short, ability could be found at any level in society, in any family, and it was clearly in the interests of progress that every individual with outstanding natural gifts should have every possible opportunity to fulfill his creative potentialities.

Conversely, the common man, the standard or substandard man, could also be found at any level in society, in any family, and it was just as clearly in the interests of progress that this great mass of unexceptional people should not be entrusted with the direction of human affairs. Wells could paint charming portraits of lower-class Englishmen, although some of them—like Kipps—were not so much "common men" as victims of the inequities of the social order. But he insisted that "common men" could not govern themselves. They had to be told what they wanted and given what they needed.[13] It was as brutally plain as that. In his novels Wells matched every lovable Hoopdriver or Kipps

11. *First and Last Things*, pp. 242–43.

12. *Anatomy of Frustration*, p. 35. "If I am something of a social leveller it is not because I want to give silly people a good time, but because I want to make opportunity universal, and not miss out one single being who is worth while": *After Democracy*, pp. 136–37.

13. " 'It is no good asking people what they want,' wrote De Windt. 'That is the error of democracy. You have first to think out what they ought to want if society is to be saved. Then you have to tell them what they want and see that they get it' ": *Shape of Things to Come*, p. 254.

with half a dozen caricatures of the dull, narrow, obnoxious, more or less uneducable mass man: the Skinners in *The Food of the Gods*, the Frapps and Ramboats in *Tono-Bungay*, the Larkinses in *The History of Mr. Polly*, Penk and Ridley in *Men Like Gods*—culminating in the pitiless full-length portrait of Edward Albert Tewler in Wells' last novel, *You Can't Be Too Careful*. Wherever the common man ruled, the parasitical entrepreneur had created a gray world of dead-level conformity. Why worry about the risk of monotony in a planned world society, asked Wells, when capitalism and democracy had already done their best to turn the world into a drab industrial slum? "Chain-shops, controlled stores and standardised production," he pointed out in 1942, had already reduced "mankind to the same dead level of everyday living. They live in the same sort of houses, wear the same sort of clothes, eat the same flabby foods and upset themselves with the same advertised medicines."[14] Professor Keppel, the psychologist in *Star-Begotten* in 1937, lost his temper altogether. The great obstacle to progress, he said, was

> the Common Fool, the Natural Man in either of his chief forms, either dispersed in mob form as the Masses, or concentrated as a Boss. . . . I hate common humanity. This oafish crowd which tramples the ground whence my cloud-capped pinnacles might rise. I am tired of humanity—beyond measure. Take it away. This gaping, stinking, bombing, shooting, throat-slitting, cringing brawl of gawky, under-nourished riff-raff. Clear the earth of them![15]

But save in rare moods like Keppel's, when a fit of exasperation drove his pen pell-mell across the paper, Wells

14. *Science and the World Mind* (London, 1942), p. 19.
15. *Star-Begotten*, pp. 178, 201. Cf. *The Holy Terror* (New York, 1939), pp. 48–50.

stopped far short of preaching the genocide of the masses. What remained was the conviction that only an elite order of volunteer aristocrats, of capable and dedicated uncommon men, could manage the revolution against the old order and manage the public business of the coming world society. And the new elite, unlike the ruling classes of the past, would be consciously a service aristocracy, of "servant-masters,"[16] responsible not to the generality of mankind, but to the evolving mind of the race.

THE STRATEGY OF WORLD REVOLUTION

The Open Conspiracy, Wells' theory of world revolution, dovetailed nicely with his thinking on democracy and leadership. Like his brief attempt to announce a new religion to the world in 1917, it will probably go down in history as a curiously interesting failure, a creed that never caught hold, although it was by no means the most wild-eyed of twentieth-century creeds. All other things being equal, the Open Conspiracy had as much chance of strongly influencing twentieth-century minds and events as the projects of Saint-Simon and Comte in the nineteenth century, which it resembled. It had some of the smell of reality about it. Open Conspirators were not to be poets or college undergraduates or the sort of people who thrive in esoteric brotherhoods. Conspirators were to be recruited from the "functional" elite discussed above, the men and women whose knowledge, skill, and creative gifts made them indispensable to modern society: scientists, engineers, the managerial class in commerce and industry and finance, physicians, civil servants, designers, teachers. The new world would be born not in mass meetings, not in locked lodge halls, but rather in the business places of the old world. The revolution

16. *Science and the World Mind,* p. 42.

would spread from factory to factory, from laboratory to laboratory, from office to office, from classroom to classroom. It would by-pass existing governments like a river changing course.

Much as he liked to represent the Open Conspiracy as a soberly realistic, workaday movement, Wells never evaded the essentially revolutionary implications of the Open Conspiracy. Like William Clissold, every year of his life made him "more certainly revolutionary."[17] The Open Conspiracy was treason to the Thing That Is, and an insult to the People Who Are. "A real world peace movement must be a revolutionary movement in politics, finance, industrialism, and the daily life alike. It is not a proposed change in certain formal aspects of life; it is a proposal to change the whole of life."[18] With as little violence as possible, the old ruling classes and masses would be shorn of their power, without respect for existing constitutions or codes of law. They would be replaced by what Karl Mannheim, as much as Wells, liked to call "functional elites."[19] When the world revolution had won its primary objectives, the old nation-states and the old capitalism would have vanished forever. In their place would rise a collectivized world society.

The project of an Open Conspiracy, under that name, was broached in *The World of William Clissold* in 1926, then treated more fully in *The Open Conspiracy* (1928). But a number of commentators, including Wells himself, have shown that the Open Conspiracy did not occur to Wells out of the blue in the 1920's.[20] The idea of an Open Conspiracy has been traced back to the New Republic in

17. *World of William Clissold, 1,* 184.

18. *Way the World Is Going,* p. 166.

19. Mannheim, *Man and Society in an Age of Reconstruction* (New York, 1940), especially pp. 81–86.

20. See *After Democracy,* pp. 10–12; Geoffrey West, *H. G. Wells,* pp. 243–55; C. H. Driver in *Edwardian England,* p. 274.

Anticipations; actually, it can be found even earlier in Wells' writings. In one of his unreprinted *Fortnightly Review* articles, for example, published in 1897, Wells challenged the intellectuals and teachers who controlled the apparatus of moral suggestion to unite and propagate a new world-faith. "One may dream," he said, "of an informal, unselfish, unauthorised body of workers, a real and conscious apparatus of education and moral suggestion, held together by a common faith and a common sentiment, and shaping the minds and acts and destinies of men."[21] Exactly what Wells expected "an informal, unselfish, unauthorised body of workers" to do was left somewhat obscure in the article, but the emphasis on loose organization and the appeal to private initiative already suggests the Open Conspiracy. In the same year, 1897, he published a short story, "A Story of the Days to Come," in which the Open Conspiracy was even more plainly foreshadowed. There is the contrast, routine in Wells' fiction, between the hard scientific mind, represented by the young doctor, and the aesthetic crank, represented by the very much *fin-de-siècle* twenty-second-century plutocrat Bindon: and the high point of the story occurs when the doctor diagnoses Bindon's fatal illness and warns his uneasy patient that a new order is dawning on earth. Bindon was a sentimentalist, and there was no place in that order for his ilk. "People with imaginations and passions like yours," said the doctor, "have to go—they have to go." Science was still young, he added. The time was coming when "you rich men and party bosses, with your natural play of the passions and patriotism and religion and so forth" would be overthrown by the scientifically trained functional classes.[22]

In *Anticipations* in 1902 Wells brought suggestions like

---

21. "Morals and Civilisation," *Fortnightly Review, 67* (1897), 268.
22. "A Story of the Days to Come," *Tales of Space and Time* (New York, 1899), pp. 312–13.

these into sharp focus. In a mood of virile confidence he predicted that the old capitalistic, nationalistic order would pull itself down by going to war. The old ruling classes would turn to the functional men, the scientifically trained men, for their salvation, and they would be betrayed. The old political order would be sabotaged and superseded by "capable operative and administrative men inspired by the belief in a common theory of social order. . . . This gray confusion that is democracy must pass away inevitably by its own inherent conditions, as the twilight passes, as the embryonic confusion of the cocoon creature passes, into the higher stage, into the higher organism, the world-state of the coming years."[23] Not, in all likelihood, through violent revolution, but through insinuation. The capable men, banded together as the "New Republican" movement, would gradually take the reins of power into their hands. They would be ordered to invent new weapons, control and reorganize national economies to meet the needs of the war effort, and even plan battles—everything would be too complex in technological warfare for the old ruling classes to remain in effective control of any significant fraction. Wells counted on an emergent political consciousness in the managerial and technical people. Little by little, they would assert their will, and they would demand a scientifically organized world society.

The New Republic would originate as a conspiratorial movement long before war actually struck:

> It will appear first, I believe, as a conscious organization of intelligent and quite possibly in some cases wealthy men, as a movement having distinct social and political aims, confessedly ignoring most of the existing apparatus of political control, or using it only as an in-

23. *Anticipations*, pp. 179–80, 189–90.

cidental implement in the attainment of these aims. It
will be very loosely organized in its earlier stages, a
mere movement of a number of people in a certain direction, who will presently discover with a sort of surprise the common object towards which they are all
moving. . . .

In its more developed phases I seem to see the new
republic as . . . a sort of outspoken secret society, with
which even the prominent men of the ostensible state
may be openly affiliated. . . . The new republicans will
constitute an informal and open freemasonry.[24]

And then, when the old order began to totter, on the brink
of war or in the throes of war, the new republicans would
close in, by-passing constitutional machinery to assume *de
facto* control of the world. Wells was to repeat this formula,
with variations and refinements in detail, in half a dozen
later books, especially in his last two Utopian novels, *The
Shape of Things to Come* (1933) and *The Holy Terror*
(1939).

In 1905 the New Republic appeared again in *A Modern
Utopia* as the "Order of the Samurai." The Samurai were
all professional men, holding some kind of advanced degree, and they all adhered to a common code of austere self-
discipline and service. Like the New Republicans and the
Open Conspirators yet to come, the Samurai had begun as
an organization for research and discussion, "but at some
stage it must have assumed a more militant organisation,
and have prevailed against and assimilated the pre-existing
political organisations, and to all intents and purposes have
become this present synthesized World State."[25] Now, it
was the managing class of the state. It had, or tolerated, no
rivals, no organized opposition, nothing to check its power.

24. Ibid., pp. 285, 298, 300.
25. *Modern Utopia*, pp. 262–63.

It had become the brains and the will of humanity, and step by step it absorbed the whole body of humanity into its discipline. It was Man growing into mature self-consciousness and taking collective possession of his planet.

In the years immediately following *A Modern Utopia* painfully unpleasant brushes with the politics of world revolution diverted Wells briefly from his prophetic course. His unsuccessful attempt to make Samurai of the members of the Fabian Society has already been noted in Chapter 1 above. More personally embarrassing, if possible, were the little Samurai groups which sprang up in England, among earnest young Edwardians, who looked—naturally enough —to Wells for leadership. The most elaborate was the joint effort of two thoroughly un-Wellsian young men, Maurice Browne and Harold Munro, later to distinguish themselves in poetry and the theatrical world. Browne and Munro collaborated in the drafting of a "Samurai Code" and founded "The Samurai Press" to publish, unprofitably, the literary efforts of the members, who tended to be poets rather than hard-headed Wellsian technocrats.[26] Wells reacted with understandable coolness, becoming the worst possible patron.

After the Fabian fiasco and the embarrassment of the Samurai movement, Wells for several years virtually repudiated his idea of an Order of Samurai and even the idea of an organized revolutionary elite. The Samurai, he declared, had been conceived under the puritanical influence of the Webbs.[27] For a time now he preferred to regard the world-state movement as a great unfolding historical force rather than as a deliberate conspiracy. In *First and Last*

26. See Maurice Browne, *Too Late to Lament* (Bloomington, Ind., 1956), pp. 85–88; and [Maurice Browne and Harold Munro,] *Proposals for a Voluntary Nobility* (Norwich, 1907), a publication of the Samurai Press.

27. Introduction to 1914 edition of *Anticipations*, p. xi.

Things, in a section entitled "Of an Organised Brother-hood," he agreed with Vernon Lee and G. K. Chesterton, two close friends, who had feared that an Order of Samurai might become in time, despite the rule of equality of oppor-tunity, a closed ruling clique, a power syndicate. There was no need, Wells thought, to imagine the world-state move-ment as an esoteric cult. It was an irresistible movement that used all sorts of people in society at every level, and he doubted that it could be organized without fatal loss to its effectiveness and appeal.[28]

In the light of other books, and in the larger perspective of Wells' whole career as a thinker, there is a good case for assuming that his reservations during these middle years of his life originated in a fear of overinstitutionalizing the Open Conspiracy rather than in any fundamental misgiv-ings about the need for a managerial elite. Wells was tem-peramentally the worst sort of man to play Leader. He was genuinely reluctant to organize or have organized in a political sense groups of men and women for even the worthiest of causes. It might be argued that he lacked an un-derstanding of politics altogether. Man was not for him a political animal. He searched all his life for higher criteria of action than laws and decrees, human or divine, and he found his higher authority in "Science" and the "Mind of the Race." If men were equipped by education with the same scientific world-view, they would automatically lend themselves to the service of the emergent world society, ac-cording to their intelligence and their capacity for creative work. Hence, although Wells perhaps never lost his confi-dence in the need for a service-elite,[29] it was not difficult for him to doubt that the service-elite had to be organized in any formal way to do its job.

28. *First and Last Things,* pp. 173–88.
29. Consider only *The Research Magnificent,* written mostly in 1914, the same year in which Wells was repudiating his idea of an Order of Samurai as something priggish and Webbian!

Much of the work of the world-state movement would, clearly, be ruined by overorganizing it. Scientific research in any field, for example, could easily be overorganized. As Wells pointed out, "The trained investigator is quite the absurdest figure in the farce of contemporary intellectual life; he is like a bath-chair perpetually starting to cross the Himalayas by virtue of a licence to do so. For such enterprises one must have wings. Organization and genius are antipathetic."[30] He had the same criticism to make of Graham Wallas' book *The Great Society* (1914). In his review in *The Nation* he accused Wallas of always resorting to organized thought—to committees, bodies of selected scholars, boards, commissions, cabinets, and what not. But it was the outsider, said Wells, the unorganized man, who invariably had the fertilizing ideas. Churches and academies could never make good their claim to a monopoly over human intellectual enterprise.[31] So Mr. Britling, who warned his American friend Direck that "what you organise you kill," and so Bishop Scrope, who unconsciously echoed Luther's doctrine of the priesthood of all believers in *The Soul of a Bishop*.[32] In any event, Wells was no political organizer. He had so little aptitude for it that he found it difficult even to prescribe formulas by which a movement with a political dimension could be organized by others more generously supplied with leader-like qualities.[33]

30. *Marriage,* p. 185.

31. "The Great Community," London *Nation, 15* (1914), p. 531. How Wells would have squared this view with his own later idea of a world brain center is far from clear.

32. *Mr. Britling Sees It Through,* p. 68; *Soul of a Bishop,* pp. 308–9.

33. "I have a strong dislike for managing, controlling or leading people. It is not my business. I want to keep my mind free, and there is nothing so exacting and enslaving as disciples and followers. They turn up, but I do my best to whip behind and get rid of them. The role of the man of science is to show the way and not lead the way." "The Greatest Opportunity the World Has Ever Had," *Sunday Dispatch,* July 27, 1941.

But the first World War demonstrated to Wells that there might not be time to wait for the normal historical process to take its course. Whether or not it was theoretically better to let the Open Conspiracy arrive spontaneously and without any sort of organization whatever, the world crisis had reached such alarming proportions that history might have to be pushed. Wells' first proposal since 1905 for a more or less self-conscious and organized world-state movement appeared in 1921, after he had had time to digest the implications of the war and the peace settlement. In *The Salvaging of Civilization* he suggested a "cult of the world state," which would take upon itself the responsibility of organizing education and the mass media of propaganda in the service of the world-state idea. It would endow schools, publish books, support social science research, fight counterrevolutionary forces in public education, attack racial and national prejudice, resist military conscription, and only when the time was entirely ripe, turn to overt political action.[34]

Finally, in 1926 in *The World of William Clissold,* he brought out a detailed set of proposals for what he now called the Open Conspiracy,[35] and he did not stray from his allegiance to some sort of project like the one sketched in *Clissold* until his final loss of faith in human prospects in 1944. But Clissold's "Open Conspiracy" was actually only a partial Open Conspiracy, as it might have developed in the mind of a progressive businessman with international

34. *Salvaging of Civilization,* pp. 37–41.

35. Wells had used the phrase a number of times before he made it familiar in 1926. The first time was in his introduction to the 1914 edition of *Anticipations:* "That conception of an open conspiracy of intellectuals and wilful people is always with me; it is my King Charles's head. . . . It is my faith. It is my form of political thought" (p. x). The phrase occurred about the same time in *Research Magnificent,* pp. 271, 447; and again in the 1917 edition of *First and Last Things,* p. 145.

business interests and contacts. Clissold spoke for Wells, but Wells, when he spoke for himself two years later in *The Open Conspiracy*, framed his proposals on an ampler scale than had his protagonist.

Still, of the two books, *Clissold* reached a wider audience. William Clissold, of "Romer, Steinhart, and Crest"—a giant metallurgical concern modeled after Brunner, Mond, and Co.[36]—belonged to a class of industrialists Wells had always considered good material for the new world order. Like every other great international business concern, Romer, Steinhart, and Crest was involved in countless manufacturing operations running this way and that over national boundaries throughout the world. These firms with international connections depended on one another, on international banking houses, and on many local industries for raw materials, machinery, skilled labor, finance capital, and markets. It followed that most of them had a heavy vested interest in world peace and free trade. It further followed, at least for Clissold, that the managers of the new world-scale business firms had to take the direction of the economy of the world into their own hands: in other words, to by-pass governments and establish an economic world order, which would also provide a solid foundation for political and social world order.

Clissold called his project for revolution the Open Conspiracy, which meant, he said,

> the establishment of the economic world-state by the deliberate invitation, explicit discussion, and co-operation of the men most interested in economic organisation, men chosen by their work, called to it by a natural disposition and aptitude for it, fully aware of its importance and working with the support of an increasing

36. See *After Democracy*, p. 100.

general understanding. . . . It is not a project to overthrow existing governments by insurrectionary attacks,
but to supersede them by disregard. It does not want
to destroy them or alter their forms but to make them
negligible by replacing their functions. It will respect
them as far as it must. What is useful of them it will
use; what is useless it will efface by its stronger reality;
it will join issue only with what is plainly antagonistic
and actively troublesome.[37]

The road to Cosmopolis could be taken only by refusing to
fight political battles on the terms of the politicians. If the
Open Conspiracy engaged in political activity at all, it
would be to oppose and remove governments which denied
their citizens the usual civil liberties—Clissold was thinking
of fascist Italy—because the Open Conspiracy could not
thrive unless it was free to educate and carry on an extensive
program of propaganda.

The work of the Open Conspirators—industrial managers, scientists, engineers, and intellectuals for the most
part—was to include a sustained campaign of re-education
through the mass media of communication, especially the
press; international interindustrial agreements to halt the
financing, manufacturing, and even invention of weapons;
and the subsidizing of a great world "literature," to replace
formal higher education. The Open Conspiracy would
grow around and over existing institutions. It would incon-
spicuously reduce them by degrees to useless appendages
tolerated, like so many features of the British constitution,
for old times' sake. At all costs the voting masses were to be
left out of the metamorphosis. "Realisation of a new stage
of civilised society," wrote Clissold, "will be the work of
an intelligent minority; it will be effected without the sup-

37. *World of William Clissold*, 2, 557, 563–64.

port of the crowd and possibly in spite of its dissent. . . . I believe the multitude, when it is suitably roused, can upset anything, but I do not believe that it can create anything whatever."[38]

In an article published in *The Banker* two years later, Wells even fitted the international banking houses into Clissold's Open Conspiracy, and offered bankers a threefold program of conspiratorial action. The financial organization of the world, by-passing governments, was to negotiate agreements leading to the stabilization of currency, the adjustment of credit supplies to break the prosperity-depression business cycle, and the withdrawal of credit to governments or armaments industries seeking to launch an arms race. It was an extraordinary article to appear in a journal as solid as *The Banker,* but Wells had friends even in the banking world, including *The Banker*'s editor, Brendan Bracken, and the American banker Thomas W. Lamont, and his article did not go entirely ignored.[39]

In the same year, 1928, Wells followed up *Clissold* much as he had followed up *Mr. Britling* during the first World War. In the earlier instance he had made a major intellectual discovery in a frankly autobiographical novel and then shortly afterward brought out a compact expository treatise on his discovery—in *God the Invisible King*. Now, he followed the suggestion of an Open Conspiracy in another frankly autobiographical novel, *The World of William Clissold,* with another compact expository treatise, which he entitled *The Open Conspiracy* and subtitled *Blue Prints for a World Revolution*. Although he could have done better, *The Open Conspiracy* was a powerful little book. It was clear, as clear as such books can be; it hit hard; and it

38. Ibid., *1*, 184, 186.
39. "Has the Money-Credit System a Mind?" *Banker, 6* (1928), 221–33. The same article appeared in the United States in the *Saturday Evening Post* (May 5, 1928), pp. 14–15.

clothed Clissold's germinal idea in enough practical detail
to make the Open Conspiracy seem a credible undertaking.
Had it first appeared a few years later, when the Great Depression was to put young people in a mood for reconstruc-
tive thinking, its impact might have been much greater.[40]

The Open Conspiracy proposed a movement substan-
tially broader than Clissold's. The Open Conspirators
would have to recognize from the beginning that their
movement had as its final objective its own transformation,
in whole or in part, into a world-directorate. It would be
open to functional men of every class, country, race, and
profession, and although it would depend for most of its
personnel on "the general functioning classes, landowners,
industrial organizers, bankers, and so forth, who control
the present system,"[41] there would also be thousands of
renegades from the classes most opposed to the world state,
from armies and navies, from governments, from the legal
profession, and from churches, and there would have to be
a great many students and intellectual folk generally in the
movement, if its ideas were to be thoroughly ventilated and
diffused as widely as possible. Nor could it be just another
movement with just another program for world salvation.
The Open Conspiracy would have to emerge as the distinctively twentieth-century form of the religious life. Like all

40. The first edition of *The Open Conspiracy* sold nearly 12,000
copies in Britain and the United States, and the first edition of *What
Are We to Do with Our Lives?*, which was actually the third edition
of *The Open Conspiracy*, sold nearly 4,000 copies. Other editions
might bring the total Anglo-American sales to well over 20,000, still
nothing earth-shaking. Wells was more successful marketing his message in the form of fiction—the British sales alone of *The World of
William Clissold* ran to more than 20,000 copies and of *The Shape of
Things to Come* to more than 60,000. (Figures supplied, with permission of H. G. Wells' executors, by courtesy of A. P. Watt & Son, London.)

41. *Open Conspiracy*, p. 63.

the historic religions, the emergent faith of the future world society would be a scheme of self-subordination to a self-transcending reality. It would have its own cosmogony, the modern scientific world-outlook. And in place of the traditional religious promise of personal immortality, Wells offered, as always, the doctrine of the immortality of the species. Like the historic world religions, the religion of the Open Conspirator would invade every phase of life and find every man a mission. Like the Western religions, it would train the vision of its believers on the coming salvation of humanity and the approach in future time of a Great Good Place: not St. Augustine's City of God, but rather a Utopian Cosmopolis.

In the very name of the movement its two chief tactical principles were disclosed. Wells would not, he thought, make the mistakes committed by most conspiratorial parties by urging the creation of some sort of secret society. The Open Conspiracy was not that kind of conspiracy. It was not to be the resort of wild-eyed, bomb-clutching fanatics. There was to be nothing Irish or Macedonian about it. The Open Conspiracy would be *open,* open to recruits of all descriptions, and bathed continually in the "light of free, abundant criticism." "It is lost," he added, "if it goes underground. Every step to world unity must be taken in the daylight, or the sort of unity that will be won will be found to be scarcely worth the winning."[42]

Still, the Open Conspiracy could be nothing less than a revolutionary conspiracy against the existing order of things. Its work would have to be trans- or para- or extra-legal. No government on earth could be expected to applaud its activities. Wells foresaw violent opposition from the professional patriots in every country, from diplomats, politicians, courtiers, and general staffs, and from all those

---

42. Ibid., pp. 33–34.

classes with a vested interest in the social status quo—arch-bishops, headmasters of public schools, professional serv-ants. He anticipated trouble with peasants and trouble with the organizers of hatred in the world: with colonial offices, Boers, "white supremacy" leaders in the American South, militant rebels of colonies or protectorates seeking a clean break with white Western civilization, and separatist fac-tions of all kinds. Anyone whose immediate interests did not coincide with the establishment of a universal world peace and overriding world controls, would find himself an enemy of the Open Conspiracy. Even if it never fired a shot in defense of its cause, the Open Conspiracy would very shortly be forced to fight a war of nerves and a war of prop-aganda on scores of fronts all over the world.

The work of the Open Conspiracy divided itself naturally into two distinct stages. During the first stage the Open Con-spirators would be concerned almost entirely with a defini-tion of their aims, the vague beginnings of organization, the explanation and propaganda of the world-state idea in all its complexity, and the establishment of close contact among educational reformers attempting to modernize education along the lines discussed in Chapter 3 above. Wells expect-ed this first stage to last for many years. It would begin as the growing awareness of a number of individuals and circles and groups of common objectives and interests. Friends would get together and find they wanted much the same things, which no existing political party could con-ceivably promise to work for. There would be steadily in-creasing agreement in principle and in detail on the pro-visional nature of the nation-state system, on the supreme need for population control, and on the wisdom of collec-tive resistance to participation in war. These three issues—world government, birth control, and resistance to military service—would be not so much the platform of the nascent Conspiracy as test issues, shibboleths by which to separate genuine true-believers from curious onlookers. They could be used to excite public controversy. They would all be important and timely and dramatic enough to win thousands of recruits to the movement and give it a measure of self-awareness. Here and there, youth groups might form; student groups; civic clubs; associations of managers, engineers, and scientists—all with a variety of names and a variety of functions. The student groups, for example, might meet to study and discuss world problems. The civic groups might help stock the local library with essential studies and background books on issues of wide contemporary interest and seek to influence local teachers.

In time, this virtually unorganized congeries of local groups might turn to more overt activities. Youth or student organizations might declare themselves unwilling to serve in armed forces in the event of conscription. Wells set great store by the issue of conscientious objection to military service. He predicted—and in this he was never a better prophet —that the issue would attract tremendous public interest. It would lead, incidentally, to "the creation of regional or national *ad hoc* committees for the establishment of a collective legal and political defensive for this dissent from current militant nationalism. It will bring the Open Conspiracy very early out of the province of discussion into the field of practical conflict."[43] Although he disliked *ad hoc* reformers as such, he insisted that at first the Open Conspiracy could not be organized as a whole, and would have to fall back on *ad hoc* committees and councils for whatever national and international organization it might have. Meanwhile, the local groups would continue their work of self-education and propaganda on a very modest scale. Members would be writing articles in newspapers and the periodical press. Study circles would be disseminating the

43. Ibid., p. 135.

scientific world-view and using books like the Wellsian educational trilogy to give their members a sound background in world history, biology, and economics. In general, this amorphous opening stage would correspond to a phase of the educational renaissance already discussed. It was of the utmost importance that the movement not be pushed any faster than its members could be educated. Wells was not proposing an uprising of ignorant and inflamed mobs. His revolution was to the usual sort of revolution what the surgeon's scalpel is to the fireman's axe.

Eventually Wells thought the movement would get around to publishing a fundamental statement of faith and policy. He suggested six articles which he felt would have to be binding on any Open Conspirator:

(1) The complete assertion, practical as well as theoretical, of the provisional nature of existing governments and of our acquiescence in them;

(2) The resolve to minimise by all available means the conflicts of these governments, their militant use of individuals and property and their interferences with the establishment of a world economic system;

(3) The determination to replace private local or national ownership of at least credit, transport and staple production by a responsible world directorate serving the common ends of the race;

(4) The practical recognition of the necessity for world biological controls, for example, of population and disease;

(5) The support of a minimum standard of individual freedom and welfare in the world; and

(6) The supreme duty of subordinating the personal life to the creation of a world directorate capable of these tasks and to the general advancement of human knowledge, capacity and power.

The admission therewith that our immortality is conditional and lies in the race and not in our individual selves.[44]

With this, or something like it, as a credo, the Open Conspiracy would finally be able to organize on the national and international level. But ties between various groups would have to be allowed to develop naturally, without any compulsion. Even after national and international groups existed, the local and regional groups might continue to function more or less autonomously.

After this proliferation of societies at various levels had initiated the Conspiracy's campaign of propaganda and reeducation, Wells foresaw a second stage in its work. Whereas the first stage would have concentrated on explanation and discussion, the second stage would be devoted to a variety of practical, constructive projects designed to strike directly at existing political, social, and economic institutions. Here the organization would have to be national and international. Some Conspirators would specialize in the "general advancement of science, the protection and support of scientific research and the diffusion of scientific knowledge."[45] Scientific men had to do their work without interference or censorship, and it was the duty of men of more general intelligence and interests to make certain that scientists had the most favorable possible working conditions. They were also to make certain that scientists had access to clear, compact reviews and analyses of twentieth-century world issues, well enough integrated to be read and understood in the limited time available to the specialized scientific man for general reading. Specific projects might include the endowment of laboratories, observatories, and experimental stations; improvements in the indexing of

44. Ibid., pp. 142–43.
45. Ibid., p. 146.

scientific reports, to speed research and eliminate unnecessary duplication of effort; the promotion of popular publications to explain the work of science and its implications for society; and the formation of *ad hoc* associations to underwrite and protect research teams.

Other Conspirators would be at work in business and industry. Specialized journals imbued with the spirit of the Conspiracy would spring up to study industrial psychology, currency and credit, and other important fields of economic research in the light of the twentieth-century world crisis, carrying out still another objective of the educational renaissance Wells insisted would have to precede world revolution. Some Conspiracy groups would be concerned with the application of biological knowledge to the economics of population, health, and food supply. Another series of groups would work in the field of education. Conspiracy families might even be forced to establish their own sectarian schools and encourage their children to marry within the movement. Members would penetrate governments, civil services, and political parties to influence government action in support of free trade, international cooperation, disarmament, and so forth. In each constituency political action committees would organize opinion locally. Pressure would be brought to bear on local candidates of the major parties to vote in the national legislature for programs supported by the Conspiracy. Still other Conspirators, in industry, trade, and banking, would be negotiating international agreements on their own initiative, in anticipation of the ultimate establishment of world economic controls. By that point Wells conceived

> of the Open Conspiracy as consisting of a great multitude and variety of overlapping groups, but now all organised for collective political, social and educational as well as propagandist action. They will recognise each

other much more clearly than they did at first and they will have acquired a common name. . . . This large loose assimilatory mass of groups and societies will be definitely and obviously attempting to swallow up the entire population of the world and become the new human community.[46]

The actual steps by which existing governments would finally be superseded and world controls established, after all this elaborate preparatory work, Wells did not choose in *The Open Conspiracy* to predict, leaving the final stage of revolution to the reader's imagination. It would depend on whether there was to be another world war, what economic conditions would prevail, and how much militant opposition the Conspiracy had encountered. But about the final objective there was to be no mistake: the Conspiracy would grow until the whole world was in its grasp, and if it did not aspire to world direction it would fail to achieve anything worth the trouble.

It was an ambitious scheme. With the earlier proposals in *The World of William Clissold,* it drew a considerable amount of attention from friends and critics. J. M. Keynes, reviewing *Clissold,* had to caution Wells that the world of industry and finance was not populated by idealists like Clissold. The book was "a huge and meaty egg from a glorious hen, an abundant outpouring from an ingenious, truthful, and generous spirit,"[47] but Keynes saw no hope of infusing the international business community with the high ideals of the Open Conspiracy. Bertrand Russell, writing to Wells on *The Open Conspiracy,* had a similar point to make about scientists. "I do not know of anything with which I agree more entirely," he said, but he warned Wells not to

46. Ibid., pp. 162–63.

47. Keynes, "Clissold," *Essays in Persuasion* (London, Macmillan, 1931), p. 357.

expect the scientists to join an Open Conspiracy; most of them were too busy flirting with the powers-that-be for national honors and prizes.[48] Bernard Shaw and Beatrice Webb both sent Wells letters of congratulation, without—at their age!—expressing any inclination to become disciples.[49] Most of the reviews were lukewarm to indifferent. The year 1928 was not conspicuously depressing. Quite the opposite. Reviewers could afford to be cheerfully cynical about schemes to save the world, and Wells' literary reputation, already in process of decay, was no longer great enough, especially among the intellectual avant-garde, to enable his new books to attract anything like the attention they might have attracted had they been written by younger, newer men.

But the idea of an Open Conspiracy did acquire a new lease on life after 1930, for which the world business depression deserved most of the credit. Wells had warned the world a number of times, as recently as 1928 in *The Banker,* about a depression. Its arrival awakened almost immediate interest in radical and revolutionary projects for recovery in every country seriously affected. In the United States, Howard Scott, a self-styled apostle of Thorstein Veblen, launched the Technocracy movement, which became especially powerful among engineers and intellectuals in the Western states and had something in common with the Open Conspiracy; and even the New Deal and the "Brain Trust" represented a radically new departure for an American government. Britain was shaken by Sir Oswald Mosley's British Fascists and by a pacifist movement of arresting vitality; Germany succumbed to the psychopathic sorcery of Adolf Hitler's Nazis. In every country where it was not brutally suppressed, communism grew by leaps and bounds.

48. Russell to Wells, May 24, 1928, in the Wells Archive.
49. Shaw to Wells, May 29, 1928; and Beatrice Webb to Wells, May 25, 1928, in the Wells Archive.

Intellectuals, young people, and the unemployed were everywhere in a mood to subscribe to schemes for scrapping the old order. Wells profited. He was able to market a second edition of *The Open Conspiracy* in 1930, a third edition extensively revised under the title *What Are We to Do with Our Lives?* in a paperback format in 1931, and still a fourth in 1935 for The Thinker's Library. The sale if not positively brisk was at least middling fair for a man whose literary reputation was on the downgrade.[50]

For all its originality, the Open Conspiracy did have an intellectual pedigree, and it can be readily compared with some of the movements that operated in the political arena of the early 1930's. Albert Guérard has noted the similarity between Wells' elite class and Voltaire's idea of an open, but organized, aristocracy of enlightened service.[51] But the best comparison is with Saint-Simon and Comte, some of whose thinking reached Wells indirectly at an early age through the Positivist movement in Great Britain. The ideal of a world state administered by a select body of industrialists and scientists and engineers appealed as strongly to Saint-Simon and Comte as it did to Wells, although Wells disliked the static quality of the Comtian Utopia and its tendency toward overinstitutionalization. The Positivist movement and the Saint-Simonian cult, which flourished in France after Saint-Simon's death, were both spiritually akin to the project of an Open Conspiracy.

In his own time Wells had the tantalizing example of the Communist party. "At the very time I was failing," he wrote in his autobiography of his failure to make Samurai of Fabians in 1906, "Lenin, under the stresses of a more pressing reality, was steadily evolving an extraordinarily similar

50. See above, p. 186, n. 40.
51. Guérard, "The 'New History': H. G. Wells and Voltaire," *Scribner's Magazine, 76* (1924), 476–84.

scheme, the reconstructed Communist Party."[52] He also compared the Open Conspiracy with the Kuomintang in China and the Fascisti in Italy.[53] But all these political movements were strongly tainted with Marxism or nationalism or both; what made them similar to the Open Conspiracy—and Wells was writing about an Open Conspiracy or something like it before he had heard of any of them—was their structure, their fanaticism, their determination to undertake the complete transformation of society undemocratically. Even the Fabian Society could be compared in one or two ways with the Open Conspiracy, in spite of its resistance to Wells' program for expansion in 1906. So patient an old Fabian as Beatrice Webb moved very near to Wells' position in the late 1920's, when, Margaret I. Cole records, she was pointing out to friends the need for "an Order, as she called it, of dedicated persons, something resembling the Jesuit Order or the Russian Communist Party."[54] It is not difficult

52. *Experiment in Autobiography,* p. 566.

53. "I am asking for a Liberal Fascisti, for enlightened Nazis; I am proposing that you consider the formation of a greater Communist Party, a Western response to Russia": *After Democracy,* p. 24. There is a preposterous letter from Sir Oswald Mosley to Wells, August 31, 1932, in the Wells Archive, in which Mosley—just then in process of organizing his British Union of Fascists—reports that he is taking Wells up on his plea for "fascism" in Britain, although he cannot promise how "liberal" it will be; along with the letter came a prepublication copy of Mosley's new book *The Greater Britain;* Mosley thought Wells would recognize some of his own teachings in it. For Wells on Mosley see *Experiment in Autobiography,* pp. 669–70, a devastating account of a Mosley rally at the Albert Hall which Wells attended, and the caricature of Mosley as "Lord Horatio Bohun" in *The Holy Terror,* especially pp. 108–13.

54. Cole, *Beatrice Webb* (London, Longmans, Green, 1945), p. 158; cf. Archibald Henderson, *George Bernard Shaw* (New York, 1956), p. 353. In their *Soviet Communism: A New Civilization?* (2 vols. New York, 1936), 2, 1131, n. 2, Sidney and Beatrice Webb compared Wells' Samurai and the Russian Communist party.

to imagine a mixture of Bolshevism and Fabianism that would resemble the Open Conspiracy, and both Bolshevist communism and Fabian socialism powerfully influenced the Webbs' thought. Among prominent American thinkers, at least vague parallels might be drawn with the work of Thorstein Veblen and Walter Lippmann.

The project of an Open Conspiracy, then, was not the only radical turning of its kind available to thinking people in the tragic years after 1930. It was one of dozens which might have been taken. But whereas it failed to attract any serious interest at all before 1930, in the Depression era— the era of the Peace Pledge, Blackshirts, the Oxford Group, and Technocracy—it had a much livelier appeal. In 1932–33 one group of liberal and radical thinkers led by C. E. M. Joad met together to found a federation aimed at coordinating the work of the innumerable *ad hoc* progressive societies then flourishing in Britain. They drew up a Basis in December 1933, much of which was taken directly from a memorandum contributed by Wells, entitled "There Should Be a Common Creed for Left Parties throughout All the World."[55] The platform of the Federation of Progressive Societies and Individuals, as it called itself, was eminently Wellsian: the Basis supported regional and world economic planning, a world currency, a world government, resistance to military conscription, a world educational system with Wellsian curricular reforms, population control, freedom of adult sexual behavior, disestablishment of the Church of England, and full guarantees of civil liberty. Its vice-presidents included Vera Brittain, Aldous and Julian Huxley, Kingsley Martin, Harold Nicolson, Bertrand Russell, Rebecca West, Leonard Woolf, and Wells. After publishing a Manifesto in 1934, the Federation struck

55. It is published in Joad, ed., *Manifesto of the Federation of Progressive Societies and Individuals* (London, 1934), pp. 12–20.

out along the usual lines followed by radical associations in England. Wells lost interest almost immediately; and in private he denounced it in effect as a miscellany of dilettantes,[56] which may have been a fair criticism. But by intention, at any rate, the F.P.S.I. started its brief career in the spirit of the Open Conspiracy.

More directly responsive to Wells' evangelism was another society founded in London in 1934, which survived until 1937 under three different names, first—Wells' vigorous animadversions notwithstanding—as the H. G. Wells Society, later as The Open Conspiracy, and finally as Cosmopolis. It was able to secure the endorsement of Olaf Stapledon, Gerald Heard, Sylvia Pankhurst, and Vera Brittain, and it grew affluent enough in time to hold a public meeting at Caxton Hall, maintain a permanent office in London, and support ten British chapters. By virtue of a chapter in Buenos Aires it became an international movement in 1935. In 1937, however, many of its members joined forces with the F.P.S.I., and the society disintegrated. Throughout its short-lived existence, the society's active members were mostly young people in their twenties and early thirties, many of them civil servants and engineers. If it was not a spectacularly successful society, it was entirely typical of its times, and evidence of Wells' persistence as an intellectual force in the 1930's.[57]

Wells continued to introduce the idea of an Open Conspiracy, under one name or another, into most of the rest of his books down to 1944. His address, "Liberalism and the Revolutionary Spirit," delivered at the Liberal Summer

56. See Wells' reply, written on the margin, to a letter he had received from the Federation's J. B. Coates, dated September 3, 1937, in the Wells Archive.

57. This account was drawn largely from letters and other materials in the Wells Archive.

School at Oxford in July 1932 and reprinted in *After Democracy,* brought the idea to a great many young people who had missed *The Open Conspiracy* itself. In *The Shape of Things to Come* (1933) the idea made its appearance as the "Modern State Movement." According to the twenty-second-century historian, the movement grew from scattered groups of technicians, scientific workers, and industrial managers during the catastrophic war years of the 1940's to become the world "Air Dictatorship" of the latter part of the century, recalling Rudyard Kipling's prophecy in two short stories written before the first World War of a world "Aerial Board of Control."[58] Professor Ernest Keppel rehearsed the arguments for an Open Conspiracy again near the end of a flimsily disguised science-fiction romance, *Star-Begotten,* in 1937. Another apocalyptic novel, *The Holy Terror,* constructed from much the same material Wells had used in *The Shape of Things to Come,* followed in 1939. Here the Open Conspiracy took the rather startling form of a political party, a reconstituted and rejuvenated British Union of Fascists, snatched from its Mosleyesque leader, Lord Horatio Bohun, by a splenetic young man who combined the talents of H. G. Wells and Adolf Hitler. After a second world war had broken out in 1944, the movement was able to infiltrate and finally take possession of all the Western governments, stop the war, and impose a world directorate.

The actual coming of the long-expected war in September 1939 did nothing to shake Wells' confidence in his theory of world revolution. He argued the case still another time in *The New World Order,* again in *All Aboard for Ararat,* and for the last time in *Phoenix: A Summary of the Inescapable*

58. Rudyard Kipling, "With the Night Mail" (1909) and "As Easy as A.B.C." (1912); cf. Michael Arlen, *Man's Mortality* (1933), and Brian Tunstall, *Eagles Restrained* (1936).

Conditions of World Reorganisation, published in 1942.[59]
It was, if anything, a more practical project in *Phoenix* than
it had been in *The Open Conspiracy*. Here Wells urged the
formation locally all over the world of two basic kinds of
Conspiracy cells, one for study, research, and propaganda,
the other in the world's industrial plants to develop "methods of working by and through the workers and management, that is to say the 'operatives,' which will deprive ownership and finance of any control whatever."[60] From these
cells would spring, in time, larger regional, national, and
international *ad hoc* groups to protect civil liberties, publish and distribute essential ideas relating to the world-state
movement, and modernize education. The propaganda and
educational cells would also expand within the framework
of the movement to coordinate the work of the industrial
Conspirators. Wells predicted a crisis between the established order and the Conspiracy as soon as the war had
ended and a peace settlement had been reached. The re-
gimes in power would now be able to devote their full attention to the Revolution. They would begin passing repressive
legislation. Some might use force illegally against the Conspirators. But the Revolution would continue to gain mo-
mentum. Radio stations, newspaper offices, power stations,
and traffic centers would be seized. Whole countries would
be captured. And when the Conspiracy had achieved power,
it would offer its opponents short shrift. Religious propaganda and sectarian schools would be prohibited; dangerous

59. See *New World Order,* pp. 84–85; *All Aboard for Ararat,*
passim. The symbolism in the latter is fairly straightforward: Wells,
in the guise of "Noah," is selecting his crew for the "Ark"—that is,
deciding what the membership requirements will be for the Open
Conspiracy, which is to keep the cause of humanity afloat on the flood-
waters of the second World War.

60. *Phoenix: A Summary of the Inescapable Conditions of World
Reorganisation* (London, 1942), p. 53.

enemies of the world state would be hunted down and executed; kings and potentates would be mediatized and stripped of authority. Wells stressed the importance of hard-headedness. Liberal and internationalist opinion was too pitifully feeble to take the world away from the tough, cynical capitalists, dictators, generals, and party bosses who held it under their thumbs. The Open Conspiracy would have to fight fire with fire.

Although *Phoenix* failed to arouse any fresh interest in the idea of an Open Conspiracy, something very much like William Clissold's version of the Open Conspiracy had been prophesied a year before in the United States by James Burnham in *The Managerial Revolution*. For a few months Burnham held the attention of critics as Wells no longer could. But in the end *The Managerial Revolution* suffered the same fate as Wells' books. No signs of a will to power have appeared among "functional" people; politicians remain as inevitable as ever, even in communist states; the Saint-Simonian vision of a managerial elite is still such stuff as dreams are made on.[61]

On the other hand, the idea of an Open Conspiracy might have taken deeper roots if someone not only younger but also more patient and politic than Wells had conceived it.

61. Not everyone would agree with this. Burnham's book has recently erupted again in a paperback edition in the United States; and C. Wright Mills offers a popular theory about the depoliticization of American and Soviet life in *The Power Elite* (New York, 1956) and *The Causes of World War Three* (New York, 1958) which argues that politicians are increasingly the captives of small ruling circles of business and military leaders. For a curious example of the influence of Wells' Open Conspiracy on Continental thought, in a book roughly contemporary with Burnham's, see Serge Chakotin, *Le Viol des foules*, Paris, 1939. Dedicated to Wells, *Le Viol des foules* called for a Wellsian-Pavlovian "psychagogic" revolution against Fascism. It appeared in an English translation in London in 1940 as *The Rape of the Masses*.

Wells' ginger group in the Fabian Society, the enthusiastic popular reception given *A Modern Utopia,* and the fair flurry of interest in *The Open Conspiracy* and its sequels in the early 1930's were all opportunities he lacked the temperament to exploit. He made the most candid confession possible in *The Common Sense of War and Peace* (1940):

> Since I began to learn about the direction of human affairs, I have been much afflicted by would-be disciples and followers. Before I took my own measure I did occasionally entangle myself with groups of people who proposed to take possession of me, interpret me and make something between a figure-head and a leader of me. These entanglements taught me one thing very clearly, that "leadership" is entirely incompatible with the clear and critical apprehension of how things are and where things are, which is the natural activity of such a mind as mine. You might just as well expect a chart and compass to steer a ship. I found out very early in life, not only that I could not "manage" people, but that I disliked in about equal measure the concessions and deceptions that are involved in *managing* anyone, and the tiresome people who obliged me to make those politic adjustments of the truth necessary to keep them in tow. I despise driven sheep, I despise dogs that fawn upon me, I despise followers and disciples.[62]

Spoiled as it is by senile vanity, the confession still spoke the truth. Wells wanted his freedom. The "scientific man" did not belong on a soap box. But the movement Wells envisioned could not have thrived as a "society" in any case, however vigorous or articulate. It had to be a movement in the historical sense, a tidal wave, an irresistible and sponta-

---

62. *Common Sense of War and Peace,* p. 8; cf. above, p. 181, n. 33.

neous outbreak of understanding. When Wells groped for words to describe his Open Conspiracy, he was in effect trying to say that unless the idea occurred independently and simultaneously to tens of thousands of able men in responsible positions all over the world, there was no hope for it. It could not be preached, written, or led into existence unless it already, in some rough form, existed in the minds of the potential elite. Wells had too much fatalism in his blood to expect history to obey H. G. Wells. He was no conjurer. Either history had reached the stage where an Open Conspiracy could become a going practical concern, or it had not.

Down at least to the middle of the twentieth century, the objective of the Open Conspiracy has remained a far more durable and widely shared ideal than the Open Conspiracy itself. All Wells' versions of the world revolution ended, as a matter of course, in the establishment of a world state. Nothing short of a world state would do. Wells is easy to dress down on the score of inconsistency, but he never wavered in a lifetime of prophesying from a resolute insistence on the impracticality of planning in less than planetary terms.

Of course Wells did not ignore the possibility of a tactical advantage from unions among peoples linked by common cultures. He was especially fond of the idea of a federation of the English-speaking peoples. They were kindred enough in their ways of life to unite, and in uniting, numerous enough and widely enough distributed around the planet to act as the possible nucleus of a world union. The project of an English-speaking superstate appeared in *Anticipations* and *Mankind in the Making*. Again, in 1935, in *The New America: The New World,* Wells looked to an Anglo-American federation as the first step in the building of a world state. It would magnetically attract other peoples, bringing into its synthetic arrangements much of northern Europe, the Hispanic world, and Asia.[63] Rud Whitlow's Common-Sense Movement campaigned for Anglo-American union as a preliminary to world government in *The Holy Terror* in 1939. Wells even went on record, shortly after the first World War, as an exponent of the idea of European federation as a bridge to the world state.[64]

But the main current of Wells' thought ran in a rather different direction from the arguments usually put forward for regional federations. As temporary and provisional arrangements, he might tolerate them. The Open Conspiracy might tolerate them. But the main business of the Open Conspiracy was to operate on a world-wide scale and produce in its upward thrust all over the world an integrated world community. True, as Wells wrote in *The Open Conspiracy* itself, the majority of Open Conspirators might be drawn from the populations of the more advanced Western powers. The initiative would rest with the "Atlantic communities."[65] But Wells warned his readers repeatedly of the dangers of setting their sights any lower than cosmopolis. Nothing less could possibly function with any degree of efficiency for any length of time under twentieth-century conditions. Everything less would necessarily be a makeshift, an expedience of the moment, to be transcended as soon as possible. Wells' point of view emerged most clearly in his criticisms of Clarence K. Streit's Federal Union movement in 1939 and 1940. There was a chance, Wells agreed, that a federal union of the Western democracies might profit the cause of world order, might not be just another League of Nations in disguise. But it could amount to little more than a pause for breath. "This Federal Union idea cannot be confined to any group of states, however exten-

63. *New America*, pp. 16–17.
64. *Salvaging of Civilization*, pp. 64–65.
65. *Open Conspiracy*, pp. 110–11, 189; cf. Comte's Western Republic!

sive. . . . It may be that as a transitional phase there may be secondary groupings of the Oslo Powers or the Latin Union or the Balkan Powers, but such groupings must be confessedly on the way to the ultimate synthesis, and they will not be safely adjusted until that synthesis is complete."[66] And, of course, the revolution could not be satisfied with constitutional reform. Streit had left out the heart of the matter: the establishment of a controlled, planned, collectivized world economy and a vast movement of propaganda and education in the service of the cause of world order. Any constitutional or unconstitutional union of the Atlantic communities that did not see itself as a small way station along the high road to world integration would scarcely matter. A simple reduction in the number of competing states in the state-system might even prove entirely irrelevant to the cause of world order.

After all, Wells was an Open Conspirator. The right way to world peace was the Open Conspiracy; and the only sane objective of the Open Conspirator was a planetary Utopia, a unified human community. "I am for the super-state," he wrote in 1924, "and not for any League. Cosmopolis is my city, and I shall die cut off from it."[67]

66. *Rights of Man,* pp. 109–10.
67. *Year of Prophesying,* p. 109.

Chapter Five:

COSMOPOLIS

UTOPOGRAPHY

In every sense Wells' career as a prophet of world order culminated in his imaginative renderings of a world Utopia. The organic cosmopolis was the embodiment in practical social action of the emergent being of humanity; preparing the world mental climate for cosmopolis was the purpose of education; establishing cosmopolis by world revolution was the function of the Open Conspiracy. In Wells the Utopographic tradition itself culminates, just as he is also one of the first writers to adapt the Swiftian device of the inverted Utopia or counter-Utopia to the anxieties of the twentieth century.[1]

Anthony West, in his recent essay on Wells, represents him in his old age as remorseful that he had coddled his readers by painting cheerful pictures of impossible future worlds. Toward the end, says West, he acknowledged the ineffectiveness of Utopian incentives and turned to jolting revelations of the hard truth in books like *The Croquet Player*.[2] Wells never admitted the futility of Utopography in any of his published writings until 1944; he was warning

1. See above, pp. 82–83.
2. West, "H. G. Wells," *Encounter, 8* (1957), 59. For more of West's argument see above, p. 82.

civilization of the possibility of disaster long before *The Croquet Player* and still writing Utopian books, like *The Holy Terror* and *Phoenix*, several years after *The Croquet Player*. But West's testimony, based in part on conversations with Wells, should be taken seriously. It does not stretch the imagination too far to fancy the latter-day Wells in a mood of exasperation, half-agreeing with his son's suggestion that he had been casting pearls before swine. All the conjurings-up of Utopia had not done much visible good. He had the best grounds for disillusionment.

But Wells could no more have gone through life without writing Utopias than he could have gone on without writing books. For better or for worse, Utopography suited Wells' ideas and instincts perfectly. All his prophecies pointed inexorably to the Utopian world city. Because Utopia would not come of its own accord, because it had to be willed into existence by the toil and courage of an Open Conspiracy of willful men, the writer of Utopias was indispensable. He enlisted true-believers in the Conspiracy by creating inspirational images of the possible future: the writing of Utopias was itself part of the propaganda work of the Open Conspiracy. The Utopographer was also the master-architect of cosmopolis, the man who fused all the hopes and plans for social amelioration of his age. Every serious Utopia, said Wells, represented an attempt at long-range social planning. There could no more be a new world without Utopias than a new house without blueprints.[3]

Wells furnished his fellow Open Conspirators with two full-dress Utopian novels, *A Modern Utopia* (1905) and *Men Like Gods* (1923); glimpses of Utopia in other novels, like *In the Days of the Comet* (1906) and *The Shape of Things to Come* (1933); and much speculation on the com-

3. See "An Apology for a World Utopia," in F. S. Marvin, ed., *The Evolution of World Peace* (London, Oxford University Press, 1921), pp. 159–78.

ing world society in nearly all his prophetic manifestoes
and journalism. *The Open Conspiracy* and *Phoenix* were
just as much Utopian books as *A Modern Utopia* itself. The
tendency of writers on Utopism to focus on fictional Utopias, to deal with Utopian novels and ignore the Utopian
element in social philosophy and religion,[4] is especially
ill-advised in a study of Wells. Everything about Wells'
thinking bears the stamp of Utopism, and a balanced picture
of his Utopia is impossible without taking all his work into
account.

Wells patently belongs in the main stream of Western
Utopism. He was a twentieth-century heir to a tradition
originating in the fourth century B.C. in Plato. But the tradition of writing Utopias or envisioning and prophesying
future ideal societies has attracted so many writers through
the centuries that there is no such thing as a "classical" or
"orthodox" Utopia. The Utopia is a device for preaching;
and just as every social philosophy is likely to embody, and
certain to imply, a Utopia, so every formal Utopia is almost
sure to embody a social philosophy. Utopias may, for example, picture a society out of space and time, a static absolute or ultimate, like Plato's Republic or the Christian
Heaven or St. Augustine's City of God, with its beginnings
in this world and its culmination and fulfillment outside of
time in the next world. Or they may idealize an infinitely
self-perfecting and self-transcending society, as many Utopias since the Enlightenment have done, reflecting Enlightenment and post-Enlightenment ideas of progress through
science or the "laws" of evolution. Wells belonged to this

4. Three representative surveys of Utopism—Lewis Mumford, *The
Story of Utopias* (1922), J. O. Hertzler, *History of Utopian Thought*
(1923), and Marie Louise Berneri, *Journey through Utopia* (1950)—
all manage, e.g., to avoid more than rare incidental references, if any,
to Condorcet, Saint-Simon, Comte, and Marx. Of the three, only
Hertzler has a section on the Christian Utopia.

school of Utopographers; like the Utopias of Condorcet, Comte, and Marx, his Utopias were not strictly ideal societies at all, but rather societies emancipated from the past, ideal in comparison to historic societies, but capable of more or less infinite progress in time. Wells emphasized this open-ended quality of Utopia more than perhaps any of his predecessors. Condorcet's Tenth Epoch, Comte's Republic of Humanity, and Marx' classless society were all in one sense secular approximations of the Christian millennium, in spirit far from free of Platonist and Christian idealism. Seeing human life and seeing it exclusively as an adventure in biological evolution and geological time, he projected Utopia on a more cosmic scale, anticipating the still more ambitious Utopography of Olaf Stapledon.

Utopias can also be classified according to their size. Plato's Republic was a Greek *polis*. Many Utopias have followed Plato's example, from Campanella's Renaissance city-state in *The City of the Sun* to the communitarian experiments suggested by Fourier and Hertzka. Other Utopias have been scaled to the size of existing national states, like Edward Bellamy's United States in *Looking Backward* or William Morris' England in *News from Nowhere*. Wells, of course, insisted on a global Utopia, again like Condorcet, Comte, and Marx, but, again, even more emphatically.

But in one respect Wells and almost all Western Utopists before him shared the same ideal. Exceptions come to mind, like Gerrard Winstanley and William Morris, but most Utopographers have organized their ideal societies along authoritarian lines. The Platonist Utopia, the Augustinian, Sir Thomas More's, the Calvinist, the Saint-Simonian, the Comtian, the Marxist, and the Wellsian Utopias all sacrifice liberty to order and democracy to authority, whether the authority of a political elite, an almighty God, or a corps of "nonpolitical" experts. The ideal society has almost always been an organically integrated society: Utopia differs from the real world in its single-mindedness, its monolithic order, its Procrustean rationality. In this part of the Western Utopographic tradition, Wells was at one with all his fellows, ancient, medieval, and modern.

The study of the Wellsian Utopia which follows draws freely on all of Wells' books, but three are especially rich in Utopian speculation: *A Modern Utopia, Men Like Gods,* and *The Shape of Things to Come.* Partly in the form of a novel, partly in the form of a Platonic dialogue, partly in the form of a treatise, *A Modern Utopia* offered a complete picture of a world society of the near future. Human nature had not yet changed, a governing class was still necessary, and scientific progress had carried only a little further than on earth. More of a sequel than an alternative to *A Modern Utopia, Men Like Gods* assumed a much later world society, with human nature under revision, no government as such, and a more advanced science and technology. Studying the two Utopias in isolation from Wells' other work might lead an unwary critic to infer that Wells had changed his mind between 1905 and 1923. But *The Shape of Things to Come* in 1933 made quite clear what was already fairly obvious from hints strewn through other books: *A Modern Utopia* and *Men Like Gods* were different stages in the life-history of the same cosmopolis. The Utopia of *The Shape of Things to Come* started out much like the puritanical world of *A Modern Utopia* and evolved by degrees into the more luminous fantasy of *Men Like Gods.* In short, as shown by the timetable of Utopian evolution in *The Shape of Things to Come,* the relationship between the two earlier Utopias was almost identical with the relationship between the dictatorship of the proletariat and the final withering away of the state in Marxist Utopography.

Not that Wells' ideas on Utopia remained rigidly consistent all through his life. Each Utopia, or brief glimpse of Utopia, reflected Wells' special preoccupations at the time of writing, and each was limited by the literary form in which he chose to give it expression. But if the timetable in *The Shape of Things to Come* can be accepted, the differences are much outweighed by the similarities. All Wells' Utopias, and especially the three principal Utopias—*A Modern Utopia, Men Like Gods,* and *The Shape of Things to Come*—are alike enough in spirit and purpose to be studied as one. And they are all labors of love, in which Wells' deepest convictions and best hopes for a solution of the twentieth-century world crisis converge in creative harmony.

The most convenient way of analyzing the Wellsian Utopia is to study, first, its system of government, or management; then its organization of work and wealth; and finally, Wells' ideas on the ultimate uses of life.

THE MANAGEMENT OF UTOPIA

Even more than the Open Conspiracy itself, Wells' Utopia lacked a political dimension. The Open Conspirators were not to clear the ground for democracy or dictatorship or any other political order of things. As one political scientist, the late Edward Mead Earle, saw very clearly, Wells believed in the possibility of by-passing the political process and political institutions altogether.[5] Critics should always feel a keen reluctance to apply the word "state" to Wells' Utopia, although Wells himself now and then talked about the "world state."[6] Utopia might not even have, strictly

5. Edward Mead Earle, "H. G. Wells, British Patriot in Search of a World State," in Earle, ed., *Nationalism and Internationalism* (New York, 1950), pp. 119–20.

6. But see *Phoenix,* p. 182: "There will never be a World State, as we apprehend a State." I chose the title of the present study with some reluctance. But taken in the broadest and vaguest sense, Wells' organically unified cosmopolis would be a "state," a body politic managed, if the paradox is admissible, without politics.

speaking, a government. In its earliest period, it would be managed by scientists, engineers, and public administrators, a fraternity more or less organized of "functional" men, a continuation of the Open Conspiracy into the new world order. In later periods the need even for public management would disappear.

As William Clissold phrased it, the Open Conspiracy in coming to world power would transform itself into a world directorate: not a world government, formed by lawful delegation of powers by sovereign states to a federal world republic, but a world directorate, unlike any government ever known in history. Governments existed to make war and conduct foreign relations. The world directorate would rather resemble the management of a giant corporation. Its work would be economic and social, not political.[7] There could be no parliament,[8] no president, no political parties; all the apparatus of democracy Wells cheerfully discarded.

Essentially, Utopia would be managed by a series of interlocking functional world controls, the progeny of those world service organizations patiently constructed by the Open Conspiracy in the revolutionary era. One world authority would manage transport, another housing, another the world police, another education, another the manufacture of staple goods, and so forth. In all the affairs of every day the staffs of the world controls would coordinate their work by means of intercontrol conferences, conducted with

7. *World of William Clissold*, 2, 566 ff.

8. Except in *The World Set Free*, where the self-appointed organizers of the new world order permitted the election of a world parliament which very shortly degenerated into a rubber stamp for specialized "scientific committees": *World Set Free*, pp. 244–48. Wells also endorsed the idea of a world parliament for a time during the first World War, in connection with his League of Nations work; and see his suggestion of a world "consumers' jury" in *Phoenix*, pp. 89–91.

the utmost informality. Wells also envisaged at first the exercise of general supervision over the world controls by some less specialized administrative body; it might even deserve the label of "governing body." In *A Modern Utopia* all positions of authority were held by members of the brotherhood of Samurai, a completely self-governing organization, which also elected mostly from its own ranks the supreme legislative assembly of Utopia. The Utopians in *The World Set Free* for a time vested supreme power in a democratically elected Parliament. In *The Shape of Things to Come* the place of the Samurai was taken by the Modern State Fellowship, the old party of world revolutionists; and a Council for World Affairs composed of Fellowship leaders coordinated the work of the world controls and formulated general policy. In *The Holy Terror* the dictator, Rud Whitlow, and his party chieftains served as the nucleus of a world directorate or council, not unlike the world council in *The Shape of Things to Come.*

But from all the Utopian books except *A Modern Utopia*, where Wells did not peer very far into the future of his Utopian constitution, it is plain that no such thing as an autocratic governing council could last for long in the enlightened mental climate of a Wellsian world civilization. Government would become rapidly obsolete, as the spirit of science and common sense and common humanity penetrated more and more deeply into Utopian life. The world councils in both *The Shape of Things to Come* and *The Holy Terror,* and the elected world parliament in *The World Set Free,* lost all their vitality and power as soon as the technical controls had succeeded in putting the world's affairs in good working order. They collapsed from lack of anything to do. In *The Shape of Things to Come,* for example, the now antiquated world council was dismissed by Emil Donadieu, the secretary of the Education Faculty, on behalf of the world controls in 2059:

"No need to govern the world," said Donadieu. "We have made war impossible; we have liberated ourselves from the great anti-social traditions that set man against man; we have made the servitude of man to man through poverty impossible. The faculties of health, education, and behaviour will sustain the good conduct of the race. The controls of food, housing, transport, clothing, supply, initiative, design, research, can do their own work. There is nothing left for a supreme government to do."[9]

In the same way, specialized governing classes would lose their privileged status and cease to function as governors, or, rather, the whole Utopian community would be assimilated into the "governing" class. The world revolutionary elite would expand, until it became synonymous with humanity itself, recalling Bernard Shaw's plea for a mob all of Caesars, a democracy of supermen.[10] This might take time. But Wells had almost unlimited faith in the power of education, science, and technology to transform and go on transforming the conditions of human life. The inferior human product would slowly be weeded out of society, not by massacres but through equalization of economic opportunity, negative eugenics, public endowment of mother-

9. *Shape of Things to Come*, pp. 376–77; cf. *Holy Terror*, p. 411. A comparison with the Marxist Utopia at this point is inevitable; but Wells admitted no debt to Marx, even for the "withering away" of the state. And cf. William Godwin on the rational millennium: "There will be no war, no crimes, no administration of justice, as it is called, and no government": Godwin, *Enquiry Concerning Political Justice*, ed. F. E. L. Priestley (3 vols. Toronto, University of Toronto Press, 1946), *2*, 528. Godwin probably reached Wells in his formative years through the medium of Shelley; Shelley is mentioned several times in the early chapters of *Experiment in Autobiography*, Godwin not at all.

10. Shaw, preface to *Man and Superman*, in *Works, 10*, xl.

hood with a sliding scale of payments depending on the quality of offspring, immense increases in the general standard of living, fundamental improvements in the quality and range of education, the total or nearly total replacement of human laborers by machinery, and so forth. The racial average would rise sharply in every generation. "Unlike all other privileged castes the world has seen," Wells said of his Samurai in *A Modern Utopia*, "it increases relatively to the total population, and may indeed at last assimilate almost the whole population of the earth."[11] In each of the later Utopias this disappearance of an elite class had already occurred or did occur before the end of the book. Its absence was especially conspicuous in *Men Like Gods*. Wells himself described the world of *Men Like Gods* as "maturer" and "further on" than *A Modern Utopia*. He now had such confidence in the scientific reorganization of society that his Utopia could afford to dispense with a separate ruling class altogether. "In 'Men Like Gods,' " he added, "all the people are Samurai. . . . [The writer] is no longer disposed to admit the necessary survival of inferior types."[12] Had Wells checked into the matter, of course, he would have found the same development clearly foreshadowed in *A Modern Utopia*, and also in *The World Set Free*.[13] Wells' ultimate society was always a functionally articulated but classless society, without a government, either of men or of laws, knowing no sovereignty but that of scientific knowledge and the collective will.

A great many practical questions remain unanswered, and Wells tried to answer them, although he often took unfair advantage of the novelist's privilege to jump from one subject to another without covering the territory in between. One of the principal duties of a governing world

11. *Modern Utopia*, p. 299.
12. Preface to the Atlantic Edition of the *Works, 28,* ix.
13. See *World Set Free*, pp. 246–48.

council, for example, the coordination of the work of the world control organizations, would in due time be discharged by the controls themselves, acting through specialized agencies. A Bureau of Reconciliation and Cooperation grew up in the Utopia of *The Shape of Things to Come,* which arranged intercontrol conferences and acted something like a supreme court. In *The Holy Terror* "conjoint sessions of the Law, Education and Biological (Health) Boards" took charge of the arbitration of jurisdictional and policy disputes, gradually relieving the world council of its responsibilities.[14]

The world governing council and governing class in the early years of Utopia had performed a still more important task: the maintenance of social discipline; and in this work, too, they were superseded. What replaced them can only be described as the control of thought and behavior from infancy by a world system of education and psychiatric "care." Most intellectually honest differences of value and opinion, Wells insisted, including the religious and philosophical differences that prevented men from reaching agreement on how to reorganize society in the face of a universally acknowledged world crisis, were "due to bad education, mental and moral indolence, slovenliness of statement and the failure to clinch issues." He had no patience with the "multitudinousness of people in these matters."[15] The world society would have even less patience. Every young mind would be trained in the schools to think scientifically. Every young mind would be indoctrinated with

14. *Shape of Things to Come,* p. 355; *Holy Terror,* p. 371.

15. *Anatomy of Frustration,* p. 13. Wells admitted that he was "exceptionally intolerant" of the elaborate differences of opinion among professional philosophers and theologians. "If I attempt to deal with them [i.e. the differences of opinion] they worry and entangle me. I cannot make the necessary reservations and adjustments": *Fate of Man,* p. 1.

the spacious world-view of modern science, especially biological science. And, because brains were as alike as eggs,
bound to come out alike if they were cooked the same way,[16]
all fundamental differences of opinion on questions of social
organization and purpose would disappear, in a matter of
generations. The educational work of the Open Conspiracy would be carried through to completion. The teachings
of the organized religions would be replaced by a doctrine
of self-transcendence in the racial adventure. Scientific
socialism and allegiance to the cosmopolitan world society
would supplant all the divisive ideologies of the defunct old
order. Once all the members of the world community
shared the same values and loyalties, the need for central-
ized control would vanish. The conscientious application of
the scientific method to every problem would indicate the
right thing to do, and properly educated Utopians would
do it, without hesitation or scruple.

In one of Wells' earlier Utopias, *In the Days of the
Comet,* this homogenization of values was accomplished by
the miracle-working vapors in a comet's tail, as it brushed
the earth's atmosphere. In most of the Utopian novels, in
Men Like Gods, for example, it was accomplished by education and psychology. The Utopian educators of *Men Like
Gods* skillfully exploited the universal urge in young people
for dedication to something larger than themselves, by cul-
tivating a deep sense of loyalty to the evolving human
species, embodied in the world society. Psychologists,
working hand in hand with educators, sublimated the animal instincts of greed and aggression, converting them into
creative, socially useful energies. The Utopian child's "curiosity flowers into scientific passion, its combativeness is
set to fight disorder, its inherent pride and ambition are

16. *The Camford Visitation* (London, 1937), p. 48; cf. Gemini
Twain in *Babes in the Darkling Wood,* p. 19.

directed towards an honourable share in the common achievement." As one of the Utopians explained to his incredulous terrestrial audience, " 'Our education is our government.' "[17]

If a citizen of Utopia developed antisocial feelings and made a nuisance of himself, if he failed to adjust to the system, he would be examined by specialists in "mental and moral health." The ugly implications of this procedure for readers of the inverted Utopias of Aldous Huxley and George Orwell either did not occur, or did not matter, to Wells—although one of his terrestrial visitors aptly compared the role of psychiatrists in Utopia to that of policemen in the modern world.[18] A more exact comparison, respecting the whole context of Wells' thinking, might have been drawn between Utopian psychiatry and the services of the priest-confessor in a Catholic society to members of his flock tempted by heresy or the appetites of the flesh.

Wells followed the same formula of government by education in *The Shape of Things to Come*. The educational system of the new world order had begun "as the propaganda of the Modern State." It had "sought to establish a new complete ideology and a new spirit which would induce the individual to devote himself and to shape all his activities to one definite purpose, to the attainment and maintenance of a progressive world-socialism." To subserve this objective, thought and behavior patterns were deliberately shaped "to the relative disregard of any other conceivable purpose." Once brought to world power, the propagandists, research workers, and educators of the Modern State Fellowship organized a world public education system, in which the training of the Fellowship was imposed on all the rest of society. "No other type of school and no other

17. *Men Like Gods*, pp. 79–80.
18. Ibid., pp. 62–63.

system of teaching was tolerated for more than half a century. Never before was man so directed and disciplined."[19]

In the end much of the censorship and rigid discipline identified with the Fellowship and its schools could be dispensed with. The Fellowship itself disappeared as a separate entity in later generations. But the educational system it had created went on functioning. No rival schools survived the years of repression to challenge its authority. Significantly, the world controls of medicine, police, and education were finally integrated into one colossal "Behaviour Control," which by implication did much the same work as the teachers and mental specialists in the Utopia of *Men Like Gods.*

The key, in turn, to the success of education in the new world order was science—conceived of as a self-correcting, self-generating source of objective knowledge that all men would accept as soon as they achieved a measure of moral and spiritual unity. Once men put themselves under the rule of science, Wells imagined that most of the world's affairs would run themselves. In any given field or project the current state of scientific knowledge and technics would suggest one right thing to do. Experts would see that it got done. The rank and file of Utopians would no more think of objecting than the rank and file of citizens in the modern world would think of questioning calendars or atlases or dictionaries. As Wells told a B.B.C. audience in 1931, on the subject of government in Utopia,

> It may be asked, Who will make the ultimate decision? There must be a king or an assembly, or some such body, to say "Yes" or "No," in the last resort. But must there be? Suppose your intellectual organization, your body of thought, your scientific men, say and prove that this, that, or the other course is the *right* one. Sup-

19. *Shape of Things to Come,* p. 398.

pose they have the common-sense of an alert and educated community to sustain them. Why should not a
dictatorship—not of this man or that man, nor of the
proletariat, but of informed and educated common-
sense—some day rule the earth? What need is there
for a lot of politicians and lawyers to argue about the
way things ought to be done, confusing the issues?
Why make a dispute of world welfare?[20]

So, in *Men Like Gods,* "Decisions in regard to any particular matter were made by the people who knew most about
that matter."[21]

The powers and limitations of science would determine
the course of life in Utopia just as the physical universe itself was governed by the laws of nature. All scientists and
engineers were men; but science was an autocratic mistress.
She demanded absolute candor and absolute obedience.
Wells had Bolaris, the Wellsian revolutionist in his short
novel *The Brothers,* prophesy that the real ruler in the
coming world order would be "necessity," the only right
way of managing things in terms of the state of scientific
knowledge. Necessity would insist, for example, "upon
much the same new industrial organization, much the same
new monetary conventions, much the same new classifications of people, much the same distribution of work and
leisure, much the same ways of travelling, much the same
countryside, and much the same education. Take it, she
says, this new world, or refuse it and perish."[22] And in science Wells obviously included the social sciences—economics, social psychology, sociology, and anthropology—in
which, as noted in an earlier chapter, he began to invest

20. *After Democracy,* pp. 202–3; cf., i.a., *Babes in the Darkling
Wood,* pp. 395–96.
21. *Men Like Gods,* p. 62.
22. *The Brothers* (New York, 1938), pp. 68–69.

more and more confidence after the first World War.[23]
Again, to quote Gustave De Windt, the theorist of world
revolution in *The Shape of Things to Come,* two scientifically respectable and antagonistic opinions about the
handling of most public affairs could not exist. " 'There is
one sole right way and there are endless wrong ways of
doing things. A government is trying to go the right way
or it is criminal.' "[24]

Wells even extended this concept of rule by science to
philosophy. The organization of intellectual life in Utopia
would preclude the possibility of serious schisms in philosophy: not only because the first Utopians would start in
life with the common beliefs and values inculcated by the
schools of the revolution, but also because at any one time
the collective human intelligence, as it evolved, could have
only one generally acceptable world-view, based on the
only one possible existing state of all scientific knowledge.
As Wells wrote in his memoir of the second World War,
'42 to '44,

> Only one body of philosophy and only one religion,
> only one statement of man's relation to the universe
> and the community, can exist in a unified world state.
> Both will expand and deepen as comprehension grows,
> but at any time that statement must embody the ulti-
> mate achievement of the mind, as completely and in
> the same manner that what is now called current
> scientific knowledge supersedes any pre-existing ideas.
> Chemistry, physiology, botany, are the same for all the
> world and are continually expanding and correcting
> themselves, and so it must be with philosophical and
> religious truth.[25]

23. See above, pp. 133–35.
24. *Shape of Things to Come,* pp. 256–57.
25. *'42 to '44,* p. 101.

Some of the naiveté in judgments like these fades—perhaps ominously—in the light of Wells' arrangements for the integration of all human mental activity in Utopia by a world "brain center." The idea has already been touched on above in Chapter 3, as it grew out of Wells' proposals for a world encyclopedia society.[26] In all of his later speculations on the organization of Utopia the project of a world brain center as a further substitute for government regularly appeared in one form or another. The existence of such a center would ensure that the state of knowledge and expert consensus at any one time had reached the same point everywhere in the world. It would be, for one thing, a world university, of which all the research schools proposed by William Clissold in his thoughts on higher education would become "the constituent ganglia."[27] It would act as a world archive, like the Utopian encyclopedic organization centered in Barcelona in *The Shape of Things to Come,* which employed seventeen million active workers throughout the world and "accumulates, sorts, keeps in order and renders available everything that is known."[28] It would help to direct and coordinate research, and it would keep educators in touch with scientific and scholarly progress. It would become, in effect, the memory system and the nerve system of the awakening mind of the race.

And what about the individual? Would he be managed and integrated out of existence? All of Wells' thinking on the problem of the individual's relationship to the species seems to reduce to the proposition that the individual was an experiment conducted by the species and that for the success of the experiment he had to be somehow "free." Not free for freedom's sake, but free for the sake of invention, research, constructive criticism, and the maximum

26. See above, pp. 162–63.
27. *World of William Clissold,* 2, 658.
28. *Shape of Things to Come,* p. 420.

development of every human potentiality likely to extend man's control over nature. Most of Wells' Utopias were equipped with charters of liberties, although not always prominently equipped. In *A Modern Utopia* all individuals were declared unique, and all were to be permitted maximum fulfillment of their uniqueness within the framework of the Utopian social order. The Utopian community guaranteed its members privacy, the right to travel freely all over the planet, sexual freedom consistent with the best interests of minors, and—except for Samurai—religious freedom. The Utopians in *Men Like Gods* in 1923 enjoyed a formal guarantee of "the Five Principles of Liberty": privacy, freedom of movement, access to knowledge, protection from deliberate falsification of knowledge, and freedom of discussion and criticism.[29] In all of Wells' Utopias, of course, individuals would also be released from all sorts of limitations on freedom imposed by the old social order. Utopia would liberate them from material want, from the conventions of Christian sexual morality, from the indignities of war, from the greed of capitalistic entrepreneurs, from the hatreds of nationalism and racism, from the tyranny of the half-educated mob and the vote-catching politician. Scholars and scientists and artists would be granted all possible freedom in their work. Individuals might, at least as individuals, openly criticize even the fundamental law of the Utopian world order, like the wandering naturist in *A Modern Utopia*.[30]

But what if groups of free individuals decided to secede

29. *Men Like Gods*, pp. 272–76. The Declaration of the Rights of Man drafted by Wells and the Sankey Committee during the second World War promised individuals in the collectivized world state a wide assortment of liberties, including all the above, and added a few more guaranteeing due process of law in proceedings against persons charged with criminal offenses. See above, pp. 46–47.

30. *Modern Utopia*, chapter 4, "The Voice of Nature."

from the world community? What if new religious sects
sprang up, in frank and open rebellion against the new
world order? What if a party of philosophers enjoying the
respect and confidence of their fellow philosophers objected
to the whole idea of a world brain center? Wells rarely
raised or answered questions of this sort. But, presumably,
in the long run, his Utopia could not tolerate or survive
organized dissent.[31] The mind of the race might be
changed; it could not be split. Critics would have to work
from within, accepting the framework of things until and
unless the climate of opinion encouraged revision. For all
Wells' enthusiastic encomia of intellectual freedom and his
own defiant independence of mind, his Utopias share many
of the ideals both of medieval Catholic and of Soviet Russian society, just as the Open Conspiracy might be likened
to the Society of Jesus or the Communist party. Nor, one
suspects, would Auguste Comte have felt out of place in at
least the earlier phases of a typical Wellsian cosmopolis.

It is no surprise to learn, for example, that in the Utopia
of *The Shape of Things to Come* Wells anticipated the
complete disappearance of all the organized religions, including Judaism and, with it, world Jewry. The world state
controlled the schools, and the schools controlled thought,
so completely that the world's Jews "were educated out of
their oddity and racial egotism in little more than three
generations," and ceased to exist as a distinct religious and
cultural body in the greater body social of mankind.[32]

31. Note that in Wells' final draft of the Sankey Declaration of the
Rights of Man, the right of association is omitted, although it had
appeared in the version approved by the Sankey Committee originally. See *Common Sense of War and Peace*, p. 85, and *'42 to '44*, p. 47,
for the two drafts. The only example of organized opposition to a
world society in being is Theotocopulos' movement in the film *Things
to Come*, and the use of the adjective "organized" here is open to
grave question.

32. *Shape of Things to Come*, p. 384.

Wells simply did not envisage the rise of any comparable new splinter groups in Utopia. Men would get into the habit of thinking and planning and working together. The racial mind would possess them all.

"One's dreamland perfection," Wells wrote in 1906, "is Anarchy."[33] How near Wells' Utopias approached anarchy in their later stages is difficult to judge, but a kind of anarchy is implicit in his fundamental assumptions.[34] He looked upon history as a progressive struggle by the collective racial mind to achieve full consciousness and self-control. When it did, individual minds all over the world would have gained a certain unity of desire, knowledge, purpose, and belief that seems perilously alien to the twentieth-century liberal intelligence. What could intellectual freedom mean in a race thinking and yearning as a single organism? Utopia in the twenty-second century in *The Shape of Things to Come* was "becoming as much a colonial organism as any branching coral or polyp, though the ties that link us are not fleshly bands, but infinitely elastic and invisible and subtle." The individual was "like an exploring tentacle thrust out to test and learn, to savour life in its fullness and bring in new experiences for the common stock," and the Utopian historian dreamed of a day when, in the supersession of "individual motives" by a "confluence of wills," the race would possess an organic common consciousness free of all traces of artificiality.[35] Wells might have been borrowing a leaf from Olaf Stapledon's *Last and First Men*.

33. *Socialism and the Family*, p. 46.
34. Anarchy, that is, in the narrow sense of freedom from the need for political life: about as much anarchy as there is liberty in Luther's "Christian liberty."
35. *Shape of Things to Come*, pp. 428–30.

But in another sense Wells was only bringing up to date the old familiar dream of Western Utopographers since Plato, that the affairs of men must be ruled by wisdom and expert knowledge. Most of the socialist Utopias of the nineteenth century, in particular, managed perfectly well without any sort of authentic political life. In the new world preached by Saint-Simon and Comte the world's business was directed by industrialists, scientists, and engineers, men of skill and knowledge. The engineers and the technicians, in effect, ruled in Cabet's *Icaria*. Bellamy's Utopia in *Looking Backward* was governed by industrial guilds. The state was to wither away entirely in the Marxist Utopia. Quite recently, B. F. Skinner has invented a Utopia, *Walden Two*, in which small-scale communities live happily and creatively without any need for government, under the control and supervision of a planning board of social engineers, specialists in the behavioral sciences, who work on a strictly empirical basis and use their subjects virtually as guinea pigs.[36] The dream persists. Wells was not the first Utopist and not the last, to insist on the sovereignty of intelligence in society. Like many other Utopographers in Western literature, he served fair warning on humanity that the rule of reason and the rule of freedom need not, even in Utopia, go hand in hand.

WELFARE IN UTOPIA

Wells did not actually devote many pages in his Utopian novels to the management of Utopia. He was too shrewd a judge of his audience to try to win converts to the cause of world order with exhaustive treatises on Utopian behavioral engineering. Without evading the question of "how," he turned most of his attention to "what." What would the

36. B. F. Skinner, *Walden Two*, New York, 1948.

Utopians do with their world order? What would world order signify in terms of human welfare?

Wells collected his thoughts on welfare in Utopia from a wide range of sources. Speculation about the creative possibilities of science and socialism for the enrichment and enlargement of life had never been more fashionable than during the 1880's and 1890's. Wells' imagination was nourished in its formative years on the books of Henry George, Edward Bellamy, Theodor Hertzka, William Morris, and many more; the references in *A Modern Utopia* and *New Worlds for Old* indicate that he had come into contact with most of the literature of Utopian socialism by the early 1900's. As the class structure of the Wellsian Utopia, in its various stages, echoed Comte and Marx, so Wells borrowed, consciously or unconsciously, from Bellamy and Hertzka in framing the social and economic policy of his Utopia. Other ideas reflect the Fabian influence. In his emphasis on the importance of aesthetically satisfying design in buildings and furnishings, he may even have betrayed a debt to William Morris. Perhaps the most striking comparison is with a passage in a book not otherwise Utopian at all: Winwood Reade's mid-Victorian classic, *The Martyrdom of Man*. In just three pages, Reade sketched the Wellsian Utopia in letter and spirit. The visions of human welfare are almost identical; no other product of the mental climate in which Wells grew to intellectual maturity is so unmistakably "Wellsian." For Reade, as for Wells after him, the key to world prosperity was science. Science, said Reade, would tap new sources of power and so extend the empire of man that he would be able to manipulate the laws of nature at will. The invention of air transport would annihilate distance and speedily extinguish national differences. United in a single world-wide industrial civilization, men would look upon the whole planet as their fatherland. Science would replace politics as the focus of interest, and hunger,

disease, and poverty would be abolished. Luxuries would
be available in abundance. The distinction between rich
and poor would become meaningless. Women would take
their place beside men as equals and companions. The
earth would be made into a garden; men would learn to
subdue their last remaining animal passions; in the end
humanity would set out to conquer the stars.[37]

This was Wells' Utopia, in embryo. It might take more
heartache, bloodshed, and sheer toil to arrive at than most
Victorians imagined. But it was possible; and it would
sweep the slate clean. The bonfires of the Beltane festivals
of *In the Days of the Comet* symbolized Wells' eagerness
for an entirely new world: all cities and buildings everywhere were pulled down, all furnishings were burned; the
men of the new era demolished and cremated the past in a
ten years' orgy of systematic razing. Although the new order
arrived less abruptly in Wells' other Utopias, they were all
ruled by the same defiant determination to begin afresh and
build a thoroughly rational world on the ampler scale made
possible by modern science. Armed with the Promethean
gifts of science, man would set no limits to his ambition.
The future opened out—infinitely.

Like most Utopian socialists, Wells founded his new
world order on the principle of collective ownership and
the abolition of class distinctions based on property. The
first task of the Utopians was to organize an economy of
abundance and to ensure that no man-made barriers of any
kind prevented any inhabitant of the world community
from sharing in its work and wealth. The Utopians would
subscribe, as Wells always had, to the socialist contention
that all land, all property, all tangible goods whatever be-

37. Winwood Reade, *The Martyrdom of Man* (London, 1872), pp.
512–15. For Reade's influence on Wells see *Outline of History, I,* vii;
but there seems to be no reference to Reade in Wells' books earlier
than 1917.

longed to the community collectively and not to its individual members.[38] The only exception would be made for personal property intended exclusively for personal use. As Urthred explained to his terrestrial guests in *Men Like Gods,* "An artist or a scientific man has complete control of all the material he needs, we all own our tools and appliances and have rooms and places of our own, but there is no property for trade or speculation."[39] The world controls would administer on humanity's behalf all the means and materials of production, planning for maximum efficiency, maximum productivity, and maximum utilization of all resources, both human and natural. The elimination of the profit motive and competing nation-states would put all the world's work on a completely rational basis. Whatever was necessary to increase the total store of useful wealth in goods and services would be done. Industrial managers, engineers, and scientists would work together in complete harmony, undeterred by profiteering investors, ministries of foreign affairs, trade unions, or parliaments.

Wells admitted that certain types of property did not lend themselves quite so well to collectivization on a world scale. World and regional controls might take over public utilities, manufacturing, mining, and the like; but he often put the organization of retail distribution and farming into a somewhat different category. Trading for speculation or "purely" for profit-making was ruled out in the Sankey Declaration, for example,[40] but at the same time Wells saw

---

38. "The Socialist holds that the community as a whole should be inalienably the owner and administrator of the land, of all raw materials, of all values and resources accumulated from the past, and that all private property must be of a terminable nature, reverting to the community, and subject to the general welfare": *New Worlds for Old,* p. 86.

39. *Men Like Gods,* p. 64.

40. See Article VI of the Declaration in *Phoenix,* pp. 189–90.

no objection to the long-term leasing of at least some types of stores and shops to private proprietors, especially those selling "fashion" or "luxury" goods and the products of craftsmanship.[41] As for farming, much of it would have to be done by small cooperatives of more or less independent farmers. In *The World Set Free* Wells represented farmers organized into self-governing guilds, maintaining their homes in nearby towns, and contracting with the world-state authorities to be responsible collectively for an agreed average yield.

In every way the world would become an economic unit, each area producing what it could produce best, subject to the general welfare. A world currency system and the complete abolition of customs duties would ensure economic integration and a leveling out of prosperity; the gap between East and West would close almost automatically. Wells suggested a number of currency systems in his Utopias, based on everything from units of atomic energy in *The World Set Free* to bank credits in *Men Like Gods*. Following De Windt's insistence that money had to be abstract, uniform all over the world, and protected by law against any sort of profit-making manipulation, the Utopians of *The Shape of Things to Come* created a world statistical organization to serve, among other things, as the world's banker. Banking became equivalent to bookkeeping.[42]

Utilizing science and technology to the full, the integrated world economy would be able in a few centuries to supply staple products and essential services in virtually unlimited quantities. But whatever the capacity of the world controls to produce, the profits of labor would be shared equitably throughout the whole population. Actual destitution would be abolished; and a minimum standard of

41. See, e.g., the intrinsically happy idea of a socialist "bazaar," ibid., pp. 129–30.

42. *Shape of Things to Come,* pp. 251–52.

living would be guaranteed to every Utopian, through some such device as a minimum wage, together with a universal system of socialized medical care, public education, and old-age insurance. But Wells rejected Shaw's idea of equal incomes. As it was phrased in the Sankey Declaration, a man might earn "such pay as the contribution that his work makes to the welfare of the community may justify or that the desire of any private individual or individuals for his products, his performances or the continuation of his activities may produce for him."[43] Popular artists, for example, might make a far better living than unpopular artists; and able people who needed extra money for their work would receive grants from the appropriate authorities. Wells even toyed with the idea of a class of rich men in Utopia, endowed by the state to indulge in free creative spending, after the example of J. D. Rockefeller and Henry Ford, whose philanthropies he had always admired.[44]

Still, in all essentials, Utopia would be a classless society. Class consciousness would disappear entirely. As already noted, there could be no permanent governing elite, and at the other end of the scale rising standards of living and negative eugenics would gradually eliminate distinctly inferior types. Every man would be a skilled, educated workman with a function to perform in the body social. Nearly all heavy or tedious work would be handled by machinery, and what little could not would be done by conscription, on the model of universal military service. Conspiracies against the public interest, from trade unions to profit-making pools and trusts, would become unthinkable in the free air of Utopia. Above all, there would be nothing left of the proletarian conscience. The Marxist Utopia was a

43. *Phoenix*, p. 189. But see Bernard Shaw, *Everybody's Political What's What* (London, 1944), p. 57, where the proposal for a minimum annual wage of £5,000 would have satisfied Wells.

44. *Work, Wealth and Happiness of Mankind*, 2, 531–33.

classless society resulting from an expansion of the proletariat, but Wells' conception "of a scientifically organized
class-less society is essentially of an expanded middle-class
which has incorporated both the aristocrat and plutocrat
above and the peasant, proletarian and pauper below."[45]
As Wells had argued in 1912, the struggle between the
leisure class and the laboring class in capitalistic society
could end in only one of three ways: in the breakdown of
society, in the establishment of a servile state of workers
managed by bureaucrats,[46] or in the evolution of an organic
social order in which labor and leisure were shared by all

45. *Experiment in Autobiography*, p. 69. It is significant that
Wells, almost alone among prominent twentieth-century British writers, hailed from the lower middle class, the class Marxists consider
most irreconcilably bourgeois. Of the following writers selected at
random—Auden, Barker, Belloc, Bennett, Chesterton, Churchill, Dickinson, Doyle, Eliot, Ellis, Galsworthy, Graves, Greene, Guedalla, Inge,
Isherwood, the Huxleys, Joyce, Keynes, Kipling, Laski, D. H. Lawrence, Masefield, Maugham, Murray, O'Casey, Orwell, Pollard, Priestley, Russell, Shaw, the Sitwells, Spender, the Stracheys, Tawney, Dy-
lan Thomas, Toynbee, the Trevelyans, Wallas, Walpole, the Waughs,
the Webbs, Rebecca West, Whitehead, and Yeats—not one originated
in the lower middle class, although a few (Barker, Lawrence, and O'-
Casey) had working-class parents. Closest to Wells in social origins,
perhaps, were Sir James Barrie, whose father was a self-employed
hand-loom weaver; Frank Swinnerton, whose father was an engraver;
and John Middleton Murry, whose father was a bank clerk. But Wells
emerged from the very heart of the petty bourgeoisie: the shopkeeping
class. For the overwhelmingly upper middle-class origins of the Victorian intelligentsia see Noel Annan, "The Intellectual Aristocracy,"
in J. H. Plumb, ed., *Studies in Social History* (London, 1955), pp. 241–
87. During the first half of the twentieth century, at least, the middle
and upper strata of the middle class have continued to supply Britain
with nearly the whole of her intellectual elite.

46. A criticism echoing Hilaire Belloc's book, *The Servile State,*
aimed at the Webbs, with whom Wells was currently not on the best
of terms.

equally, through the scientific organization of production and, if necessary, a universal year or so of compulsory labor service.[47] Utopia, obviously, would choose the third course.

So blessed with prosperity and inner harmony, the world commonwealth, Wells thought, would be able to offer its citizens a life of infinite richness, freedom, and adventure. The Utopians would be able to call the whole world their home; they could find work anywhere; they would be free to travel anywhere on the globe without any restrictions whatsoever; a universal second language, like Basic English, would solve the problem of communication. The Utopians would be great tourists and great migrants, heirs to all the world in all its variety and beauty. To charges that his Utopia would be a dull, mechanical, uniform world, Wells always replied that it would be just the opposite. No longer forced to live the cramped, monotonous, narrow, traditional life of this or that region, individual Utopians would be released to join in the whole vital adventure of civilization. They would work less, travel more, and choose from an immeasurably wider assortment of interesting occupations. There would be no tedious poverty, no grinding, soul-destroying heavy labor, no bondage to the soil.[48]

And Utopians would live longer, healthier lives. Medical science would conquer disease, prevent needless deformity, and prolong the human life span by several decades. Although Wells' Utopians never got as far as Shaw's in *Back to Methuselah,* the greater length of life and the abundance of life's goods would produce a wiser, less hurried, less in-

47. *Social Forces in England and America,* p. 154.
48. For Wells' refutation of the charge that his Utopia would be "dull" see *World Brain,* pp. 23–24, and *Things to Come,* pp. xii–xiii. A typical assault on the Wellsian Utopia may be read in Donald Davidson, "The Shape of Things and Men," *American Review,* 7 (1936), 225–48.

secure race of men than walked the earth in the twentieth century. Crime rates would sink phenomenally.[49]

Wells' Utopias were not always designed to win the confidence of liberals, but in one important respect they were consistently libertarian. In Utopia society would cease to pry into the sexual life of responsible adults, except to safeguard the rights of children. Almost every novel, whether Utopian or not, that Wells ever wrote sooner or later worked around to an indictment of the Victorian sexual code. He insisted on complete sexual freedom for himself, and he offered his Utopians the same freedom. Men and women would be put on a footing of absolute equality—the New Woman of the 1890's and the Edwardian era would take her place beside the New Man. There would be a real de-emphasis of sex in Utopian society. In the more relaxed and creative atmosphere of Utopia, prostitution, the journalism that thrives on sexual scandal, the blatant use of sex in advertising, and pornography would all wither away. As one of the Utopians explained in *The Dream,* "We take love by the way as we take our food and our holidays, the main thing in our lives is our creative work."[50] That was Wells' position in a nutshell. Sex was play, as harmless and refreshing as a picnic, and the sooner society stopped inflicting Victorian sexual taboos on its adult members, the better. Men and women might pair. Marriage was even the usual thing in *A Modern Utopia,* although it had disappeared in *Men Like Gods.* But men and women would hold no claims over one another. Pairing and mating, Wells suspected, were animal functions, necessary perhaps for a time in early maturity, but not part of the life of the fully grown, intellectually mature Utopian. Stephen Wilbeck, Wells' alter ego in *Apropos of Dolores,* prophesied that family-

49. See, e.g., *Shape of Things to Come,* pp. 420–23, for crime statistics in Utopia.
50. *Dream,* p. 73.

raising would be a "pre-adult phase" in the ampler world to come. "That fully adult human being towards whom destiny moves," he said, "will not pair at all."[51]

It is easy to imagine the women in Wells' life trying to persuade him that women were naturally possessive, craving only one man's love and care, and Wells holding out for a change in female psychology under Utopian conditions.[52] Women would enjoy complete equality with men, they would all be educated, they would be able to choose stimulating careers, and Utopia would provide for their children. This last point was especially important. Women in the old social order had to have husbands and keep husbands because they could not otherwise support their children. A large percentage of marriages "succeeded" solely for the sake of offspring. But in Utopia women would be completely protected, either through a legally binding contract between the natural parents or through outright endowment of motherhood, or both. In *A Modern Utopia* the world state made it a criminal offense for a man and woman to have children unless they earned a fixed minimum income, were free of serious hereditary defects, and did not fall below a certain minimum standard of health and intelligence. The parents then contracted with the state and with each other to raise and educate the children, as a debt owed to society. Subsidies were to be paid to a mother in case of real need or as a bonus for the production of exceptionally gifted children. In *Men Like Gods,* an individual was automatically credited at birth with a sum sufficient to maintain and educate him until his mid-twenties, thus relieving the parents of all financial responsibility. Either way, the mother did not need a lifetime husband and sexual

51. *Apropos of Dolores,* p. 277.
52. See the conversations between Clissold and Clem in *The World of William Clissold* and between Wilbeck and Dolores in *Apropos of Dolores*. Both in all likelihood have a high autobiographical content.

behavior could be completely divorced from the problem of child-raising. What sex life adults led was their private affair; the state intervened only in the interests of children, and it was especially eager to maximize the number of births of high quality.

As the Utopians would transform themselves, altering human nature, so they would transform the planet on which they lived. An Englishman and the son of an English gardener,[53] Wells could think of no better way to convey his idea of Utopia than to call it a garden. Like a garden, the planet would be drilled and subdued to human purposes and human ideas of beauty. The energies formerly poured away in war would be concentrated against the obstinacy of nature.

There would be, first of all, a great reorganization of urban and industrial life. Mines and factories would be set far apart from residential areas. Scientifically planned urban developments would replace the congested cities of the old world. The whole planet could then be weeded and reconditioned. In *Men Like Gods,* the Utopians exterminated every "ugly" and "noxious" species of life that could be dispensed with safely. The larger wild animals were domesticated as pets, and horticultural science produced innumerable new species of plants for human use. In *The Shape of Things to Come,* scientists were working on weather control, earthquake and volcano control, explorations of the earth's crust at extreme depths, and "geogonic planning." Wild life would be protected, soil conserved, new forests planted. "The whole land would be like a garden," Mr. Barnstaple surmised in his early days in Utopia, "with every natural tendency to beauty seized upon and developed and every innate ugliness corrected and overcome."

53. Wells' father had been a gardener before taking the crockery shop in Bromley, Kent, where Wells was born. Cf. the descriptions of Utopian England in William Morris' *News from Nowhere.*

Life would march with a terrifying swiftness. A hundred years of progress as modern men understood progress "could not compare . . . with the forward swing of these millions of associated intelligences in one single year."[54]

Progress would, in fact, lead humanity beyond Utopia itself. Even Utopia was only a phase in a larger adventure. Life had ultimate uses beyond man's dreaming.

THE ULTIMATE USES OF LIFE

Wells has often been charged with preaching a grossly materialistic Utopia, and some of his work seems to bear out his critics. In 1935, for example, Alexander Korda filmed a motion picture, using Wells' own script, of *The Shape of Things to Come,* under the title *Things to Come.* Buck Rogers was popular in those days; and in a rare mismating of genius, Wells and Korda contrived to produce a Buck Rogers kind of film. Even Hollywood's recent butchery of *The War of the Worlds* does not really measure up to it.

To a large and curious audience, swollen since Wells' death by millions of television viewers, *Things to Come* unveiled a tasteless vision of Utopia as machinery, tended by mechanical men. The heroes and heroines were hacked into human form like cardboard dolls. The spirit of Utopia was caught in a cinematographic collage of thumping, humming, shrieking machines. One of the characters from *The Shape of Things to Come,* Ariston Theotocopulos, in the original novel a designer frustrated by the world council's austere insensitivity to art, figured now in the film script as a sinister demagogue with reactionary designs on human "progress." In the end, the daughter of the president of the world council and her lover volunteered to man an experimental rocket to the moon. An angry mob led by Theoto-

54. *Men Like Gods,* pp. 170–71.

copulos stormed the launching site, too late, as the lovers
were fired into space, symbolizing the restless vitality of
Utopia. Wells had never been guilty of so much concentrated bathos. Michael Roberts took the opportunity in
The Spectator of observing that in Mr. Wells' "sombre
world" there would be no art, no music, no spiritual life,
nothing but soulless science, autocratic technicians, and
meaningless material progress.[55]

This had always been a stock objection to Wells' Utopias,
but it tended to be taken more seriously in the changing
mental climate of the 1930's. To a younger generation far
more concerned than in Wells' Edwardian heyday with the
plight of the individual in the machine age, and mistrustful
of science, the world state in *Things to Come* could have
seemed positively repulsive, a sort of grotesque confession
from Wells himself that Aldous Huxley's *Brave New World*
or E. M. Forster's *The Machine Stops* had hit the mark.

Things to Come was Wells' worst, most lopsided Utopia,
conceived in haste to hammer home one simple message to a
mass audience incapable of digesting more than one idea at
a time; and yet it is fair to ask how much it did not, after all,
convey of the essence of Wells' thoughts on the ultimate
uses of human life. Did he value anything above material
welfare and the exploits of science? The question has to be
approached gingerly.

Clearly, a thinker so committed to the evolutionary outlook as Wells could not conceive of a static Utopia. That
much is certain. Utopians would always be hurling themselves, like the young lovers in *Things to Come*, into new
adventures. The price of complacency—witness the Eloi in
The Time Machine—was degeneration. The flow of life
never faltered. But just where, for the rest of time, it might
carry *Homo sapiens* Wells did not in the ordinary line of his

55. Michael Roberts, "Mr. Wells' Sombre World," *Spectator, 157*
(1936), 1032–33.

duties as a Utopographer choose to predict. The same impulse which led him to imagine the world as a fruitful, smiling garden tended by colossal machines and enterprising scientists often failed at the level of ultimates. Still he did find a place for ultimates in his scheme of values: that is what matters, and fortunately enough clues exist in one place or another to assemble a reasonably convincing refutation at least of the tired old story that Wells was an arch materialist wishing a mechanical fate worse than death on hapless humanity.

He did not by any means, for example, ignore the aesthetic dimension of life in Utopia, *Things to Come* notwithstanding. He had always cultivated an acid contempt for the doctrine of art as an end in itself, for professional critics of art, for aesthetic withdrawal from life.[56] At the same time he was far from a model Philistine. Man and nature, he said,

---

56. The short stories, including most of Wells' best, are often transparent parables of the perils of *ars pro arte*. Wedderburn in "The Flowering of the Strange Orchid" was nearly killed by a fascinating carnivorous orchid. The Chelsea artist Harringay was tempted by the devil to sell his soul for an "indubitable masterpiece" in "The Temptation of Harringay." "The Beautiful Suit" related the fatal passion of a small boy for fine clothes and moonlight. Lionel Wallace in "The Door in the Wall" met a similar death, searching for an enchanted garden remembered from childhood. "The Pearl of Love" dramatized the absurdity of substituting aesthetic means for spiritual ends. *The Sea Lady* distinguished between public service, however unpleasant, and the fatal lure of beauty, embodied in a mermaid. In the same vein is William Clissold's childhood experience with forget-me-nots and sedge leaves in *The World of William Clissold, 1,* 33–34. And cf. all the aesthetes satirized in Wells' fiction, from the poet Aubrey Vair in "In the Modern Vein" and Bindon in "A Story of the Days to Come," to Harold Crumb in *Christina Alberta's Father,* Theodore Bulpington in *The Bulpington of Blup,* Rowland Palace in *Brynhild,* and Professor Trumber in *The Camford Visitation.* Hardly any of Wells' novels manage without at least one such caricature, a kind of composite of Richard Le Gallienne, Ford Madox Ford, and Henry James.

brimmed with beauty, real or potential, although beauty
could not readily be isolated, analyzed, criticized, or picked
to pieces. The sensation of beauty came to a man spontaneously. All beauty, he wrote in *A Modern Utopia,* was really
kinetic or momentary. The Greek temple, for example, was
"a barn with a face that at a certain angle of vision and in a
certain light has a great calm beauty."[57]

There would be artists in Utopia, and, even more important to Wells, there would be designers. The Utopians
would insist that everything in use be beautifully designed,
even machinery. They would have a practiced eye for harmony of form, proportion, and function. One of the chief
failings of the world council in the early years of the world
commonwealth in *The Shape of Things to Come* was its indifference, even hostility, to the aesthetic needs of man. A
cheap stage villain in the film version, the designer Ariston
Theotocopulos had a hero's part in the novel. In his notebooks Theotocopulos accused the world council of having
no feeling for the artist's functions; it would allow engineers to grind out a building and then call in designers
to "decorate" the misshapen results, to "sugar the pill,"
as if art and life were alien to one another. There had
been a real need, perhaps, for discipline and austerity
in the early years of the revolution. But "we are Stoics,"
said Theotocopulos, "that we may be Epicureans." And
when the world council was finally overthrown in a
bloodless *coup d'état,* the Utopians in a declaration of
independence from its authority rejoiced that "the struggle
for truth and that indescribable necessity which is beauty
begins now."[58] In another book, two years later, Wells had
his hero agree with Theotocopulos that world peace, economic efficiency, universal education, "all these things we
find in the long run have but one objective, to make the

57. *Modern Utopia,* p. 233.
58. *Shape of Things to Come,* pp. 369, 375, 378.

world safe for artists."[59] The socialist world society anticipated in *Phoenix* would be crowded with rival schools of art. "In a world which is beginning to dare to love beauty," Wells predicted, "there will be a thousand conceptions of beauty, intensities of rivalry, unjust detraction and a great amount of critical publication."[60]

As he explained during the second World War, his ideal man was not so much the grubbing scientist as the full-blooded, fully rounded man who loved truth and beauty as inseparables and spent his life in pursuit of "reality," wherever he might find it—a man, in short, like Leonardo da Vinci. In their own time the Leonardos in history

> lived like strangers from some mightier planet. In such a Renaissance as we can anticipate, they would have been at home among their peers. Every vital artist is an experimenter in form, in the latent possibilities of material, in our mental reactions to new combinations of sounds or textures. Art and poetry as something antagonistic to scientific thought, will seem a preposterous opposition.[61]

Science and art turned out, on closer examination, to share the same end goal. Both represented the immortal element in mankind exploring the universe, gathering strength, and wisdom, and power.[62]

Throughout Wells' Utopias runs a suggestion, and some-

59. *Anatomy of Frustration*, p. 204; cf. *Shape of Things to Come*, p. 375.

60. *Phoenix*, p. 132.

61. *Guide to the New World*, p. 147.

62. See *Open Conspiracy*, p. 56; *Anatomy of Frustration*, p. 204. And yet there are many other passages in Wells' work in which he seems to feel, with his world councilmen in *The Shape of Things to Come*, that art is only frosting on the cake of science, and truth infinitely more important than beauty. See, e.g., *The Happy Turning*, pp. 49–50.

times more than a suggestion, that *Homo sapiens* would in the course of millennia evolve into a being qualitatively different from modern man. Material progress would never slow to a halt; and yet the search for truth and beauty could in time become a chief occupation of a race emancipated from inequality and material want. As the racial average rose and machinery replaced human labor, more and more individuals would be able and available to undertake purely creative work. The Utopians would be strangely and wonderfully hard. The brooding, anxious introvert would vanish from the gallery of human personality types.[63] Three thousand years ahead of modern man, the Utopians of *Men Like Gods* "were passing beyond man towards a nobler humanity. They were becoming different in kind." "They may be good," he added in 1941, "by our current orientation of things; they may be evil. Why should they not be in the nature of our good and much more than our good—'beyond good and evil?' "[64] Purged of his lower animal nature, living as a single organism with a single collective will and mind, man might do fantastic things—reshape the planet to his tastes, colonize the stars, eugenically accelerate the evolution of his own brain and body, and even solve the immemorial riddles of metaphysics and religious experience. Wells set no limits upon discovery.

> Day by day, this little planet and at length perhaps this strange, scattered, starry universe, will be yielding the secrets of its mastery to the organised World Brain of an awakened and co-operative mankind. I cannot anticipate discovery. I cannot foretell the possible triumphs of a continuing universal assault upon reality by minds made clean and fearless. That will become the chief business of our race; the exploration of that

63. *Shape of Things to Come*, p. 359.
64. *Men Like Gods*, p. 95; *You Can't Be Too Careful*, p. 298.

super-rational system to which we are necessarily akin, which we realise more and more underlies our existence and all existence, which is in us and yet transcends us.[65]

These are not—need it be said?—the reflections of a materialist, pure and simple.

Whether he was reaching for the stars or, more typically, looking into the immediate future, it remains only to note that Wells' Utopias were intensely personal statements of his own dreams. Science, Promethean humanism, progress, the mind of the race—all ruled in Utopia. In place of the unplanned, unjust, taboo-ridden, divided world in which he had grown, rankling with indignation, to manhood, would rise a scientifically managed and organically unified Leviathan populated by wiser and more beautiful H. G. Wellses, bubbling over like himself with creative *élan,* lusty, extraverted, curious about the whole various world, peripatetic, essentially intolerant of other world-views or other ways of life than their own.

Personalizing Utopia made it easier for Wells to write with sincerity and conviction. Like Mr. Barnstaple of *Men Like Gods,* he fell in love with it. [66] Like Mr. Barnstaple, he yearned to live in a rational integrated world civilization, with the aching yearning of a man who knows it beyond his reach, which has its Christian parallel, for a very recent ex-

65. *Guide to the New World,* pp. 147–48.
66. Mr. Barnstaple's "spirit had made him an uncomfortable rebel throughout his whole earthly existence. He loathed political parties and political leaders, he despised and rejected nationalism and imperialism and all the tawdry loyalties associated with them; the aggressive conqueror, the grabbing financier, the shoving business man, he hated as he hated wasps, rats, hyenas, sharks, fleas, nettles and the like: all his life he had been a citizen of Utopia exiled upon Earth": *Men Like Gods,* p. 205.

ample, in the ecstasies of Ransom in C. S. Lewis' Utopia *Perelandra*. There is no element of fraud or deception in a well-made Wellsian Utopia; each is a faithful rendering of Wells' own dreams, and in each his scolding, school-mastering career as a prophet of world order finds its ultimate justification.

Chapter Six:

H. G. WELLS And The
TWENTIETH CENTURY

THE PROPHET AS A FAILURE

Wells' prophetic career has been studied in the five preceding chapters without much deliberate effort to judge its effectiveness. As a critic of the institutions and mores of Victorian England, as a novelist and journalist and encyclopedist, his success was fairly obvious. With Bernard Shaw, Graham Wallas, Sidney and Beatrice Webb, Bertrand Russell, and many others, he helped to mobilize the intellectual attack on the Victorian social order; and most of the England of his childhood had disappeared by 1946, the year of his death. Nor can his success as a literary man, measured against the usual standards—critical interest, royalties, number of published works—be seriously questioned. As Beatrice Webb wrote to Wells in 1936, "You have romped through the world, living the life you liked, and doing the work you intended to do, amid a multitudinous applause." But her letter came in response to a copy Wells had just sent her of *The Anatomy of Frustration,* in which she detected more than a little of that bitterness and exasperation which finally cost Wells his faith in even the possibility of world order in the last chapter of his life. How, she wondered, could Wells feel frustration? "I think," she added, "you exceed all bounds of expectation."[1]

She was probably right. But in at least one light, Wells'

---

1. Beatrice Webb to Wells, October 20, 1936, in the Wells Archive. Quoted by permission of the Passfield Trustees.

career—all his triumphs notwithstanding—can very well be evaluated as a humiliating personal failure. Wells saw the attack on the Victorian social order as only an episode in a larger struggle, in England and throughout the world, between a vast complex of forces tending toward world integration and world order and another complex of forces tending in the opposite direction. The emancipation of women or the more equitable distribution of wealth or the regulation of industry by government was all to the good. But Wells asked for much more. Surveying his prophetic career in 1944, when he wrote *Mind at the End of Its Tether,* he saw no signs that mankind was anywhere near to achieving a world Utopia. It had, in fact, blundered blindly into a cul-de-sac from which there was no escape. All of his attempts to proselyte the intellectual avant-garde of the generations which came to maturity in the years after 1914 had failed. The Open Conspiracy had not materialized, either directly in answer to his books or as a great spontaneous wave of enlightened militant action. No circle of able Wellsians had gathered at his feet (not that Wells would have tolerated disciples). He had appeared in print so often and spread himself so thin that while he lived his name registered at least vaguely in the mind of nearly every literate inhabitant of the Western world; he was everywhere—but his influence by the same token was fitful, patchy, and imponderable; and since his death in 1946, his already declining prestige has dwindled to almost nothing. At least in the United States, it is quite possible nowadays to meet university-educated people who have never heard of the man.

All things considered, he probably did succeed in instilling a little of his moral urgency and many of his thoughts on world crisis and world order into millions of Western minds. But before summing up the nature and extent of his success as a prophet, it might be wise to investigate the nature and extent of his failure.

Insofar as he was a failure, he failed because he lost the attention of the younger generation, from literary critics and fellow novelists to leaders of new directions in political thought. Like most of the members of his generation who had been popular before the first World War, he suffered the fate, as he neared sixty, of being considered old hat. Although he may have lost some ground during the war, young people first began to desert him en masse in the 1920's. In the 1930's he kept interest percolating in his work only by pouring out a steady stream of new books and enjoying a still considerable literary reputation for some of his early work—especially the short stories and science fantasies of the 1890's. But the majority of younger thinking people turned to new idols.[2]

The anxieties felt by intellectuals in the 1920's and 1930's, both those shared by Wells, and others he did not feel, brought to the foreground a generation of moody, mercurial, brilliant writers, who had new messages to convey in new idioms. In spite of his continuing intellectual fertility, it was more exciting to follow the spiritual peregrinations of John Middleton Murry from liberalism through mysticism to Christian pacifism, or of Aldous Huxley from moral hedonism to mysticism, or of John Strachey from Toryism through fascism to Marxism, than to listen to an old Edwardian radical like H. G. Wells. To make matters worse, James Joyce, Gertrude Stein, D. H. Lawrence, Ern-

2. See Geoffrey West's assessment of Wells' audience in 1930: "With the doubtful exception of Bernard Shaw, no living writer of [Wells'] calibre gains so wide a hearing from the man in the street, yet his influence with the post-war intelligentsia of England and America is all but imperceptible. Sinclair Lewis one might point to as having drunk of the fountain, but though the more representative British figures of the Sitwells, Aldous Huxley, Lawrence and Joyce may have paid their tributes to that unfailing spring of humour and imagination and wisdom, they seek other sources for their refreshment": West, *H. G. Wells,* pp. 278–79.

est Hemingway, and scores of gifted contemporaries were experimenting in forms of literary expression that gave Wells' writing by comparison a sonorous mid-Victorian ring. The feeling grew that Wells had run his course, just at that point in his career as a prophet of world order when, in books like *The Open Conspiracy* and *The Shape of Things to Come,* his thoughts on the world crisis had fully matured.

Down to about 1930 there was not much open critical acknowledgment of the enormous gap that had gradually widened between Wells and most of his juniors. But after 1930 his press clippings took a decisive and permanent turn for the worse. Large numbers of intellectuals had always snubbed him, conservative and radical alike. But only after 1930 did the decline in his fortunes become generally obvious enough to prompt critics to write articles about it. C. Hartley Grattan divided Wells' public in 1931 into three classes: "passionate admirers among men slightly younger than himself, suspicious but attentive men of thirty-five to forty, and the indifferent young." To young people, said Grattan, Wells was "simply a gabbling old dodo of sixty-four who occasionally gallops down from the heights with a new revelation of the future. . . . He does not speak the language of the rising generation. They read him only as an easy way to comprehend a dying type of mentality, and they are not stirred to action or belief by anything he may say."[3] An exaggeration, but it contained several grains of truth. More charitable and yet to the same effect was Malcolm Cowley's description a few years later of Wells as "the survivor of a prehistoric time, a warm, ponderous, innocent creature ill adapted to the Ice Age in which we live, and yet overshadowing the smaller animals that shiver behind rocks without ever venturing into the open. They have a bitter wisdom that he lacks, but they are not of his stature." The

3. Grattan, "Good-Bye to H. G. Wells!" *Outlook* (New York), *157* (1931), 178–79.

Wellsian Utopia belonged "to the happy days before the War." Now it was less alive than Lenin's corpse in Red Square.[4]

Reviews of Wells' books became more and more perfunctory through the 1930's. Sales dropped. The typical prophetic book or propaganda novel was lucky to sell four or five thousand copies. As Stanley Kauffmann pointed out in 1940, Wells during the early years of the century had been

> one of the two or three great inspirers of youth in Great Britain and the United States. . . . Today, a new book by Wells usually elicits the feeling that "the old man is still writing" or the "well, well, I thought he was dead" reaction. . . . For the most part, they are brought out, reviewed kindly though much in the spirit above, advertised briefly, and forgotten. . . . When he speaks, it is not because he is entreated but because he is tolerated for old times' sake. . . . The influence of Wells has declined sharply since about 1925.[5]

The most striking thing about Wells had been his power to kindle the imagination and devotion of youth. Now, Kauffmann noted from his own personal experience, students paid no attention to him. A reference to an idea of Wells' in conversation yielded no response.

Kauffmann might have added that Wells was also failing to take an interest in youth. The young people in his novels after 1920 were still, in all their essentials, late Victorian or Edwardian young people. Except for a few vividly nineteen-twentyish types in novels written in the late twenties and early thirties under the influence of a brilliant friend and fellow author, Odette Keun—in novels like *The Bulping-*

4. Cowley, "Outline of Wells's History," *New Republic, 81* (1934), 23.

5. Stanley Kauffmann, "Wells and the New Generation: The Decline of a Leader of Youth," *College English, 1* (1940), 573–74.

ton of Blup—Wells stuck with an astonishing lack of insight to the same aspiring heroes and heroines he had created before the first World War. He touched bottom in 1940 with Gemini and Stella in *Babes in the Darkling Wood*—an Edwardian couple in their every word and thought and mannerism, born thirty years too late, portrayed with an unintended comic note as representative young English people caught up in the tragedies of the second World War.

This indifference to changing habits of speech and manner may help to explain why Wells lost younger readers in his later years, but the whole problem of his failure as a prophet of world order, insofar as he did fail, is much more complex. Many explanations suggest themselves, but no one single explanation seems even remotely adequate except the obvious catch-all that a hundred H. G. Wellses could not have saved Western civilization from whatever fate has overtaken it in the twentieth century. But why did Wells' prophetic labors meet with so feeble and disappointing a response, especially after about 1925 and especially among thinking people of the younger generation?

Certainly he need not be singled out from the rest of his own generation. Few fared any better with their posterity, and most not as well. For a living writer to remain the darling of his public longer than ten or twenty years, no matter how productive he may continue to be, is rare. Like styles of art and dress, writers run the risk of going out of fashion after even the briefest season of popularity.

But just as Wells had been branded a futurist by conservative opinion in Edwardian times, so after the first World War he tended to be seized on by younger thinkers as a convenient illustration of all that was *démodé* in the ideas and beliefs of the Victorians and Edwardians. Their use of Wells was seldom fully justified, but he made, with whatever justice, a serviceable scapegoat. His mind had been formed in the thought-world of the late nineteenth century; his fundamental assumptions betrayed him. Enough has already been said in previous chapters to suggest how much he owed T. H. Huxley, the nineteenth-century Utopian socialists, the Positivist movement, William James, William Ernest Henley, and Victorian rationalism. Although he had a livelier sense of the limitations of science, progress, common sense, and socialism than many of his Victorian teachers, it was easy, after the traumatic experiences of the first World War, to look on Wells as a spokesman for exploded hopes and broken promises.

He talked about progress, for example. Not automatic or providential progress: only a certain potentiality in the resources of the human intelligence, and especially of science, for realizing a sane, ordered world society. But it was enough that Wells talked about progress. The disenchanted intellectuals of the Western world after 1914 used him freely as a symbol of nineteenth-century optimism in its most extreme form. And still do. "Wells was the last of the encyclopaedists," says Christopher Dawson, putting Wells still further back in time, "—a belated child of the Enlightenment who still preserved its faith in progress and humanity and science with all its optimism and naïveté, even in the hostile climate of post-war Europe."[6] C. Hartley Grattan had made the same point in his article on Wells in 1931. Wells had a typical modern mind of "the pre-war variety. . . . The post-war minds have been disciplined and disillusioned. There is no longer a widespread belief in the inherent goodness of man. No critical thinker today is convinced that progress will *immediately* issue in anything at all. . . . And so H. G. Wells is losing his grip upon the thoughtful public."[7] These are both unjust distortions of Wells' actual position, as anyone who takes the trouble to read his work carefully may

6. Dawson, "H. G. Wells and the Outline of History," *History Today*, *1* (1951), 29.
7. Grattan, "Good-Bye to H. G. Wells!," p. 198.

find out for himself. But most thinkers who have committed themselves in print on Wells share the same misconception. There is even an adjective—"Wellsian"—which means just what Arnold J. Toynbee has in mind when he says that the English middle classes in the year of Queen Victoria's Diamond Jubilee believed in the arrival of a state of permanent felicity in the world, believed, in short, that they were "Wellsian rationalists living in a scientific age."[8]

What drew the critics' fire more than anything else, perhaps, was Wells' persistent use of the Utopian device. His glimpses of Utopia in books like *The Outline of History* and, of course, the beatific visions in *Men Like Gods* and the closing pages of *The Shape of Things to Come* were bitterly received by the postwar intelligentsia. No one but Wells and Shaw among the major writers had the audacity to publish Utopias after 1914; and although Wells' later Utopias were inspirational books and not naive prophecies, the distinction could easily be overlooked. Wells thought "men" would some day be "like gods," so the story ran. Wells imagined this was "the shape of things to come." The old man was fooling himself! The majority of the intellectuals turned in the opposite direction: to the writing and agonized appreciation of inverted Utopias, like Wells' own *fin-de-siècle* novel *The Time Machine*.

The inverted Utopias of the twentieth century nearly all follow the same pattern, whether written by reactionary thinkers like G. K. Chesterton or left-wing liberals like George Orwell. In nearly every instance some fiendish travesty of a Wellsian superstate—and often the writers have Wells specifically in mind—has established itself over groan-

8. Toynbee, *Civilization on Trial* (New York, Oxford University Press, 1948), p. 17. Ironically, Wells was just in that year writing *The War of the Worlds,* to jolt Victorians out of their complacency. For other representations of Wells as a prophet of automatic progress see above, p. 81.

ing humanity. The individual becomes a slave or a robot. The new masters of the world aim at the annihilation of spiritual values, at the glorification of power and machinery, at the extirpation of intellectual and artistic freedom. Since Chesterton's *The Napoleon of Notting Hill* (1904) the authoritarian, mechanized, inverted Utopia has been conjured up in novels and stories like Robert Hugh Benson's *Lord of the World*, AE's (George William Russell's) *The Interpreters*, Zamyatin's *Nous autres*, E. M. Forster's "The Machine Stops," Aldous Huxley's *Brave New World*, Karel Čapek's *War with the Newts*, C. S. Lewis' *That Hideous Strength*, George Orwell's *1984*, and scores of recent science-fiction— or anti science-fiction—novels along the lines of Kurt Vonnegut's *Player Piano*.[9]

The counter-Utopias have helped to dramatize a whole new collection of fears and anxieties endemic in twentieth-century minds, fears and anxieties Wells often did not really share. He saw the world crisis in biological terms: man's lower animal nature, full of greed, jealousy, and animal inertia, struggling against his quintessentially human ambition for collective progressive evolution. The individual, in the final analysis, was a means to the racial end. Wells' juniors have differed. Science and technics—according to Wells, forces without moral content that supplied mankind with a chance at Utopia—have taken on a nightmarish cast.

9. Wells sometimes put in a personal appearance in twentieth-century counter-Utopias: he is the "Prophet" in Victor Rousseau's *The Apostle of the Cylinder* (1918), and he is Horace Jules, the Director of the National Institute of Co-ordinated Experiments, in C. S. Lewis' *That Hideous Strength* (1946). That Orwell's *1984* was in some measure a reaction against Wells and Wellsian "optimism" can be surmised from his charge during the second World War that Wells was a "nineteenth-century Liberal" whose innocent faith in progress made him temperamentally unable to admit even the possibility of an Axis victory: Orwell, *Critical Essays*, pp. 86–87.

The modern intelligence may see in "the Machine" not only a bloodthirsty killer in war but, even worse, a taskmaster regimenting and stereotyping the helpless individual, stamping out human values, debasing human souls, applying the discipline of the assembly line to every aspect of human life.

Wells also had no terror of the tendency in Western civilization toward "bigness" in government, business, and social organization. Rather, in fantasias like *The Food of the Gods,* he gloried in the "change of scale" that had overtaken humanity. Bigness was intrinsically good. It made for efficiency, increased productivity, an enlargement in the range and scope of the individual life. It heralded the coming of the single integrated world society. Again, his juniors have taken up radically different positions. The twentieth-century experience has suggested that bigness may be intrinsically evil: an octopus, an affliction of fascism, communism, and capitalism alike, which, many sensitive intellectuals nowadays suspect, threatens to swallow up the individual. Wells grew up in a mental climate supersaturated with collectivistic social philosophies. Living in an age when collectivism is being tried on a grand scale at the sometimes disastrous expense of personal freedom and dignity, many of his juniors have turned back to a defiant individualism.

Wells is also caricatured by his juniors as an apostle of old-fashioned rationalism, of "the faith that man is at root rational," says Kingsley Martin, "that poverty, war and disease can be conquered by education and the application of scientific knowledge to human society."[10] The caricature is at least half-true. It goes as far back as Max Beerbohm's famous Edwardian cartoon showing "H. G. Wells and his Patent Mechanical New Republic, and the Spirit of Pure

10. Martin, "H. G. Wells," *New Statesman and Nation,* 32 (1946), 115.

Reason crowning him President."[11] Although Wells had no illusions about the animal aspect of man's nature and although he was duly impressed by the revelations of Freudian, and more particularly, Jungian, psychiatry, it remains perfectly true that he hinged most of his hopes on the triumph of human reasonableness and common sense. His emphasis always fell on the possibilities of reason rather than on the high incidence of unreason; whereas most recent intellectuals, without necessarily approving of unreason any more than Freud or Graham Wallas approved of it, let the emphasis fall the other way.

The last few decades of the twentieth century have witnessed, too, a revival in religiosity among serious-thinking men. The "neo-Orthodox" Protestantism of Karl Barth and Reinhold Niebuhr, the neo-Thomism of Etienne Gilson and Jacques Maritain, the Christian testaments of every kind of fashionable modern writer from C. E. M. Joad to Nicholas Berdyaev and Arnold J. Toynbee all illustrate a searching out of new orientations in which Wells had no part whatever. He considered himself a religious man, but his religion was more the nineteenth-century Positivist religion of humanity than any current faith. Far from having any sympathy with the new religiosity, he dealt with it as obscurantism, a continuation into the twentieth century of the decaying faith of his Victorian forefathers. He was especially critical of the new mysticism of P. D. Ouspensky, Gerald Heard, and Aldous Huxley. The mystics were "defeatists," he argued, seeking a "comfortable retreat from the world," lowering "the vitality of many impressionable youngsters who might have been won to the service of the revolution."[12] He had a trace of mysticism in his own make-

11. Reprinted in Thomas Seccombe, "H. G. Wells," London *Bookman, 46* (1914), 21.
12. *Phoenix,* pp. 49–50.

up, kept carefully under control, but he could not appreciate it in others. And one by one, men who might have been Wellsians turned to the satisfactions of more esoteric gospels. Joad, himself a Shavian and Wellsian until middle age, ended his somewhat erratic life a professing Christian. Wells' own biographer, Geoffrey West, became a Wellsian early in life, compiled a bibliography and subject index of Wells' writings in his mid-twenties, and wrote his biography of Wells before he was thirty. But within a few years of the appearance of this frankly eulogistic biography he had fallen under the spell of John Middleton Murry and published a far from Wellsian confession, *Calling All Countries: A Post-War Credo,* in which he described Wells as inadequate for his spiritual needs. Murry, he confessed, was saying things Wells had never dreamed of and could not understand. Wells was all right as far as he went, but he didn't go far enough. He was not tuned in, West thought, to the "higher" realities.[13] As Gerald Heard—a member of the H. G. Wells Society in the mid-1930's—pointed out several years ago in *The Saturday Review of Literature,* Wells' faith marked the end of an age, "the end of Utopianism, that specific mythos of the Modern Age, the Faith which took the place left by the gap when the Dantesque Divine Comedy closed with the close of the Middle Ages."[14]

In much the same vein Wells could be accused of fostering Western cultural imperialism, at a time when Western intellectuals were growing more and more sympathetic to Eastern philosophy and religion. Belloc and Chesterton never tired of censuring Wells for his sham cosmopolitanism. He was, they said, a suburban Victorian cockney to the fingertips, and his so-called cosmopolis only a Victorian sub-

13. West, *Calling All Countries: A Post-War Credo,* London, 1934; cf. C. E. M. Joad, *The Recovery of Belief,* London, 1952.

14. Heard, "H. G. Wells: The End of a Faith," *Saturday Review of Literature, 31* (1948), 9.

urb magnified to planetary proportions.[15] A German scholar, W. Halfmann, writing in the early 1920's, used Wells as a prize illustration of "Anglo-Saxon imperialism" in British letters. Wells was the culminating figure, he said, in a line that reached all the way from Bentham to Carlyle and Kipling.[16] And again, it is perfectly true that Wells had very little understanding or appreciation of any culture but his own. He knew and loved England,[17] he knew something of America, and a little of Continental Europe; he preached political and economic equality for all the peoples of the world, and he had no patience with colonialism or racism; but Asians and Africans would probably have contributed little more than their genes and chromosomes to the Wellsian world commonwealth. His Utopias were all cast, like *A Modern Utopia* by his own admission, "in the mood of the Western peoples." Utopian man would not face the struggle with nature in the ascetic spirit of the East: rather he would set himself bravely to the task of subduing and mastering nature, in the Promethean spirit of the West.[18]

15. See, e.g., Belloc's books on *The Outline of History*, cited above, p. 145, n. 41, and G. K. Chesterton, "Mr. Wells as a Bishop," *New Witness*, reprinted in *Living Age*, 295 (1917), 294–97.

16. W. Halfmann, "H. G. Wells' Vereinigung von Imperialismus und Pazifismus und ihre Grundlagen in der englischen Literatur," *Englische Studien*, 59 (1925), 193–259.

17. "I have a passionate pride in being of the breed that produced such men as Shakespeare, Milton, Bacon, Cromwell, Newton, Washington, Darwin, Nelson and Lincoln. And I love the peculiar humor and kindly temper of an English crowd and the soft beauty of an English countryside with a strong, possessive passion. I find it hard to think that other peoples matter quite as much as the English. I want to serve the English and to justify the English. Intellectually I know better, but no man's intelligence is continually dominant; fatigue him or surprise him, and habits and emotions take control": *Washington and the Riddle of Peace*, p. 13.

18. *Modern Utopia*, p. 8.

And when he spoke, as he often did, of the brilliant future appointed for the Eastern races, he meant simply, as he wrote in *Social Forces in England and America,* that "an awakened Asia will be reorganising its social and political conceptions in the light of modern knowledge and modern ideas"—in other words, Western knowledge and Western ideas.[19] Fresh from a reading of the first volumes of Toynbee's *A Study of History,* he told the China Society in 1935 that the nonsense about an "eternal separation of East and West" had no basis in fact. The East was neither mysterious nor monolithic. There were a number of Eastern societies and they were all moving closer and closer to the West, joining forces with the West in the struggle for a universal world commonweal and a higher standard of common life.[20] But Wells made quite clear elsewhere that the passivity and mysticism and other-worldliness embedded in most Eastern faiths would have no place in the Great State of the future.[21] In an age when Western intellectuals are re-examining with a deepening distrust the "mood of the Western peoples" and opening their minds more than ever before to Eastern religious insights, Wells' rejection of the characteristically Eastern varieties of religious experience identified him all the more with the baldly self-reliant rationalism of the nineteenth century.

Wells might still have held his public if he had remained more loyal to one or the other of the two distinctively nineteenth-century social philosophies which have preserved, if not strengthened, their prestige among twentieth-century

19. *Social Forces in England and America,* p. 381; cf. Wells' prophecy of a radiant future for a China which "turns her face to the new learning of the West" in *Soul of a Bishop,* p. 189.

20. Typescript of an unpublished speech in the Wells Archive.

21. See his criticisms of Chinese and Indian religion in *Fate of Man,* pp. 177–78, and *Crux Ansata: An Indictment of the Roman Catholic Church* (Harmondsworth, Middlesex, 1943), p. 43.

intellectuals: liberal democracy and socialism. He could not fully subscribe to either. He incorporated liberal democratic ideas into his thinking, and he never quite lost touch with the socialist movement, but his fundamental assumptions and his obstinate independence of mind and character kept him at an appreciable distance both from liberal democratic orthodoxy and from the various leading schools of socialist doctrine.

In the context especially of the 1930's, Wells' acute hostility to Marxism cost him the support of thousands of younger men powerfully attracted to Marxism whether inside or outside the discipline of the Communist party. He differed crucially with the Marxists on the idea of the class struggle, and just as he alienated liberals and democrats by the authoritarian character of his Utopias, so he earned the tag of "class enemy" among Marxist socialists for his idea of a classless Open Conspiracy—which was to conspire, not against malefactors of great wealth, but against the nation-state system, drawing its membership principally from the middle and upper levels of the bourgeoisie itself.

According to Trotsky, Lenin after his historic conversation with Wells in 1920 dismissed Wells as an incurable bourgeois and Philistine,[22] and every Marxist critic since Lenin has followed the same line. D. S. Mirsky defined Wells in 1932 as "an instrument for the grafting of an Imperialist ideology on to the petty bourgeois," all the more to be feared because he seemed on the surface an opponent of capitalism.[23] Christopher Caudwell pointed out in his *Studies in a Dying Culture* that Wells had never been able to understand the interests of any class but his own, the petty bourgeoisie, which turned him against the working classes

22. Leon Trotsky, *Lenin* (New York, 1925), p. 173.
23. D. S. Mirsky, "Mr. Wells Shows His Class," *Labour Monthly, 14* (1932), 384.

and forced him willy-nilly into effective alliance with the upper bourgeoisie, to which every petty bourgeois yearns to belong. Wells did not understand the modern world at all, since the petty bourgeoisie, "the only class Wells understands, is simply the dust flung off by the impact" of the two great opposing forces in the class struggle.[24] Nor were Wells' Marxist critics entirely wrong. It is perfectly clear that he had no feeling for, no understanding of, the working class. The peasantry of the East and the agricultural proletariat of the West were still more foreign to him. His aim was to convert the world into one vast educated bourgeoisie.

It may be argued, of course, that Wells would have had to surrender his intellectual integrity to make common cause with any of these powerful trends in twentieth-century thought. He could not have cut his connections with the nineteenth century, writhed in existentialist agony, preached Bellocian localism, swallowed mysticism, bolted to Buddhism or Christianity, put his faith in simple democracy, or embraced the brawny Bolshevik worker-hero— could not have done so and remained recognizably H. G. Wells. But he alienated still another and perhaps larger body of opinion, in which most of the rest participated, by surrendering another kind of integrity: his integrity as a literary artist.

Something of the story of Wells' quarrel with art has already been suggested in Chapter 5.[25] His steadily increasing preoccupation with the propaganda of world order especially after 1914 did result in dozens of poor, thin novels; in a profusion of hastily conceived prophetic books; in much journalism written for the moment to snatch something use-

24. Caudwell, *Studies in a Dying Culture* (London, 1938), p. 82. For another Marxist interpretation of Wells see the section entitled "Cellophane Utopia," in A. L. Morton, *The English Utopia* (London, 1952), pp. 183–94.

25. See above, p. 239, n. 56.

ful to the cause of world order from the latest headlines. "Save for an incidental lapse or so," he admitted in 1930, "I have never taken any very great pains about writing. I am outside the hierarchy of conscious and deliberate writers altogether. I am the absolute antithesis of Mr. James Joyce."[26]

The literary critics have been prompt to agree with him. Since the 1920's his stock among the critical profession has dropped almost to zero, whereas Joyce has rocketed to heights Wells never reached even in Edwardian times. A typical estimate, repeated over and over again in all the standard histories and critiques of twentieth-century English literature, may be studied in J. W. Cunliffe's *English Literature in the Twentieth Century*. According to Cunliffe, Wells did his best work before 1912, in books like *Kipps*, *Tono-Bungay*, and *The History of Mr. Polly*. Since then his stories had been smothered in propaganda. His imaginative spontaneity now and then flickered again, but it was almost extinct. As for the journalism, of course, that was "evanescent."[27] Less professorially, D. H. Lawrence's review of the first volume of *The World of William Clissold* expressed the same judgment. *Clissold* was no novel, said Lawrence, "because it contains none of the passionate and emotional reactions which are at the root of all thought, and which must be conveyed in a novel. This book is all chewed-up newspaper, and chewed-up scientific reports, like a mouse's nest."[28] There is no need to multiply examples. Most literary people, and a good many sensitive readers appalled by Wells' apparent waste of his genius, wrote Wells off their books long ago, and there are few hints of a Wellsian revival, except for recent reminders to the critical pub-

---

26. Wells in introduction to West, *H. G. Wells*, p. 13.

27. Cunliffe, *English Literature in the Twentieth Century* (New York, 1933), pp. 139–62.

28. Lawrence, *Selected Literary Criticism*, ed. Anthony Beal (New York, Viking, 1955), p. 138.

lic that he was the arch-Philistine who taunted poor old Henry James in *Boon*.[29]

Actually, there was nothing indefensible about Wells' purposes even from the purely literary point of view. As J. Isaacs has noted, Wells deserves credit for having turned the novel in a radically new direction. He may have been surpassed by later writers, but he pioneered in the creation of the peculiarly twentieth-century novel of ideas or discussion, in which, according to Wells' own formula, the novelist takes "the whole of life" for his field of action.[30] Wells' rebellion against the self-conscious artistry of the Henry Jameses and the George Moores and his insistence on the novelist's right to deal directly with ideas and issues were not, one suspects, the real reasons for his failure as a literary artist, and for the very real loss of prestige and respect he suffered among fellow writers and intellectuals generally. His failure was rather one of execution. A good novel of ideas, like Thomas Mann's *The Magic Mountain* or Aldous

29. See especially Leon Edel and Gordon N. Ray, eds., *Henry James and H. G. Wells,* Urbana, Ill., University of Illinois Press, 1958. The editors conclude, pp. 38–41, that "the old master of Rye and Chelsea" had the final word, which is not at all clear from their very fair and full documentation of the James-Wells debate. A still more Jamesian position is taken by E. K. Brown in "Two Formulas for Fiction: Henry James and H. G. Wells," *College English, 8* (1946), 7–17. For a short objective account of James vs. Wells consult Vincent Brome, *Six Studies in Quarrelling,* pp. 75–102. There is even a vigorously anti-Jamesian, pro-Wellsian review of the Edel-Ray volume by Kenneth Rexroth, "The Screw Turns on Mr. James," *Nation, 187* (1958), 76–77.

30. Isaacs, *An Assessment of Twentieth-Century Literature* (London, 1951), pp. 22–24. For Wells on the English novel see the talk he gave to the Times Book Club in 1911, which may be studied, slightly revised, in *Social Forces in England and America,* under the title "The Contemporary Novel," pp. 173–98. See also "The Novel of Ideas," a preface to *Babes in the Darkling Wood,* pp. ix–xv.

Huxley's *Eyeless in Gaza,* requires fully as much art, as much patience and skill and genius, as any other kind of novel. Most of Wells' later work and a good percentage of his earlier was poured out at a furious pace,[31] without the thoughtful care it deserved, slapped together anyhow, peopled with jerky, unfinished bit players and heroes or heroines in shining intellectual armor, pitted against silly, dreary, or contemptible villains. His vigorously extraverted personality, his headlong impatient verve, his gift for fantasy, and his comic genius—so effective a combination in his best early novels—somehow never quite jelled for the manufacture of discussion novels. He could not execute a completely sober and at the same time completely convincing book. All of this disastrously reduced his influence among thinking men as a prophet of world order. And he labored under the further disadvantage of having settled down in the early years of the century into a style and a vocabulary which, for some purposes at any rate, had passed out of fashion between 1920 and 1930. It lacked pungency, it was somehow too full and honest, it had an awkward way in critical moments of sounding more like Tennyson than like Lawrence or Hemingway; and this, too, helped to damn him in the eyes of the younger generation.

One final category of failings should be mentioned: call them tactical errors in the career of a world revolutionist.

31. It all began perhaps in 1895, after the great success of *The Time Machine.* Wells wrote three novels and fifteen short stories in eleven months that year; as he explained in a letter to an unidentified recipient, November 25, 1898, in the Yale University Library, "When the *Time Machine* came out (Spring, 1895) I was a journalist living from hand to mouth & I thought it wiser to turn out a succession of striking if rather unfinished books & so escape from journalism than to let myself be forgotten again while I elaborated a masterpiece." Once in the habit of "turning out a succession of striking if rather unfinished books," he went on doing more of the same, at the same pace, all his life.

There is, for example, his notorious inability to lead or work with other people,[32] and the sometimes morally repugnant character of his private life. Anyone who goes inquiring about Wells among the British intelligentsia in mid-twentieth century is likely to discover that his irascibility, promiscuity, and bad manners are much more vividly recalled than his thoughts on profound subjects. Catholic critics fancy that Wells opposed their church because it did not approve of his sexual exploits.[33] Montgomery Belgion has recently dismissed all of Wells' books on world order as the mewlings of a colossal infant, insensitive to any desires or feelings but his own. Wells as prophet was "Baby Wells," who wanted a world made to order for him, with legalized free love because he was promiscuous, with no class distinctions because he hated the English upper classes, and so forth. As Belgion argues, all the heroes in Wells' novels are Wells himself—and he is not far from the truth.[34] It would take no prodigious effort to find a character talking and thinking as Wells thought, often with a life history based on events in Wells' own life, in every novel he published.

At any rate, it was easy to see in H. G. Wells a thoroughly unspiritual, even egotistical man, frustrated and embittered

32. See above, p. 202.

33. For a good illustration see Robert Speaight, *Life of Hilaire Belloc,* p. 399. The late Sir Robert Ensor went so far as to tell Anne Fremantle that Wells' row with the Fabian Society was caused solely by his sexual misconduct with the daughters of fellow Fabians. See Anne Fremantle, *This Little Band of Prophets: The British Fabians* (New York, 1960), pp. 163–64.

34. Belgion, "H. G. Wells," *Writers and Their Work, 40* (London, 1953), especially pp. 13–29. But then Belgion neglects to observe that nearly all social prophets are guilty of the same egocentricity; and still more, he neglects to point out that Wells' personal needs and desires and prejudices were shared by millions of his contemporaries.

in youth, living a sensual, irresponsible adult life, without any of the personal gravity, dignity, or charity which might, presumably, improve a prophet's chances of being taken seriously. Certainly Wells' incapacity to cooperate with others or supply anything like personal leadership cost him much potential influence, in the Fabian Society and on many other occasions when opportunity seemed to knock, all through his life.

Another charge brought against him almost from the first was his apparent inconsistency as a thinker. He was accused of shifting recklessly from one position to another, of abandoning every force or cause or movement in which he took an interest. "Each new message of his," S. P. Sherman observed as long ago as 1917,

> cancels his previous messages. He has no base of supplies; he keeps open no line of communication with the past. He is still the grandiose and romantic dreamer bent upon bringing forward a brand-new scheme for the salvation of the world. A few years ago it was world-Socialism; a little later it was world-aristocracy; today it is world-theocracy. What it will be tomorrow no man knows, but every man can guess that it will be something different and equally evanescent.[35]

And as a disillusioned Wellsian, Odette Keun, complained in 1934, it was tragically disconcerting "to expect from a social thinker a system to which you can rally and which you can put into execution, and receive instead a swamping cataract of rushing broken notions." Wells shifted and changed, she said, "almost from one moon to another, his ground, his angle, and his solutions," shattering the confi-

35. Sherman, *On Contemporary Literature* (New York, Holt, 1917), pp. 80–81. Sherman was probably referring to *New Worlds for Old* (1908), *The Research Magnificent* (1915), and *God the Invisible King* (1917).

dence of "the men and women who aspired to be his disciples."[36]

Again, Wells can be justly accused of a tactical error in his campaign for world order. With an impatience and nervous enthusiasm altogether characteristic of the man, he had the habit of spending a few years emphasizing one problem or project, supporting one or more movements which attracted his attention and sympathy, and then turning a few years later to some other aspect of his campaign, withdrawing support, rewording and reworking his own position, shifting his emphasis, allowing himself to be attracted by other movements. His fundamental ideas and his basic approach to the problem of world order never changed appreciably down to 1944, but he sowed confusion among his followers. Even in a world used to its intellectuals' making impetuous turnabouts, Wells' repeated shifts of emphasis and allegiance diminished his effectiveness, and all the more so because he pretended to be a "scientific man." That all his New Republics, world socialisms, emergent deities striving to world theocracies, educational renaissances, Open Conspiracies, World Encyclopedias, and world guarantees of political and economic rights added up to the same almost rigidly consistent vision of an integrated world society did not help the individual reader struggling from year to

36. Odette Keun, "H. G. Wells—The Player," *Time and Tide, 15* (1934), 1309. Cf. criticisms of Wells' inconsistency in Francis Hackett, *Horizons* (New York, 1918), p. 132; Hesketh Pearson, *Modern Men and Mummers* (New York, 1922), p. 173; Maurice Hewlett, "Mr. Wells on the Millennium," *Forum, 67* (1922), 185–86; and many more. One critic in the 1930's even took the trouble to defend Wells against the charge of inconsistency, a sure indication that he needed defending: see H. E. L. Mellersh, "Religion and Mr. H. G. Wells: His Unchanging Faith," *Socialist Review, 2* (1930), 259–67. Another similar defense appeared earlier in F. H. Doughty's *H. G. Wells: Educationist,* pp. 24–25.

year to reconcile his latest utterance with the one just before it.

But perhaps, after all, the main reason Wells failed to exert a deeper and more lasting influence over thinking men was his unwillingness or inability to concentrate his energies on a conspicuously direct and systematic appeal to the elite groups who would, ultimately, have to manage a Wellsian world revolution.[37] As Aldous Huxley pointed out some years ago, there is no comparison between the effect on history of a Bentham, a Marx, or a Sorel, and the effect of Wells. Bentham, Marx, and Sorel were read by a few people of genius who translated their ideas into reality; Wells' audience was immense, but he failed to reach the right people.[38] A few careful, comprehensive, powerfully written, soundly executed, well-documented novels of ideas and treatises on crisis, revolution, and world order, books worth reprinting and rereading, would have multiplied Wells' impact many times over in the years after 1914. Any one such "classic" might have had the weight of fifty of the slight, slipshod volumes he habitually produced. The intellectuals were looking for new orientations. For all his connections with the discredited immediate past, Wells had something to offer. But he never focused long enough on any one project; he dissipated his energies. Misled perhaps by his early commercial successes, he overextended himself in a hopeless appeal to the common sense of the common

37. Cf. J. Salwyn Schapiro on Wells in a review of *The Outline of History:* "Toward the great problems of the world his imagination makes a magnificent stride; but his intellect cannot keep pace with it. Hence in the realm of ideas he is suggestive, not creative. He arouses, he stimulates, he throws out fine hints, he suggests new ways of looking at things; but he is utterly incapable of being the architect of any new system of thought, be it political, social, moral, or philosophical": Schapiro, "H. G. Wells's 'Outline of History,' " in B. A. Heydrick, ed., *Types of the Essay* (New York, Scribner's, 1921), p. 232.

38. Huxley, *The Olive Tree* (New York, 1937), pp. 14–15.

man. He attempted to combine a popular, entertaining, loose-spun style of exposition with thinking of a depth and urgency well over the heads of people who look to literature primarily for its entertainment value. As Wells himself put it, in discussing his novels in his autobiography, "The fastidious critic might object," but, so he imagined, "the general reader to whom I addressed myself cared no more for finish and fundamental veracity about the secondary things of behaviour than I. I did not want to sweep under the mat for crumbs of characterization, nor did he want me to do so. What we wanted was a ventilation of the point at issue."[39]

Wells mistook his audience. The general reader was far less important than the fastidious critic, and in the end neither one would have him. The general reader wanted fewer ideas, the critic finer writing. An elitist in theory, Wells in practice acted as if he knew nothing at all about the migration of ideas and values in a society. In theory he knew as well as anyone that they form at the top, among elites, and sift down through little by little. In practice, he tried at one and the same time to formulate a general program of social action and to act as his own intellectual middleman: educator, popularizer, encyclopedist, journalist, distributing the goods of his intellect judiciously through all the layers of society. The work he cut out for himself proved altogether too immense. For a few years in the Edwardian decade he had critics, avant-garde, general public, and all by the ear, and his personal influence in those years in demolishing a variety of obsolescent Victorian values, attitudes, and tastes cannot be questioned. After that, as a prophet of world order, his personal influence inexorably declined. His very popularity with the general reader may have cheapened him in the eyes of the avant-garde, as C. E. M. Joad thought unsolicited popularity in the 1920's cheapened Shaw.[40] As Wells extended himself further and fur-

39. *Experiment in Autobiography,* p. 418.
40. Joad, *Shaw* (London, 1949), p. 9.

ther, his voice grew weaker and weaker. Everywhere he touched he left something of himself, and something of those late nineteenth-century ideas he had incorporated into his own thought. But he could not accomplish all he set out to accomplish. Like a morning mist scattered by the warmth of the sun, he remains an ingredient in our mental atmosphere in mid-century; but he is no longer a visible ingredient.

THE PROPHET AS A SUCCESS

For all these reasons, in all these ways, Wells failed. Taken on his own terms, he failed. But taken on the less exacting terms of history, he also succeeded. It matters only a little to the historian of ideas that Wells' warnings and proposals and Utopias were not accepted as a single system by a self-consciously Wellsian intellectual movement, or that his name no longer means much to young people. It it almost irrelevant that Wells fell short of literary greatness. If he threw away golden opportunities (and he did), if he lacked the ideal personality for a prophet of world order (and he did), still he has an assured place in Western intellectual history, and he is still, however indirectly and anonymously, a force in modern thought. Dozens of eminent commentators have described Wells as the most influential thinker of his generation, or divided the honor between Wells and Shaw.[41] Not all for the same reasons, however.

41. Good illustrations may be found in André Maurois, *The Edwardian Era,* trans. Hamish Miles (New York, 1933), p. 289; C. H. Driver in F. J. C. Hearnshaw, ed., *Edwardian England,* pp. 272–73; Kingsley Martin, in his obituary notice of Wells in *New Statesman and Nation, 32* (1946), 115; Julian Huxley, "H. G.," *Spectator, 177* (1946), 161; Sinclair Lewis, "A Generation Nourished on H. G. Wells," New York *Herald Tribune Weekly Book Review* (October 20, 1946), pp. 1–2; Eric Goldman, *Rendezvous with Destiny,* p. 230; and Joseph Wood Krutch, *The Measure of Man,* p. 18.

There has been, in fact, no adequate appreciation of Wells' contribution to twentieth-century thought, especially of Wells as an interpreter and prophet of the twentieth-century world crisis.

Perhaps the main reason for the reluctance of critics to pay the prophetic Wells his due is the alarming difficulty of measuring his real influence. Wells happened to specialize in ideas that have since become, for whatever reason, platitudinous—ideas like the "abolition of distance," the "change of scale," the "race between education and catastrophe," the "unity of history," the need for a "world state," the coming of a "world economy," the "time lag between the physical and the social sciences." As R. A. Scott-James has written, "Before [Wells] was dead, his views had been absorbed and digested so thoroughly that they became truisms —the younger generation was inclined to pass him by as a man talking platitudes. That gives us the measure of his success. Just as the British Liberal Party taught all Britons to be Liberals and all but perished because its work was done, so with Wells."[42] How, for example, to measure the influence of *The Outline of History?* It stretched thousands of minds, reached millions of homes; but it would take a regiment of Harvard sociologists with I.B.M. machines and perhaps a platoon of psychoanalysts to begin to discover what impact the book actually had. Even they would make only a beginning.[43] Because Wells was rarely appreciated or advertised by critics in the last quarter century of his life, because he was at least half a popular as well as a serious writer, and because he tended to become a symbol of the nineteenth century among the avant-garde in spite of his

42. Scott-James, *Fifty Years of English Literature, 1900–1950* (London, Longmans, Green, 1951), pp. 32–33.

43. See D. C. Somervell, *English Thought in the Nineteenth Century* (London, 1929), p. 9, for the even knottier problem of weighing the influence of Wells' novels.

life-long rebellion against the Victorian *ancien régime,* his influence has been miscellaneous and even anonymous. Although tens of thousands of books written in English since 1900 on subjects of general interest make some glancing reference to Wells, a sizable percentage of them are baldly ignorant references. To a quite extraordinary degree, Wells is a writer known mostly by rumor and hearsay. But a few fairly patent reasons may be adduced to explain why Wells probably did succeed in reaching people with some substantial portion of his prophetic message. There are even reasons why generations not yet heard from or not yet born may find much more in Wells than it is currently fashionable to find.

First of all, most obvious of all, and least appreciated of all, he was the first twentieth-century writer to predict and dramatize the political, economic, social, and religious crisis in contemporary Western civilization. As the present study has tried to show, he was a student of the crisis before the debacle of 1914–18. In his prewar novels and journalism he issued warnings by the dozen on nearly all the critical aspects of that still generally unsuspected age of disaster and disorder into which the West and all the world, after a half-century of precarious stability, was then being pitched. There had been ominous obscure rumblings in the nineteenth century, storm signals in Nietzsche, Burckhardt, Matthew Arnold, Danilevsky, Nordau, Brooks Adams. But Wells was far more explicit and worked at a much closer range than any of these. After the first World War nearly all of his books were devoted to studies and dramatizations of the breakdown of contemporary civilization. He familiarized millions of readers with at least the bare notion of a world-wide, civilization-wide crisis; and, although in time he was superseded, at least for the intellectual avant-garde, by Spengler, Berdyaev, Toynbee, Schweitzer, and scores of fellow prophets, he had contributed more than he is usually

credited with contributing to the now universal consciousness of a crisis in civilization. If his philosophy of history is
no longer fashionable, at least he put his public in a receptive state of mind. He conditioned early twentieth-century minds to think in terms of catastrophe.[44] He also invented the modern science-fiction novel and the modern
counter-Utopia, which lately have grown into major vehicles for the expression of the gravest fears and anxieties of
twentieth-century man.[45] It cannot be a coincidence that of
all Wells' books except *The Outline of History* in the
United States, only the science-fiction novels and short stories are still in heavy demand; and *The Time Machine,* the
earliest and best known of the scientific romances, is the
first authentic nightmare Utopia in recent modern literature.

If not the whole program, at least some parts of Wells'

44. One veteran of the first World War, Ford Madox Ford, insisted
many years later that Wells' novels had so thoroughly conditioned him
to the horrors of scientific warfare that when he actually experienced
them on the field of battle he felt numb, apathetic, and resigned:
Ford, *Portraits from Life* (Boston, 1937), p. 122.

45. The historians and devotees of science-fiction tend to look on
Wells as the first major science-fiction writer, although, of course, the
honor might easily go to any of several nineteenth-century writers,
including Jules Verne and Edward Bellamy. But it is true that in tone,
technique, and range Wells' scientific romances are much nearer contemporary science-fiction than either Verne or Bellamy. In Verne, for
example, science plays second fiddle to adventure, and what science
there is, is much more practical and prosaic than in Wells' romances
or in the work of contemporary science-fiction writers. See the appreciation of Wells in L. Sprague de Camp, *Science-Fiction Handbook*
(New York, 1953), pp. 58–63; and for a typical testimonial—by Groff
Conklin, one of the leading anthologists of science-fiction—see *Galaxy
Science Fiction* (December, 1954), p. 108. For critiques of science-
fiction and its place in contemporary society consult Basil Davenport,
Inquiry into Science Fiction (New York, 1955) and Kingsley Amis,
New Maps of Hell: A Survey of Science Fiction, New York, 1960.

formula for world reconstruction have managed to survive, and his influence here should not be underestimated. His passion for science as an instrument of human salvation and his work as a popularizer of science cut him off from the sympathies of many sensitive twentieth-century intellectuals. But science, scientific work, and scientists still enjoy much prestige in Western society, and even more relatively in the communist societies of Eastern Europe and Asia. Science is still looked on by a substantial fraction of thinking men as a savior and emancipator, and Wells in his own time was one of the most widely read exponents of the scientific attitude. His influence, direct or indirect, on such public teachers and champions of science in England as Sir Richard Gregory, Julian Huxley, J. B. S. Haldane, J. D. Bernal, and Lancelot Hogben was considerable. There is no calculating how much enthusiasm and reverence for the achievements and possibilities of science he instilled into the public mind.

In *World Brain* and other books published in the 1930's, Wells was also one of the first important recent thinkers to call attention to the problem of the integration of knowledge, which has attracted the interest of a growing number of scholars, including philosophers of history like Henri Berr, the founder of the *Centre internationale de synthèse* in Paris, and Erich Kahler; and philosophers of science like Otto Neurath, Philipp Frank, Lancelot Law Whyte, F. L. Kunz, and Oliver L. Reiser. Wells' personal contribution here may have been slight; he was more an integrator of knowledge by example than by precept.[46] But it is one more ingredient in his formula of response to the world crisis which has not gone "out of date" and probably never will, as long as science and scholarship go on producing knowl-

46. But see the acknowledgments to Wells in recent pleas for intellectual integration in C. E. M. Joad, *Decadence* (London, 1948), p. 364, and Oliver L. Reiser, *World Philosophy* (Pittsburgh, 1948), pp. 41–42.

edge at a rate faster than it can be digested and assimilated.

Of greater and more permanent significance are Wells' thoughts on world government and an organically unified world society. Unlike most of the socialists and liberals of his early days, he always insisted on the inevitability of some kind of world state should humanity survive its twentieth-century time of troubles. He preached the world state as early as 1902 in *Anticipations,* and in nearly every book he wrote throughout his life. As much as any man, he prepared the climate of opinion in Britain and America for a postwar League of Nations between 1915 and 1918. Certainly much more than any other single man he was instrumental in creating the climate of opinion in which the various world government societies founded since 1939 have flourished in the West. He was almost alone as a prophet of world organization in 1902. Today, says Herbert J. Muller, "All would agree . . . that the major practical task of our civilization is to establish some kind of world order strong enough to maintain peace." The need for a world government is a "commonplace conclusion."[47]

But the new prophets of world order, like Wells, often go far beyond mere schemes for world government. In the writing of Arnold J. Toynbee, Pitirim A. Sorokin, F. S. C. Northrop, Lewis Mumford, Erich Kahler, and many other widely read and widely discussed contemporary prophets, the altogether Wellsian dream of an organically integrated world society, a society unified spiritually, intellectually, and culturally as well as politically and economically, finds articulation at a depth and in a spirit sometimes far removed from Wells' own work, and yet often to the same

47. Muller, *The Uses of the Past* (New York, Oxford University Press, 1952), p. 357. For a useful survey of the world government movement between 1939 and 1950 see Frederick L. Schuman, *The Commonwealth of Man,* New York, 1952.

practical effect.[48] The evidence for much direct influence is negligible. Still, Wells and these contemporary prophets of world synthesis, all a full generation or more younger, have obviously acted as spokesmen of the same anxious aspirations in the twentieth-century mental climate.

The interest generated in mid-twentieth century by the arguments of a Toynbee or a Northrop or a Mumford for some kind of integrated world civilization may also suggest that Wells was successful in teaching his serious readers to adjust their thinking to world perspectives. No other writer at least of his generation was as energetic as Wells in working to make the twentieth-century mind world-conscious. World-consciousness and world-mindedness, he insisted, were necessary preconditions of world order. He hammered at "world" themes in all his writing. The idea of a world crisis, the writing of world history, the movement for world government, the concept of a world economy, the prophecy of a world Utopia—all have significant origins in his work. In one sense, his whole life was dedicated with a commendable pertinacity to convincing his fellow men of the planetary proportions of life in the twentieth century. Those proportions are now painfully familiar to every educated mind. They were far from familiar when Wells began pointing them out more than sixty years ago.

Since the sheer logic of survival will force men of every faith and culture to commit themselves to more and more

48. Pleas for an integrated world civilization may be studied in most of the published work of the authors cited, in Toynbee's *Study of History;* in Sorokin's *The Crisis of Our Age* (1942) and *The Reconstruction of Humanity* (1948); in Northrop's *The Meeting of East and West* (1946) and *The Taming of the Nations* (1952); in Mumford's *The Condition of Man* (1944) and *The Transformations of Man* (1956); in Kahler's *Man the Measure* (1943) and *The Tower and the Abyss* (1957). See also, i.a., Julian Huxley, *Evolution and Ethics* (1947); Hugh Miller, *The Community of Man* (1949); and William Ernest Hocking, *The Coming World Civilization* (1956).

far-reaching experiments in world integration in the years ahead, the long fifty-year span of Wells' prophetic career is a kind of bridge, a bridge of ideas, between the perspectives of nineteenth-century Western civilization and the coming world society. The shape of things to come is still unclear. To use Karl Popper's language, the world society may be more nearly a "closed" society, on Catholic, communist, or even Wellsian lines, than an "open" society.[49] It may not be the kind of world in which the twentieth-century liberal could feel comfortable. For all its harmony and spaciousness, the Wellsian Utopia never was. But it will be one world. Ruled by priests, commissars, industrial managers, or electoral majorities, it will be one world. And whether it chooses to remember him or not, in its rhythms and contours, its ethos and aspirations, there will always remain indelible traces of H. G. Wells.

49. Popper, *The Open Society and Its Enemies*, Princeton, N.J., 1950.

A CHECK LIST OF THE PRINCIPAL WORKS OF H. G. WELLS

Titles marked with an asterisk are especially valuable sources for a study of Wells' thought.

*After Democracy, 1932: London, Watts.

All Aboard for Ararat, 1940: London, Secker and Warburg; (1941) New York, Alliance.

*The Anatomy of Frustration, 1936: London, Cresset; New York, Macmillan.

Ann Veronica, 1909: London, Unwin; New York, Harper.

*Anticipations of the Reaction of Mechanical and Scientific Progress upon Human Life and Thought, 1902: London, Chapman and Hall; New York, Harper.

Apropos of Dolores, 1938: London, Cape; New York, Scribner's.

The Autocracy of Mr. Parham, 1930: London, Heinemann; Garden City, N.Y., Doubleday, Doran.

Babes in the Darkling Wood, 1940: London, Secker and Warburg; New York, Alliance.

Bealby, 1915: London, Methuen; New York, Macmillan.

*Boon, 1915: London, Unwin; New York, Doran.

The Brothers, 1938: London, Chatto and Windus; New York, Viking.

Brynhild, 1937: London, Methuen; New York, Scribner's.

The Bulpington of Blup, 1933: London, Hutchinson; New York, Macmillan.

The Camford Visitation, 1937: London, Methuen.

Certain Personal Matters, 1897: London, Lawrence and Bullen.

Christina Alberta's Father, 1925: London, Cape; New York, Macmillan.

The Common Sense of War and Peace, 1940: Harmondsworth, Middlesex, Penguin Books.

*The Conquest of Time, 1942: London, Watts.

The Croquet Player, 1936: London, Chatto and Windus; (1937) New York, Viking.

Crux Ansata: An Indictment of the Roman Catholic Church, 1943: Harmondsworth, Middlesex, Penguin Books.

*Democracy under Revision, 1927: London, Hogarth Press (also published in *The Way the World Is Going*).

The Discovery of the Future, 1902: London, Unwin.

The Dream, 1924: London, Cape; New York, Macmillan.

The Elements of Reconstruction, 1916: London, Nisbet.

*An Englishman Looks at the World, 1914: London, Cassell; (as *Social Forces in England and America*) New York, Harper.

*"Exasperations: The Last Testament of H. G. Wells," c. 1945 (unpublished MS in the Wells Archive, University of Illinois).

*Experiment in Autobiography, 1934: 2 vols. London, Gollancz; New York, Macmillan.

*The Fate of Homo sapiens, 1939: London, Secker and Warburg; (as *The Fate of Man*) New York, Alliance.

The Fate of Man: see The Fate of Homo sapiens.

Faults of the Fabian, 1906: London, privately printed for the members of the Fabian Society.

First and Last Things, 1908: London, Constable; New York, Putnam; rev. ed. 1917, London Cassell.

The First Men in the Moon, 1901: London, Newnes; Indianapolis, Bowen-Merrill.

The Food of the Gods, 1904: London, Macmillan; New York, Scribner's.

'42 to '44: A Contemporary Memoir upon Human Behaviour during the Crisis of the World Revolution, 1944: London, Secker and Warburg.

The Future in America, 1906: London, Chapman and Hall; New York, Harper.

God the Invisible King, 1917: London, Cassell; New York, Macmillan.

Guide to the New World, 1941: London, Gollancz.

The Happy Turning, 1945: London, Heinemann; (with *Mind at the End of Its Tether,* 1946) New York, Didier.

The History of Mr. Polly, 1910: London, Nelson; New York, Duffield.

The Holy Terror, 1939: London, Joseph; New York, Simon and Schuster.

In the Days of the Comet, 1906: London, Macmillan; New York, Century.

In the Fourth Year, 1918: London, Chatto and Windus; New York, Macmillan.

The Invisible Man, 1897: London, Pearson; New York, Arnold.

The Island of Dr. Moreau, 1896: London, Heinemann; New York, Stone and Kimball.

Italy, France and Britain at War: see *War and the Future.*

Joan and Peter, 1918: London, Cassell; New York, Macmillan.

The King Who Was a King, 1929: London, Benn; Garden City, N.Y., Doubleday, Doran.

Kipps, 1905: London, Macmillan; New York, Scribner's.

Love and Mr. Lewisham, 1900: London, Harper; New York, Stokes.

Man Who Could Work Miracles, 1936: London, Cresset; New York, Macmillan.

Mankind in the Making, 1903: London, Chapman and Hall; (1904) New York, Scribner's.

Marriage, 1912: London, Macmillan; New York, Duffield.

Meanwhile, 1927: London, Benn; New York, Doran.

Men Like Gods, 1923: London, Cassell; New York, Macmillan.

Mind at the End of Its Tether, 1945: London, Heinemann; (with *The Happy Turning,* 1946) New York, Didier.

Mr. Belloc Objects to "The Outline of History," 1926: London, Watts; New York, Doran.

Mr. Blettsworthy on Rampole Island, 1928: London, Benn; Garden City, N.Y., Doubleday, Doran.

Mr. Britling Sees It Through, 1916: London, Cassell; New York, Macmillan.

A Modern Utopia, 1905: London, Chapman and Hall; New York, Scribner's.

The New America, the New World, 1935: London, Cresset; New York, Macmillan.

The New Machiavelli, 1911: London, Lane; (1910) New York, Duffield.

The New World Order, 1940: London, Secker and Warburg; New York, Knopf.

New Worlds for Old, 1908: London, Constable; New York, Macmillan.

The Open Conspiracy: Blue Prints for a World Revolution, 1928: London, Gollancz; Garden City, N.Y., Doubleday, Doran.

The Outline of History, 1920: 2 vols. London, Newnes; 2 vols. New York, Macmillan.

The Outlook for Homo sapiens, 1942: London, Secker and Warburg (a revision and amalgamation of *The Fate of Homo sapiens* and *The New World Order*).

The Passionate Friends, 1913: London, Macmillan; New York, Harper.

The Peace of the World, 1915: London, The Daily Chronicle.

Phoenix: A Summary of the Inescapable Conditions of World Reorganisation, 1942: London, Secker and Warburg; Girard, Kan., Haldeman-Julius.

The Research Magnificent, 1915: London, Macmillan; New York, Macmillan.

The Rights of Man, 1940: Harmondsworth, Middlesex, Penguin Books.

Russia in the Shadows, 1920: London, Hodder and Stoughton; (1921) New York, Doran.

The Salvaging of Civilization, 1921: London, Cassell; New York, Macmillan.

Science and the World Mind, 1942: London, New Europe.

The Science of Life (with Julian Huxley and G. P. Wells), 1931: 2 vols. London, Cassell; 2 vols. Garden City, N.Y., Doubleday, Doran.

The Scientific Romances of H. G. Wells (an anthology of the best science-fiction novels, with an important introduction by Wells), 1933: London, Gollancz; (as *Seven Famous Novels,* with *Men Like Gods* omitted, 1934) New York, Knopf.

The Sea Lady, 1902: London, Methuen; New York, Appleton.

The Secret Places of the Heart, 1922: London, Cassell; New York, Macmillan.

Select Conversations with an Uncle, 1895: London, Lane; New York, Merriam.

Seven Famous Novels: see *The Scientific Romances of H. G. Wells.*

*The Shape of Things to Come, 1933: London, Hutchinson; New York, Macmillan.

A Short History of the World, 1922: London, Cassell; New York, Macmillan.

The Short Stories of H. G. Wells, 1927: London, Benn; (1929) Garden City, N.Y., Doubleday, Doran (includes all the short stories through 1926).

Social Forces in England and America: see *An Englishman Looks at the World.*

Socialism and the Family, 1906: London, Fifield; (1908) Boston, Ball.

The Soul of a Bishop, 1917: London, Cassell; New York, Macmillan.

Stalin-Wells Talk; the Verbatim Record and a Discussion by G. Bernard Shaw, Wells, Keynes, Ernst Toller, and Others, 1934: London, New Statesman and Nation.

Star-Begotten, 1937: London, Chatto and Windus; New York, Viking.

The Story of a Great Schoolmaster, 1924: London, Chatto and Windus; New York, Macmillan.

Tales of Space and Time, 1899: London, Harper; New York, Doubleday and McClure.

Things to Come, 1935: London, Cresset; New York, Macmillan.

This Misery of Boots, 1907: London, Fabian Society; (1908) Boston, Ball.

The Time Machine, 1895: London, Heinemann; New York, Holt.

Tono-Bungay, 1909: London, Macmillan; New York, Duffield.

Travels of a Republican Radical in Search of Hot Water, 1939: Harmondsworth, Middlesex, Penguin Books.

The Undying Fire, 1919: London, Cassell; New York, Macmillan.

War and the Future, 1917: London, Cassell; (as *Italy, France and Britain at War*) New York, Macmillan.

The War in the Air, 1908: London, Bell; New York, Macmillan.

The War of the Worlds, 1898: London, Heinemann; New York, Harper.

The War That Will End War, 1914: London, Palmer; New York, Duffield.

Washington and the Hope of Peace, 1922: London, Collins; (as *Washington and the Riddle of Peace*) New York, Macmillan.

Washington and the Riddle of Peace: see *Washington and the Hope of Peace.*

The Way the World Is Going, 1928: London, Benn; (1929) Garden City, N.Y., Doubleday, Doran.

What Are We to Do with Our Lives? (Rev. ed. of *The Open Conspiracy*), 1931: London, Heinemann; Garden City, N.Y., Doubleday, Doran.

What Is Coming? 1916: London, Cassell; New York, Macmillan.

The Wheels of Chance, 1896: London, Dent; New York, Macmillan.

When the Sleeper Wakes, 1899: London, Harper; New York, Harper. (Rev. ed. entitled *The Sleeper Awakes,* 1910: London, Nelson.)

The Wife of Sir Isaac Harman, 1914: London, Macmillan; New York, Macmillan.

The Wonderful Visit, 1895: London, Dent; New York, Macmillan.

*The Work, Wealth and Happiness of Mankind, 1932: 2 vols. London, Heinemann; (1931) 2 vols. Garden City, N.Y., Doubleday, Doran.

*World Brain, 1938: London, Methuen; Garden City, N.Y., Doubleday, Doran.

*The World of William Clissold, 1926: 3 vols London, Benn; 2 vols. New York, Doran.

The World Set Free, 1914: London, Macmillan; New York, Dutton.

A Year of Prophesying, 1924: London, Unwin; (1925) New York, Macmillan.

You Can't Be Too Careful, 1941: London, Secker and Warburg; (1942) New York, Putnam.

The only important collected edition of Wells' writings is *The Works of H. G. Wells:* Atlantic Edition (28 vols. London, Unwin, and New York, Scribner's, 1924–27), prepared by Wells himself. The Atlantic Edition contains most of his work through 1924, but not all, and in many of the nonfiction titles whole sections or chapters are sometimes deleted.

For scholarly purposes the chief value of the Edition is the preface Wells wrote for each volume.

In the present study, the ordinary procedure has been to use the first American edition, where one exists; otherwise, the first British edition.

BIBLIOGRAPHICAL NOTE

1. BIBLIOGRAPHICAL AIDS

Two bibliographies of Wells' writings were published in the mid-1920's: Fred A. Chappell, *Bibliography of H. G. Wells* (Chicago, 1924), far from complete and not always accurate; and Geoffrey H. Wells, *H. G. Wells: A Bibliography, Dictionary and Subject-Index* (London, 1926), which is fairly reliable and nearly complete, through 1925. See also the bibliography in Georges Connes, *Etude sur la pensée de Wells* (Strasbourg, 1926), pp. 492–99; and, especially, the bibliographies in Vincent Brome, *H. G. Wells* (London, 1951), pp. 241–45, and Montgomery Belgion, *H. G. Wells*, Writers and Their Work, 40 (London, 1953), pp. 37–43. Although still not complete, the bibliographies in Brome and Belgion have the advantage of running through to the end of Wells' life. Among standard reference books, Fred B. Millett, *Contemporary British Literature* (3d ed. New York, 1935), contains a good section on Wells, useful particularly for secondary sources, on pp. 501–8. A complete, up-to-date Wells bibliography is badly needed.

2. PRIMARY SOURCES

The most important collection of Wells papers is now the Wells Archive at the University of Illinois. Composed mostly of books and papers acquired from the estate, the Archive holds several thousand letters, of which the majority are letters received by Wells; the manuscripts and/or typescripts of most of Wells' books, including a few unpublished works; and collections of first editions, press clippings, appointment books, photographs, and other materials. The Archive also has photostatic copies of many letters by Wells held in other libraries. For the purposes of the present study the materials in the Wells Archive were valuable but not nearly so valuable as Wells' published writings. Wells was not a great letter-writer; on serious subjects his letters contain almost nothing he did not say, fully and frankly, in print.

All of the published work, including the short stories and the novels, should be studied carefully for his thinking on the problem of world order. (An alphabetical check list of the principal titles appears above, pp. 277–85.) Although most of Wells' important newspaper and magazine articles were reprinted in collections like *Social Forces in England and America* and *A Year of Prophesying*, more than 300 articles have never been reprinted in book form. A good many of these are listed in Geoffrey H. Wells' bibliography, pp. 73–79, and described on pp. 87–251 passim.

3. SECONDARY SOURCES

Wells' work has called forth an immense critical literature, most of it mediocre. The majority of the studies cited here, the best of hundreds which might be mentioned, do not deal directly with Wells as a prophet; most see him from the perspectives of the 1920's and 1930's, when his work was not yet finished and his place in the history of recent thought difficult to assess. Nor are many of them as broadly conceived and ambitious as their titles might seem to promise. But they all help, not only in interpreting Wells himself but also in gauging his influence.

Of the biographies the best is still Geoffrey West (pseudonym of Geoffrey H. Wells, no relation by either surname), *H. G. Wells: A Sketch for a Portrait*, London, 1930. Antonina Vallentin, *H. G. Wells: Prophet of Our Day*, trans. Daphne Woodward (New York, 1950), is an album of book reviews strung together by a narrative that sometimes verges on historical fiction. Vincent Brome's *H. G. Wells* (London, 1951) makes bright reading, but cannot fully qualify as a scholarly work. A biography which may very well be definitive is now being written by Gordon N. Ray.

Critical books useful for a study of Wells' thought include Van Wyck Brooks, *The World of H. G. Wells* (New York, 1915), an interesting but premature attempt to locate Wells in contemporary English literature; William Archer, *God and Mr. Wells* (London, 1917), a Rationalist Press Association assault on *God the Invisible King;* Edouard Guyot, *H.- G. Wells* (Paris, 1920), sensible and sound; Hilaire Belloc, *A Companion to Mr. Wells's "Outline of History"* (London, 1926), a rancorous exercise in Roman Catholic polemics; Georges Connes, *Etude sur la pensée de Wells,* massive and unenlightening, but at least a forthright attempt to study the whole range of Wells' thought down to 1925; F. H. Doughty, *H. G. Wells: Educationist* (London, 1926), a solid piece of work on Wells' role as a critic of English education; Vincent Brome, *Six Studies in Quarrelling* (London, 1958), in which four of the six studies concern Wells; and Leon Edel and Gordon N. Ray, eds., *Henry James and H. G. Wells* (Urbana, Ill., 1958), a convenient compilation of memoirs, essays, and letters with a long introduction by the editors, pp. 15–41. Wells' friendship with Arnold Bennett is discussed and fully documented in Harris Wilson, ed., *Arnold Bennett and H. G. Wells,* Urbana, Ill., 1960. Wells provoked about thirty other books and pamphlets over the years, but few of them turned out to be useful for the present study. Of recent unpublished doctoral dissertations, two should be mentioned: Moses W. Steinberg, "Formative Influences on the Thought of H. G. Wells," University of Toronto, 1952; and Robert P. Weeks, "H. G. Wells as a Sociological Novelist," University of Michigan, 1952.

There are also several good interpretative essays in books and periodicals, more stimulating on the subject of Wells as a prophet and thinker than all the books written about him put together. See especially René Seguy, "H.-G. Wells et la pensée contemporaine," *Mercure de France, 95* (1912), 673–99; H. L. Mencken, "The Late Mr. Wells," *Prejudices, First Series* (New York, 1919), pp. 22–35, a vitriolic attack on Wells' "messianic" complex; H. E. L. Mellersh, "Religion and Mr. H. G. Wells: His Unchanging Faith," *Socialist Review, 2* (1930), 259–67; C. Hartley Grattan, "Good-Bye to H. G. Wells!" *Outlook* (New York), *157* (1931), 178–79, an acute inquiry into the decline of Wells' popularity; Odette Keun, "H. G. Wells—The Player," *Time and Tide, 15* (1934), 1249–51, 1307–9, and 1346–48, an overwrought but often penetrating criticism written by a one-time close friend; Carl Becker, "Mr. Wells and the New History," *Everyman His Own Historian* (New York, 1935), pp. 169–90, one of the best reviews of *The Outline of History;* Christopher Caudwell, "H. G. Wells: A Study in Utopianism," *Studies in a Dying Culture* (London, 1938), pp. 73–95, the Marxist approach; Stanley Kauffmann, "Wells and the New Generation: The Decline of a Leader of Youth," *College English, 1* (1940), 573–82; and George Orwell, "Wells, Hitler and the World State," *Critical Essays* (London, 1946), pp. 83–88. Since Wells' death four substantial critical essays have appeared: Sir Arthur Salter, "H. G. Wells, Apostle of a World Society," *Personality in Politics* (London, 1947), pp. 120–37, a suggestive sketch of Wells' life and work, with an emphasis on his prophetic career; Edward Mead Earle, "H. G. Wells, British Patriot in Search of a World State," in Earle, ed., *Nationalism and Internationalism* (New York, 1950), pp. 79–121, workmanlike and scholarly, the first fruits of research that would have culminated in a full-length book if Professor Earle had lived to write it; William J. Hyde, "The Socialism of H. G. Wells in the Early Twentieth Century," *Journal of the History of Ideas, 17* (1956), 217–34; and Anthony West, "H. G. Wells," *Encounter, 8* (1957), 52–59, a carefully written argument designed to disclose the pessimism in Wells.

This is not the place to attempt anything like a comprehensive survey of all the fields of learning that might be explored in making a study of Wells' thought, but a few titles of special value should be mentioned. For the history, and more particularly the intellectual history, of England in the late nineteenth and early twentieth centuries, Ernest Barker, *Political Thought in England from Herbert Spencer to the Present Day*, London, 1915; R. C. K. Ensor, *England, 1870–1914*, Oxford, 1936; and Esmé Wingfield-Stratford, *The Victorian Sunset* (London, 1932) and *The Victorian Aftermath* (London, 1933), are all excellent. For the interwar era, the standard history is Charles Loch Mowat, *Britain between the Wars, 1918–1940*, London, 1955. English literature in Wells' time is studied profitably in Holbrook Jackson, *The Eighteen Nineties*, London, 1913; H. V. Routh, *English Literature and Ideas in the Twentieth Century*, London, 1946; William York Tindall, *Forces in Modern British Literature, 1885–1946*, New York, 1947; R. A. Scott-James, *Fifty Years of English Literature, 1900–1950*, London, 1951; and J. Isaacs, *An Assessment of Twentieth-Century Literature*, London, 1951. Isaacs' book is especially commended to students of intellectual history. For socialism in Britain consult Edward R. Pease's old standby, *The History of the Fabian Society*, London, 1916; Anne Fremantle's engaging new book *This Little Band of Prophets: The British Fabians*, London, 1960; and the last three volumes of G. D. H. Cole's monumental *History of Socialist Thought, 1789–1931*, 5 vols. London, 1953–60. Two fairly recent and fairly good studies of English Utopism are V. Dupont, *L'Utopie et le roman utopique dans la littérature anglaise* (Paris, 1941), an encyclopedic survey;

and A. L. Morton, *The English Utopia* (London, 1952), a Marxist analysis.

Finally, and perhaps most important of all, are the books of and about people like Sir Ernest Barker, Hilaire Belloc, Arnold Bennett, G. K. Chesterton, Sir Richard Gregory, Frank Harris, William Ernest Henley, Thomas Henry Huxley, Aldous Huxley, Sir Julian Huxley, Henry James, William James, C. E. M. Joad, Harold Laski, Bertrand Russell, Bernard Shaw, Frank Swinnerton, Graham Wallas, and Beatrice and Sidney Webb. Of all the titles suggested by this formidable list, among just the biographies and critical works, some of the most helpful in studying Wells and his times include Robert Speaight, *The Life of Hilaire Belloc* (London, 1957), no kinder to Wells than Belloc himself was; W. H. G. Armytage, *Sir Richard Gregory* (London, 1957), full of material on Wells—Gregory was one of Wells' oldest friends and most extravagant admirers; Alan Wood, *Bertrand Russell: The Passionate Sceptic,* London, 1957; Archibald Henderson, *George Bernard Shaw* (New York, 1956), perhaps the best of the many good Shaw biographies; C. E. M. Joad, *Shaw* (London, 1949), an engaging critical study; and Margaret I. Cole, *Beatrice Webb,* London, 1945. The work of some of the great Victorians and nineteenth-century Americans who most influenced the direction of Wells' thinking is examined in William Irvine, *Apes, Angels, and Victorians: The Story of Darwin, Huxley, and Evolution,* New York, 1955; Cyril Bibby, *T. H. Huxley,* London, 1959; and Ralph Barton Perry, *The Thought and Character of William James,* 2 vols. Boston, 1935. Also worth mentioning are the recent biographies of two great *fin-de-siècle* British editors who numbered Wells among their "men" and gave him much useful encouragement in the critical early years: Vincent Brome, *Frank Harris,* London, 1959; and Jerome Hamilton Buckley, *William Ernest Henley,* Princeton, N.J., 1945.

INDEX

Wells' works have been entered under their respective titles.